BROWNING'S STAR-IMAGERY

BROWNING'S STAR-IMAGERY

The Study of a Detail in Poetic Design

By C. WILLARD SMITH

1965

OCTAGON BOOKS, INC.

New York

Reprinted 1965
by special arrangement with Princeton University Press

OCTAGON BOOKS, INC.
175 FIFTH AVENUE
NEW YORK, N. Y. 10010

LIBRARY OF CONGRESS CATALOG CARD NUMBER: 65-25890

Printed in U.S.A. by
NOBLE OFFSET PRINTERS, INC.
NEW YORK 3, N. Y.

To Florence Webster Smith

FOREWORD

THIS study of a detail in Robert Browning's poetic design was suggested by a preliminary investigation of Browning's versification that progressively seemed to draw my attention to a related interest in the poet's imagery. In its present form the study is a complete revision of a doctoral dissertation, *The Image of the Star in Browning's Poetry: a Study of a Detail in Poetic Design,* presented to the faculty of Princeton University in 1937.

It is a pleasure to acknowledge the generous assistance and criticism of Professor Gordon Hall Gerould, of Princeton University, and of Professor Harry Wolcott Robbins, of Bucknell University.

C.W.S.

Department of English
Bucknell University
May, 1941

CONTENTS

BROWNING'S STAR-IMAGERY

INTRODUCTION

Poetic imagery is one of the most characteristic elements of Robert Browning's art. But rarely, if ever, does Browning employ this descriptive power to adorn his poetry with purely ornamental detail; he prefers to use it as one of his most effective means of expression. The poetic image was for him the *oblique way of telling truth, of doing the thing that shall breed the thought*. His clearest explanation of this principle is in the twelfth division of *The Ring and the Book*, beginning at line 841:

> Why take the artistic way to prove so much?
> Because it is the glory and the good of Art,
> That Art remains the one way possible
> Of speaking truth, ...
> . . . . wherein man nowise speaks to men,
> Only to mankind,—Art may tell a truth
> Obliquely, do the thing shall breed the thought,
> Nor wrong the thought, missing the mediate word.
> So you may paint your pictures, twice show truth,
> Beyond mere imagery on the wall,—
> So note by note, bring music from your mind,
> Deeper than ever e'en Beethoven dived,—
> So write a book shall mean beyond the facts,
> Suffice the eye and save the soul beside.

The purpose of the present study is to accept the suggestion of these lines to examine with some care the nature and the functions of one of Browning's favorite images, the image of the star. That this image in particular was intended by the poet to *mean beyond the facts* is stated clearly in the Preface to the first edition of *Paracelsus* where the poet has commented upon his artistic method as follows: "It is certain, however, that a work like mine depends on the intelligence and sympathy of the reader for its success,— indeed were my scenes stars, it must be his cooperating fancy which, supplying all chasms, shall collect the scattered lights into one constellation—a Lyre or a Crown." These words, it seems to me, may serve as an introduction to the principal thesis of the present study of a detail in Robert Browning's poetic design, for they imply not only the poet's apparent pleasure in using the image of the star in the composition of many poems, but also his conception of the relationship of imagery to total poetic form.

A formal investigation of the works of Robert Browning is hardly necessary to prove what even a casual familiarity with his poetry may conceivably suggest, that the image of the star was, among the hundreds of poetical images he employed, a constant favorite. This image was pictorially and spiritually related to the general vision of light with which the poet was intensely preoccupied throughout the greater part of his poetic career. The first of

Browning's critics to pay particular attention to this imagistic preoccupation was Algernon Charles Swinburne, whose interest was expressed in sentences like the following:

> The difference between the two [Chapman and Browning] is the difference between smoke and lightning; and it is far more difficult to pitch the tone of your thought in harmony with that of a foggy thinker than with that of one whose thought is electric in its motion. To the latter we have but to come with an open and pliant spirit, untired and undisturbed by the work or the idleness of the day, and we cannot but receive a vivid and active pleasure in following the swift and fine radiations, the subtle play and keen vibration of its sleepless fires; and the more steadily we trace their course the more surely do we see that all these forked flashes of fancy and changing lights of thought move unerringly around one centre and strike straight in the end to one point. Only random thinking and random writing produce obscurity; and these are the radical faults of Chapman's style of poetry. We find no obscurity in the lightning, whether it play about the heights of metaphysical speculation or the depths of character and motive; the mind derives as much of vigorous enjoyment from the study by such light of the one as of the other. The action of so bright and swift a spirit gives insight as it were to the eyes, and wings to the feet of our own; the reader's apprehension takes fire from the writer's, and he catches from a subtler and more active mind the infection of spiritual interest; so that any candid and clearheaded student finds himself able to follow for the time in fancy the lead of such a thinker with equal satisfaction on any course of thought or argument; when he sets himself to refute Renan through the dying lips of St. John or to try conclusions with Strauss in his own person, and when he flashes at once the whole force of his illumination full upon the inmost thought and mind of the most infamous criminal, a Guido Franceschini or a Louis Bonaparte, compelling the black and obscene abyss of such a spirit to yield up at last the secret of its profoundest sophistries, and let forth the serpent of a soul that lies coiled under all the most intricate and supple reasonings of self-justified and self-conscious crime. And thanks to this very quality of vivid spiritual illumination we are able to see by the light of the author's mind without being compelled to see with his eyes, or with the eyes of the living mask which he assumes for his momentary impersonation of saint or sophist, philosopher or malefactor; without accepting one conclusion, conceding one point, or condoning one crime. It is evident that to produce any such effect requires above all things brightness and decision as well as subtlety and pliancy of genius; and this is the supreme gift and distinctive faculty of Mr. Browning's mind. If indeed there be ever any likelihood of error in his exquisite analysis, he will doubtless be found to err rather through excess of light than through any touch of darkness.[1]

It was impossible to proceed very far in the present study without noting that Browning's use of the star-image was closely related to his use of many other images of light and to his general conception of poetic form. Furthermore, as a result of examining the functions of the star-image in *Pauline,*

[1] Algernon Charles Swinburne, "Essay on the Poetical and Dramatic Works of George Chapman," *The Works of George Chapman,* Vol. II, London: Chatto and Windus, 1875.

Paracelsus, and *Sordello,* it became apparent that the image of the star was related aesthetically to Browning's use of many varieties of imagery besides those associated with the general vision of light. It became clear also that these star-images possessed both a symbolic and structural significance which made them artistically inextricable from the texture of these poems. It seemed appropriate, therefore, to define the purpose of the present analysis as an attempt to see the significance of the following related artistic phenomena: (1) the frequency of the appearance of the star-image in Browning's poetry, (2) the symbolic meanings of the star-images, (3) the structural functions of these images, (4) the relation of the star-image to the total or enveloping designs of the poems in which it occurs, and (5) the relationship of Browning's use of the star-image to his general development as an artist.

A chronological plan of procedure therefore became essential to the expository outline required for the presentation of the observations which follow. Beginning with the early poems, I have examined Browning's use of the star-image in every poem in which it occurs, with the exception of those poems which are based upon translation from the Greek, and which, in a sense, constitute a special problem of analysis. Occasionally it has been necessary to digress from the main path of investigation for the purpose of examining certain elements of Browning's artistic practice which, while not in themselves explanatory of his use of the star-image, supply a kind of evidence that is of assistance to an explanation of some of the peculiarities of his imagistic technique.

Among the many critical studies and commentaries upon the poetry of Robert Browning the subject of Browning's imagery has been frequently noted, with most attention, perhaps, in C. H. Herford's *Robert Browning,* Part II, "Browning's Mind and Art," John Kester Bonnell's "Touch Images in the Poetry of Robert Browning," and Professor Paul de Reul's *L' Art et la Pensée de Robert Browning.* The present study, therefore, makes no claim to priority in the examination of imagery in Browning's poetry. Such value as it may possess depends upon the possibility of its adding to the observations already made, but chiefly upon the degree of success which it attains in showing the relationship of the poet's use of the star-image to his conception of total poetic form and to his development as an artist.

CHAPTER I

PAULINE, PARACELSUS, AND STRAFFORD

PAULINE, 1833

PRELIMINARY work in this study of the use of the star-image in Browning's poetry had not proceeded very far when it became clear that the star, as well as the moon, the flower, the sea, and other images equally significant, possessed certain qualifications that recommended it for particular examination. Apparently it was not only an image of light, and therefore especially favored by the poet, but also an image of integral importance to Browning's thought, an image of wide distribution appearing in a great number of Browning's poems, from the beginning to the end of his literary career. It therefore seemed best, for expository reasons, to make use of the chronological plan thus suggested, for by this means it would be possible not only to record in an orderly way the numerous instances of Browning's use of the star-image, but also to observe the differences in its use in various stages of the poet's development.

The first poem to be examined, therefore, is *Pauline,* in which eleven clearly marked images of the star occur. Both readers and critics of Browning poetry seem to agree in the opinion that *Pauline* is an interesting poem, but that it is also unusually puzzling, ill-formed, and "obscure." Browning himself said some rather uncomplimentary, if not harsh things about it. *Pauline* is likely to impress one as a series of passages, of unequal poetic quality, that fail to produce either a coherent or a unified effect. While our study may thus seem to begin inauspiciously, it will be seen later, I think, to have begun with this advantage at least: that an examination of the star-images in *Pauline* reveals to an interesting degree a structural unity that otherwise remains hidden. Premature though this statement may be, lacking as it now does all supporting evidence, it may serve both as a beginning and as a suggestion of the course our discussion will follow. Furthermore, it should be noted that, while the star-image remains always the principal object of study, it has been impossible to ignore the importance of other related details in the design of *Pauline* and in the designs of all the other poems to be discussed. In the attempt to understand Browning's use of the star-image it has been necessary to study in each instance the relation of this to other significant details in the poet's total design.

The first passage in which the star-image occurs in *Pauline* is the one composed of the first twenty-seven lines of the poem, the invocation. The image appears specifically in the following line:

From out thy soul as from a sacred star! (15)

Thus drawn from its immediate context it fails to be unusually interesting; it seems merely to complete the simile of which it is a part, and perhaps to suggest an agreeable picture. The real significance of the "sacred star" depends upon its association with other images and ideas in the passage. A hint of this association may be given by extending the quotation to include six lines:

> But what can guard thee but thy naked love?   (10)
> Ah dearest, whoso sucks a poisoned wound
> Envenoms his own veins! Thou art so good,
> So calm—if thou should'st wear a brow less light
> For some wild thought which, but for me, were kept
> From out thy soul as from a sacred star!

In reading these lines one's inclination is to prefer the rather unpleasant though vigorous image of the "poisoned wound" as the most effective in the passage. An examination of the poem as a whole nevertheless shows the effect of the "poisoned wound," however sensational, to be momentary rather than lasting in its power to impress the reader. The star-image, on the other hand, is repeated often enough, as the poem continues, to acquire, through iteration, a cumulative force that increases the significance of each of its appearances. In the first eleven lines of the poem Pauline is represented as a woman. The effect of the image of the "sacred star" is to introduce one of what we might call the essential "obscurities" of the poem. When we read *Pauline,* we can never be quite sure just what our attitude towards Pauline herself should be. Is she woman or divinity? We conveniently decide that she is now one, now the other, and sometimes both. The "sacred star" is the first clear sign of the fusion of these conceptions. The effect of the "poisoned wound" and the "sacred star" is to represent the self-conscious young poet who trembles lest his confession envenom the purity or tarnish the brilliance of his ideal. These and other elements of imagery in this passage suggest to me that Browning here intentionally brought them together, representing, as they do, both womanliness and divinity, into one of his characteristic "obscurities." A less sympathetic regard for the struggles of the young poet would perhaps charge him with carelessness and mental confusion.

In spite of the intrusion of certain other pictorial elements which tend to obscure its clarity, the image of Pauline as a woman is maintained for the first eleven lines of the poem. Then the "sacred star" accomplishes the transformation. Pauline assumes the attributes of a divinity whose radiance the brooding poet fears he may darken. The poetical transition is achieved, in a manner implying the artistic intention of the poet, by the preparatory suggestions of the words, "calm" and "light," which in no sense deny the woman, but at the same time introduce the goddess and the star. In succeeding lines of the passage such phrases as "quivering lip" and "whose brow burned beneath the crown," help to sustain this imagistic and thematic fusion.

A complete resolution of this passage into its elements of imagery would reveal an over-abundance of shapes and forms, approximately one to each line, a veritable cluster of images. These imagistic clusters *can* be separated into single elements, or resolved into meaning, if the reader like the poet can work "on one leg." After taking the trouble to perform such an analysis, we should discover, however, that most of these images, though interesting in themselves, and often descriptively beautiful, are of momentary rather than of lasting importance to the poem as a whole. But in the instance of the "sacred star" we may be certain, I think, that we are looking upon a poetic detail which belongs structurally as well as imagistically to the poem as a whole, and which lasts in the mind's eye long after images of momentary importance have vanished.

Another reason, of course, for the lasting quality of the star-image is the frequency with which it occurs in *Pauline*. This iterative characteristic may be noted in eleven literal instances. The image is also clearly suggested by the connotations of words in other lines of the poem. If these connotative suggestions should be counted as instances of the star's appearance, the number would rise to at least twenty. Some of these connotations precede the literal appearance of the image and thus prepare the reader to receive its full effect; others follow the image to recall it to the reader's mind and to help in sustaining its force.

The next passage to be considered contains examples of such connotative suggestions. The passage to which I refer begins:

> Sun-treader, life and light be thine forever!   (151)

and continues to,

> To see thee for a moment as thou art.   (205)

In his distress the poet has turned to Shelley ("Sun-treader") for renewal of his inspiration. He attributes to Shelley the same luminous quality that he associates with Pauline:

> But thou art still for me who have adored   (168)
> Tho' single, panting but to hear thy name
> Which I believed a spell to me alone,
> Scarce deeming thou wast as a star to men!

The suggestions preparatory to this specific appearance of the star-image are such phrases as: "Sun-treader," which may well mean "star," "light," "they [thy songs] stand, thy majesties," "The air seems bright with thy past presence," and "spell," in which the poet's diction shows the selection of certain words often associated with stars. The four lines quoted above are followed by a succession of some of the most charming images in the poem: the "sacred spring" and "fountain head," the girl whose lips bloom like "a mountain berry," and the return to the "sun-treader" to conclude the apostrophe with an image of light.

Browning's preoccupation with the star-like influence of Shelley pervades the succeeding passage, the luminous quality of his vision once more coming to focus in images of the star:

> I am a watcher whose eyes have grown dim   (227)
> With looking for some star which breaks on him
> Altered and worn and weak and full of tears.

and,

> I am to sing whilst ebbing day dies soft,   (252)
> As a lean scholar dies worn o'er his book
> And in heaven the stars steal out one by one
> As hunted men steal to their mountain watch.

As the reader approaches the first of these images, he may become aware of its presence through the preparatory suggestion of such lines as:

> Remember me who flung   (209)
> All honour from my soul, yet paused and said
> "There is one spark of love remaining yet,
> "For I have nought in common with him, shapes
> "Which followed him avoid me, and foul forms
> "Seek me, which ne'er could fasten on his mind;
> "And though I feel how low I am to him,
> "Yet I aim not even to catch a tone
> "Of harmonies he called profusely up;
> "So, one gleam still remains, although the last."

It is also interesting to note that Browning has introduced here an auditory image which he proposes to blend with the vision of light. The "tone of harmonies" is a theme wholly compatible not only with poetry, but also, through venerable tradition, with the stars of heaven themselves. Browning's gratitude to Shelley cannot but express itself through a mingling of the images of light and music:

> Thy sweet imaginings are as an air,   (221)
> A melody some wondrous singer sings,

so that when his "eyes have grown dim with looking for some star," we can easily imagine his ear to have strained for Shelley's music.

As the passage continues, the swift succession of various kinds of images produces a profusion in which the star-image is almost forgotten. When it appears again in the guise of simple description,

> And in heaven the stars steal out one by one,   (254)

the symbolic force, which it had begun to acquire through its association with Shelley and Pauline, has been diminished. Enough of it remains, however, to raise the line above the merely pictorial level. If this passage is examined closely, a structural transition may be noted which suggests the necessity of a change in the symbolic force of the image. Browning is about to use the star-image for another purpose. He has previously made it the "sacred star" of Pauline's divinity, the "star to men" of Shelley's inspiring achievements; now it is to become the "lode-star" of God's guiding truth:

> And of my powers one springs up to save   (281)
> From utter death a soul with such desire
> Confined to clay—. . . . .
>
> . . . .
> A mind like this must dissipate itself,
> But I have always had one lode-star; now,
> As I look back, I see that I have halted
> Or hastened as I looked towards that star—
> A need, a trust, a yearning after God:
> A feeling I have analyzed but late,
> But it existed, ...

Obviously, the implications have been changed for any symbolic value which the star-image may have begun to possess. But if the leading motive of the poem, the poet's quest for light and for the control of his powers, be recalled, this change in imagistic effect may be seen to be harmonious with Browning's fundamental design. The more limited significance of the star's first appearance has been translated into an expanded symbol of the light of poetry, embracing the conceptions of inspiration, mortal achievement, and the law of God.

The next appearance of the star-image, because of its separation from the "lode-star" by eighty lines, and from the specific instance which follows it by thirty-one lines, seems at first glance to possess a significance only remotely connected with the other images. Yet its occurrence in the descriptive verse

> Till stars look at them and winds call to them   (372)

is entirely appropriate to assist in sustaining the vision of light that has been created with added emphasis by the "lode-star." Lines in the poem occurring between the "lode-star" passage and the passage just quoted carry this suggestion of heightened emphasis, most noticeably in verses like the following:

> . . . . but sense supplies a love   (311)
> Encircling me and mingling with my life.
> These make myself: I have long sought in vain
> To trace how they were formed by circumstance,
> Yet ever found them mould my wildest youth
> Where they alone displayed themselves, converted
> All objects to their use: now see their course!

Browning is talking about the poet's (his own) experience with the senses; but if the expression of this idea is imaginatively considered, it will be observed that he has chosen words which hold to more than a casual association with stars: "Encircling," "mingling," "trace," "formed by circumstance," "displayed," "converted," "see their course." When we find that for "mould my wildest youth," Browning wrote originally (1833 version), "*turning* my wild youth," we not only discover a word which agrees better with "converted" in the next line, but also another hint of his originally sustained preoccupation with the ("turning") "lode-star."

As the passage continues, the imagery of light is further sustained by phrases such as: "my first dawn of life," "halo-girt," "sunset," "morn broke clear as those On the dim clustered isles of the blue sea," "heaven was lampless save where poesy shone out," "glittering mountain-tops," "glancing sea," "forests steeped in light," "far-flashing sun," finally concluding with the wedding of light and music, a blending of themes which we have already noted in other passages:

> For music . . . . (365)
> . . . . is like a voice,
> A low voice calling fancy, as a friend,
> To the green woods in the gay summer time:
> And she fills all the way with dancing shapes
> Which have made painters pale, and they go on
> Till stars look at them and winds call to them
> As they leave life's path for the twilight world
> Where the dead gather.

For a few more lines the theme of music and light is sustained, but the focus of attention then shifts to the light of the stars:

> As on the works of mighty bards I gazed, (385)
> . . . . I rather sought
> To rival what I wondered at than form
> Creations of my own; if much was light
> Lent by the others, much was yet my own.
> . . . . all my powers
> Burst out. I dreamed not of restraint, but gazed
> On all things: schemes and systems went and came
> And I was proud (being vainest of the weak)
> In wandering o'er thought's world to seek some one
> To be my prize, as if you wandered o'er
> The White Way for a star.

Of the eleven literal appearances of the star-image in *Pauline,* this is the eighth. The three that follow, important though they are to our present investigation, depend for their effects much less upon their own force than they do upon their association with the other eight. These, through a comparatively regular iteration, have acquired a cumulative importance and symbolic force that give the last three stars a significance which they would not otherwise possess. From this point in the poem to the end, our examination of the star-image does not lead us into the matter of the poem as it did previously. Structurally and imagistically considered, the function of the last three star-images is to recall the several themes developed in the first half of the poem, to secure thereby a greater unity, and a cumulative heightening of effect. The function of these three star-images is therefore different both in kind and in degree from the dominant imagery of the stars in the first four hundred lines of the poem.

Having permitted myself the luxury of the phrase, let me explain the sense in which I use *dominant imagery*. While the phrase itself is understandable, its application to the star-image in *Pauline* may be questioned. The question of dominance is a matter upon which even friends are likely to disagree, whether they are thinking of imagery or of government. It is with government of a poetical kind, as much as with imagery, in mind, that I have chosen to call the star of the first four hundred and three lines of *Pauline* a dominant image. The star-image is the one artistic element in these lines that combines within itself the presence of Pauline, Shelley, and "A need, a trust, a yearning after God": the "sacred star," the "star to men," and the "lode-star," the three entities with which the poet is intensely preoccupied. The quest for light, the matter of the first part of the "confession," is thus fittingly symbolized by a clear image of light.

As the poem progresses through two hundred and fifty-three lines to the next literal appearance of the star, there are many instances of verbal or connotative suggestion that keep the image going and hold before the reader the vision of light. Several of these are of so delicate a nature as not to stand extraction from their contexts; others, like the following, are quite clear in quotation, especially in the instance of those words that I have italicized:

<blockquote>

And thus I sought   (504)

To chain my spirit down which erst I freed
For *flights to fame*: I said "The troubled life
"Of genius, seen so gay when working forth
"Some trusted end, grows sad when all proves vain—
"How sad when men have parted with *truth's peace*
"For falsest fancy's sake, which waited first
"As an obedient spirit when delight
"Came without fancy's call: But alters soon,
"Comes darkened, seldom, hastens to depart,
"Leaving a heavy darkness and warm tears.
"But *I shall never lose her;* she will live
"Dearer for such seclusion. But *I catch*
"*A hue, a glance* of what I sing: so, pain
"Is linked with pleasure, for I ne'er may tell
"Half *the bright sights which dazzle me*; but now
"Mine shall be *all the radiance*: let them fade
"Untold—*others shall rise as fair, as fast!*
"And when all's done, *the few dim gleams* transferred,"—

. . . .

"And when all's done, how vain seems e'en success—
"The vaunted *influence* poets have o'er men!"

</blockquote>

It is only the latter part of this quotation which distinctly carries the image of light, and which clearly suggests the star in the words: "hue," "glance," "bright sights," "dazzle," "radiance," "fade," "rise as fair," "dim gleams transferred," and "influence." I have purposely included the preliminary lines to submit at least one notation of the image that becomes more important than the star in this division of the poem. This is the image of the chain, a figure well suited to the subject of conflict between passion and restraint which here engrosses the poet's attention. Furthermore, these preliminary lines show the contrasting shadows with which Browning heightens the effect of his images of light.

The specific star-image occurs again just after the close of the famous description of Andromeda:

> quite naked and alone; a thing   (665)
> I doubt not, nor fear for, secure some god
> To save will come in thunder from the stars.

Its effect, as previously stated, depends largely upon its power of recalling the dominant imagery of the stars of preceding passages, but its metonymic suggestion of heavenly power of itself raises the image above the level of ornamental description.

The next appearance of the star-image takes its place in a rapid succession of images of various kinds. Its rôle is, therefore, of no greater importance than that of any other element in the passage:

> I can live all the life of plants, and gaze   (716)
> Drowsily on the bees that flit and play,
> Or bare my breast for sunbeams which will kill,
> Or open in the night of sounds, to look
> For the dim stars; I can mount with the bird
> Leaping airily his pyramid of leaves
> And twisted boughs of some tall mountain tree
> Or rise cheerfully springing to the heavens;
> Or like a fish breathe deep the morning air
> In the misty sun-warm water; or with flower
> And tree can smile in light at the sinking sun
> Just as the storm comes, as a girl would look
> On a departing lover—most serene.

It should here be noted, parenthetically, that if the other images represented in this passage were traced through the poem (especially those of the insects, the sun, trees, water, clouds, and the girl), we should probably discover an artistic significance for each of them equaling, to a degree, the artistic significance of the star, though none, I think, would equal the star's in importance.

One more star-image appears as the poem approaches its end. Implicit in this image is an expression of final resolution appropriate to the idea of conclusion. At the same time, it is charged with a sudden and cumulative reference to the stars that precede it. Furthermore, this star unites structurally with other images of importance, a fact which heightens its force and assists both poet and reader in establishing a greater unity of design. The lines in which it occurs are the best explanation of these effects:

> There were bright troops of undiscovered suns,   (911)
> Each equal in their radiant course; there were
> Clusters of fair far isles which ocean kept
> For his own joy, and his waves broke on them
> Without a choice; and there was a dim crowd
> Of visions, each a part of some grand whole:
> And one star left his peers and came with peace
> Upon a storm, and all eyes pined for him;
> And one isle harbored a sea-beaten ship,
> And the crew wandered in its bowers and plucked
> Its fruits and gave up all their hopes of home;
> And one dream came to a pale poet's sleep,
> And he said, "I am singled out by God,
> "No sin must touch me."

There is no necessity to labor the point which the quotation makes clear; for the effort to be argumentatively convincing would entail the repetition of explanations already presented, ultimately requiring the quotation of the entire poem.

The more detailed the analysis of the star-image becomes, the more patently emerges the design of its structural relationship to the whole of *Pauline,* the more tantalizingly appears the complexity of its relationship to other images whose importance is often as great. During the process of studying the functions of the star-image, I have been aware constantly of the structural and symbolic force that other images often acquire. I have previously paused to mention only one of them formally, the image of the chain. There are many more that should be carefully examined if the imagistic design of the poem were to be known more certainly. Consequently, I have attempted to guard against attributing more than a just degree of importance to the images of the star, but at the same time, I have allowed the evidence of my analysis of them to crystallize into what I consider to be reasonable conclusions.

The evidence points, I think, to Browning's having either consciously or subconsciously assigned to the star-image a structural function. This opinion is strengthened by observing the functional similarity of other noteworthy images. It is possible, therefore, to submit the conventional opinion, with which our analysis began, to further modification, in addition to that which has been supplied incidentally. We cannot explain away the unequal poetical quality of *Pauline,* but we can be certain that a fundamental design for the poem existed in Robert Browning's mind, however imperfectly he may have realized his design in final composition. It is a design of images, a considera-tion of which still points to the poet's imperfect execution. But we safely may conclude that the unity of *Pauline,* such as it is, may be found more readily by an examination which assumes that its imagery, rather than its logical division, contains the elements of poetical structure and form.

We are accustomed, in working out the construction of a poem, to make logical order the criterion of our analysis. Usually there is enough of logical plan in a poem to make our task agreeable and our findings satisfactory, but, in the critical method which we thus employ, there is little that differentiates the process from that type of analysis we should apply to the scientific essay, in which we have every right to expect a high degree of logical "unity, co-herence, and emphasis." It is quite possible that the discovery of the "outline" of a poem like *Pauline* might be accomplished more successfully by a method similar to the one we should require for the examination of a painting or a piece of music, especially when the author happens to be a young man who, through inheritance and training, had already acquired a taste for, and a degree of proficiency in, drawing and musical composition.

Such an approach to the poem does not remove its "obscurity," but suggests that the critic must read the poem in another way. He must become a traveler in a landscape crossed and recrossed by a net-work of paths and by-paths that radiate from and encircle the hill-tops of imagery. The hill-tops mark the traveler's progress and assure his arrival at his destination. The poet is like an enthusiastic novice sailing his boat against the wind and tide, now rounding a mark with evident pride in his seamanship, only to discover later that he has redoubled his course. His interest in the shifting currents of his progress adds pleasure to his experience. When he finally picks up his moor-ings in a lubberly fashion, to the amusement of the accomplished amateur and the shuddering disdain of the professional yachtsman, his chagrin is lost in the delight of achievement. There is no real reason why Browning should have later repudiated his unmistakable originality with the kind of sentences that may be found in the prefaces to the collected works of 1868 and 1888: "The first piece in the series, I acknowledge and retain with extreme repugnance. . . . ," "Twenty years' endurance of an eyesore seems more than sufficient: my faults remain duly recorded against me. . . ." Have we not noticed in *Pauline* how the star-images alone point to some of the loveliest passages of poetry he has written?

PARACELSUS, 1835

In contrast to *Pauline, Paracelsus* is a well-planned poem. When he wrote it, Browning evidently followed a literary model that set before him a pattern of well-marked divisions of time, place, and action. It is possible, therefore, in discussing the functions of the star-image in *Paracelsus,* to begin with a preliminary consideration of the total form of the poem, and to suppose that by this means an expository advantage may be gained for the discussion of the moment.

This dramatic poem is arranged in a series of five clearly differentiated sections, or "scenes," which correspond to the five acts of the well-known design for poetical drama. The "acts" of *Paracelsus* are separated by specific periods of time and by distinct, though sequential differences in action and setting. These, as well as other elements in the design of *Paracelsus,* show unmistakably that Browning intended to give his work both symmetry and proportion. In contrast to his work on *Pauline,* the literary craftsmanship of *Paracelsus* is noticeably superior.

This observation will hold, I think, even when we turn our attention specifically to the study of Browning's use of star-images in *Paracelsus.* The orderliness with which they have been distributed within the narrative outline of the poem makes it possible to compose a fair synopsis of *Paracelsus* merely by giving a brief, though certainly an unpoetical interpretation of each of these images in the order of their appearance. This fact alone suggests that the results of a more detailed analysis may well corroborate the opinion we already are inclined to hold: that the star-images of *Paracelsus* are both structurally and symbolically significant.

The synopsis runs as follows, showing, as it goes, the pattern of distribution of the star-images in the poem:

PART I, Paracelsus Aspires: Scene.—Würzburg; a garden in the environs. 1512

(1)   As if, where'er you gazed, there stood a star!   (66)
marks the beginning of Paracelsus' resolve to know, and his feeling that the love of Festus and Michal for each other will ever be a comfort to him, a star to which he can look for peace and reassurance in the face of discouragements that will come his way. It is because he forgets the quality of life, which this star signifies, for the over-radiant splendor of Aprile's *Love* that comfort and peace are lost to him until the end of his life when he once more realizes the beauty of human love in the ever-devoted friendship of Festus.

(2)   But to become a star to men forever;   (527)
signifies the mark of Paracelsus' ambition, the end of his striving.

(3)   What was a speck expands into a star,   (557)
represents the expansion of Paracelsus' soul through his newly imagined vision of life beyond the reach of common men, the abounding hope and confidence with which he begins his quest for new knowledge.

PART II, Paracelsus Attains: Scene.—Constantinople; the house of a Greek Conjurer. 1521

(1)   Or sapphirine spirit of a twilight star,   (425)
is an image of mythological charm (one of the ardors for which Aprile lacks the power of expression) that points out to Paracelsus an aspect of beauty

which all the powers of *knowing* cannot realize unless assisted by *love*. It is in this part of the poem that Paracelsus learns that *knowledge* and *love* (power and beauty) must be united in the soul of a "star to men."

(2)   Even as a luminous haze links star to star,   (476)
advances the theory of poetry and artistic creation which Aprile teaches Paracelsus.

(3)   The stars that sparkled o'er them, night by night,   (552)
represents the beauty of the realm whence Aprile would gather "herbs" for his followers, an image that further clarifies Aprile's conception of the function of poetry.

PART III, Paracelsus: Scene.—Basil; a chamber in the house of Paracelsus. 1526

(1)   Saw in the stars mere garnishry of heaven,   (183)
suggests that natural man is incapable of appreciating the power of new truth, just as he is incapable of extraordinary insight into the beauties of nature.

(2)   The night, late strewn with clouds and flying stars,   (1000)
        Is blank and motionless:
marks the conclusion of Paracelsus' confession to Festus. His vain struggles have spent themselves; blankness covers his mind.

(3)   Diluted, grey and clear without the stars;   (1033)
represents the condition of Paracelsus' mind after his confession, a mind bereft of shining light, but also freed from the inconstant (and by implication, worthless) super-radiance of shooting meteors. Paracelsus is moved to hope that he may yet attain constant splendor.

(4)   Yet see how that broad prickly star-shaped plant,   (1039)
is a symbol of Paracelsus himself, an image of his hope that he may attempt the heights of renewed ambition.

PART IV, Paracelsus Aspires: Scene.—Colmar in Alsatia; an Inn. 1528

(1)   *Sic itur ad astra!*   (1)
is the watchword of a new life. Paracelsus has regained confidence.

(2)   That neither noontide nor starshine   (467)

(3)   Each helm made sure by the twilight star,   (477)

(4)   So the stars wheeled round, and the darkness passed,   (484)
harmoniously intensify the dominant image of the song in which they occur. It is the song of a voyage that symbolizes the blank disillusionment to which Paracelsus' second wave of aspiration compels him.

PART V, Paracelsus Attains: Scene.—Salzburg; a cell in the Hospital of St. Sebastian. 1541

(1)   A halo round a star . . . .   (65)

signifies the glory to which Festus thinks Paracelsus might have attained with God's help.

(2)   With magical music, as they freight a star   (115)
          With light,

shows Paracelsus, in his extremity, still clinging to the thought of Aprile and the over-radiance of his tragic example. Paracelsus seeks to convince himself that a similar glory shall enfold him at his death.

(3)   Oh Persic Zoroaster, lord of stars!   (187)

is an image associated with the general idea of achievement, the subject of the passage in which it occurs, although its exact meaning is difficult to interpret. (See below, pp. 35-37.)

(4)   A soft star trembles through the drifting clouds.   (208)

is the signal announcing the final spiritual attainment of Paracelsus; at last he is to shine steadily through the clouds that have darkened his life.

(5)   While only here and there a star dispels   (745)

stands for the final sober judgment of Paracelsus: that the hope of man's finally becoming Man is clear in the rise of certain individuals who increasingly dispel the "darkness."

(6)   As from the over-radiant star too mad   (889)

signifies the final renunciation of the extreme behavior, the inconstant impetuosity of both Paracelsus and Aprile.

Obviously the twenty items listed above are not intended to constitute an adequate outline of the five parts of *Paracelsus;* they are set down to show how much of the development of the poem may be seen in the images of the star alone, or, more exactly, in the passages to which the star-images organically attach themselves. In addition to these instances of the star's appearance, many more that are suggested through verbal connotations of the star might have been included, thereby increasing their number, at a conservative estimate, to approximately thirty. The even distribution of the star-images within the several divisions of the poem points at once to their structural significance, as the meanings to which they attach themselves signify their symbolic importance.

In the above synopsis I have deliberately included the "scenes." I have done so for two reasons. The first reason is that the "scenes" clearly show one of the essential differences between the style of *Pauline* and the style of *Paracelsus.* To use Browning's own phrase in a slightly altered form, *Pauline* is *confessional* poetry, while *Paracelsus* is poetical drama of *character in action.* Even though *Paracelsus* may not seem to succeed in freeing itself sufficiently from the confessional mode to become purely dramatic in form, it does so to a noticeable degree. For the moment, it is at least necessary to recognize the dramatic intentions of the author. The second reason, corollary to the first, is that the scenes themselves are a part of the imagery of *Paracelsus,* for they have been conceived with dramatic intent, rather than with historical accuracy in mind. When questions arise as to what may be the dominant image of one of the "acts," the scene in which the action takes place must be given full attention. Had Browning decided, or in this instance attempted to compose a first-rate play for the stage, there would be no question of the importance of his "garden in the environs of Würzburg," "house of a Greek Conjurer," "chamber in the house of Paracelsus," "an Inn," and "a cell in the Hospital of St. Sebastian."

Our analysis must be affected, then, by a realization of the superior construction of *Paracelsus,* by a recognition of its approach to the dramatic form, and by the acknowledgment that the poet's confessional manner may not be at variance with, but actually of assistance to the peculiar dramatic form that is presented in this work. Otherwise, there is no necessity for changing our method of investigation; so that we may continue to examine the star-images in the order of their appearance.

The significance of the first image does not become clear until the iterative nature of the star-image in *Paracelsus* is known. It is not until succeeding divisions of the poem have been read that we recognize the beauty of the idea the first star signifies: the essential beauty of the love of man for man.

Festus, Michal, and Paracelsus are talking together of the daring ambitions that Paracelsus confesses. Observing the strange look in Paracelsus' eye, Festus says:

> Now, Aureole, stay those wandering eyes awhile!   (61)
> . . . .
> . . . . that look
> As if, where'er you gazed there stood a star!
> How far was Würzburg with its church and spire
> And garden walls and all things they contain,
> From that look's far alighting?
> > *Paracelsus.*   I but spoke
> And looked alike from simple joy to see
> The beings I love best, shut in so well
> From all rude chances like to be my lot,
> That when afar, my weary spirit,—disposed
> To lose awhile its care in soothing thoughts
> Of them, their pleasant features, looks and words,—
> Needs never hesitate, nor apprehend
> Encroaching trouble may have reached them too,
> . . . .
> But, unobstructed, may at once forget
> Itself in them, assured how well they fare.

In other words, the happiness of his friends and his love for them will be for Paracelsus a serene star which he may contemplate in time of distress.

The loftiness of Paracelsus' incipient desire is represented in the second star-image of Part I:

> But to become a star to men forever;   (527)

We have noted the "star to men" in our examination of *Pauline*, where it represented Shelley. Perhaps Browning may wish to suggest here a Promethean similarity between his two heroes. The third star continues to reveal the mind and the ambitions of Paracelsus with the interesting difference that, while the first two show states of mind, the third image represents the mind in action at a moment of sudden and expanding realization; it is the image of a star in the process of becoming a star:

> If there took place no special change in me,   (549)
> How comes it all things wore a different hue
> Thenceforward?—pregnant with vast consequence,
> Teeming with grand result, loaded with fate?
> So that when, quailing at the mighty range
> Of secret truths which yearn for birth, I haste
> To contemplate undazzled some one truth,
> Its bearings and effects along—at once
> What was a speck expands into a star,
> Asking a life to pass exploring thus,
> Till I near craze. I go to prove my soul!
> I see my way as birds their trackless way.
> I shall arrive! what time, what circuit first
> I ask not: but unless God send his hail
> Or blinding fireballs, sleet or stifling snow,
> In some time, his good time, I shall arrive:
> He guides me and the bird. In his good time!

Paracelsus has heard "a still small voice from without"; he becomes animated with ambition and convinced he will "arrive"; the speck expands into a star! Throughout the long passage, for which the quotation above may be regarded as a conclusion, the meaning of the lines has been chiefly autobiographical, both for Paracelsus and for his creator, Robert Browning. Again associations with *Pauline* are clear, not only through the confessional quality of the lines, but also through the reappearance of several images familiar to the reader of *Pauline*, the star being one of them. Furthermore, the method of preparatory suggestion which sometimes introduces the star (and which may be observed to have been used frequently in the earlier poem) here produces a setting appropriate to the appearance of the image. Evidence of Browning's use of this method may be seen in his choice of such words as the following: "steadfast," "hue," "loaded with fate," "mighty range," and "undazzled."

The "speck" expanding "into a star" is the last specific appearance of the star-image in *Paracelsus*, Part I. We have noted its literal appearance at points corresponding to the beginning, and the approximate middle of this division of the poem. It would be gratifying to discover its presence at or near the end, since any further evidence of the structural importance of the image would support such claims as have been made previously in regard to the organic necessity of the image in this poem. I think such a discovery is possible in the notable passage that concludes Part I, a sequence of approximately one hundred lines, where the star appears, not literally, but through connotations in the poet's choice of words. The quotation that follows has been drawn from this passage:

> But, friends,   (725)
> Truth is within ourselves; it takes no rise
> From outward things, whate'er you may believe.
> There is an inmost center in us all,
> Where truth abides in fullness; and around,
> Wall upon wall, the gross flesh hems it in,
> This perfect, clear perception—which is truth.
> A baffling and perverting carnal mesh
> Binds it, and makes all error: and to *know*
> Rather consists in opening out a way
> Whence the imprisoned splendour may escape,
> Than in effecting entry for a light
> Supposed to be without. Watch narrowly
> The demonstration of a truth, its birth,
> And you trace back the effluence to its spring
> And source within us; where broods radiance vast,
> To be elicited ray by ray, as chance
> Shall favour: chance—for hitherto, your sage
> Even as he knows not how those beams are born,
> As little knows he what unlocks their fount:
> And men have oft grown old among their books
> To die case-hardened in their ignorance,
> Whose careless youth had promised what long years
> Of unremitted labour ne'er performed:
> While, contrary, it has chanced some idle day,
> To autumn loiterers just as fancy-free
> As midges in the sun, gives birth at last
> To truth—produced mysteriously as cape
> Of cloud grown out of the invisible air.

The clustering of images in these lines is readily apparent. Independently or separately considered, these images produce one of Browning's characteristic "obscurities," for they include such various pictures as: "wall upon wall" of "gross flesh," "carnal mesh" with its binding strength, "imprisoned splendour" (obviously a light, possibly a star), "spring" and "source," brooding "radiance," rays, the birth of "beams," the fountain, "autumn loiterers," "midges in the sun," "a cape of cloud," and "invisible air." But, when joined to the idea which they express—that is, the origin of truth—they become unified artistically by their similar functions.

Unless they are so regarded, with full recognition of their common artistic function, their imagistic force disintegrates, and they stand an enumeration of comparisons with little more than pleasantly descriptive effects. The touchstone to a proper perception of them may be found in lines 733-744, where the poet clearly states his intention to blend them harmoniously. Our attention falls upon these lines first, because they are reminiscent of a similar blending of themes of light and music in *Pauline* (201-229),[1] except that in this instance the blend is one of light and flowing water. The details of blending may be seen in the words that the poet has used: "imprisoned splendour," "light," "trace back the effluence to its spring And source within us," "radiance," "ray by ray," "beams," and "unlocks their fount." Consequently, the question which cannot be answered satisfactorily by the analysis of a similar instance in *Pauline,* the question whether Browning produced such an effect consciously or merely as a result of his own confusion, can now hope to find an answer that at least approaches the truth. The superior organization of *Paracelsus,* the security of its design, the structural and symbolic importance of its star-images, which we have already observed and shall continue to observe, point, in this instance, to the poet's thoroughly conscious craftsmanship.

That he worked thus knowingly may be further explained by the analysis of another aspect of the cluster of images before us. If these images should be considered once again as individual pictures, separated from their common function, a most interesting chain of logical association becomes clear. Starting with the idea of a "center," Browning proceeds inevitably to the "wall" which encloses the "center"; a wall "hems" in truth; so does a "mesh," but a mesh also "binds." Truth, then, is a prisoner, and "imprisoned splendor" which must "escape"; escape, perhaps, as water flowing from a "spring." A mysterious hand "unlocks" the prison "fount." It is the mysterious hand that no one can explain, for truth comes to "autumn loiterers as fancy free As midges in the sun" as often as it does to men who have "grown old among their books." Apparently allowing his imagination to run free through this chain of associations, Browning has never permitted his fancy to run away with his thought. He is simply, or perhaps not so simply, thinking in images. He has withstood their invitation to irresponsible freedom. There is control from the beginning to the end of this passage in the word and the idea— "truth."

Should one find that in the poetry of later periods of his development Browning repudiated this method of blending and clustering his images, it would not mean, necessarily, that his art had improved because it had lost some of its former "obscurity"; it would mean, only, that he no longer wrote

[1] See above, p. 10.

in this way. Close attention to passages of this kind must certainly increase the reader's delight in *Paracelsus,* and surely lead the way to a better understanding of criticisms that followed hard upon the poem's publication—to the point, possibly, of answering some of those that were adverse.

Paracelsus, Part II, begins with a soliloquy representing Paracelsus in distress over his misgivings regarding his attainment. Consequently, light is deliberately removed from the scene of his discouragement, "the house of a Greek Conjuror":

> Over the waters in the vaporous West   (1)
> The sun goes down as a sphere of gold
> Behind the arm of the city, which between,
> With all that length of domes and minarets,
> Athwart the splendour, black and crooked runs
> Like a Turk verse along a scimitar.
> There lie, sullen memorial, and no more
> Possess my aching sight!

The first suggestion of the star-image (if, indeed, it be the star at all, for it quickly changes into a different variety of the images of light) appears as a thing vaguely recalled, no longer shining clear before Paracelsus' once ardent eye:

> For some one truth would dimly beacon me   (161)
> From mountains rough with pines, and flit and wink
> O'er dazzling wastes of frozen snow, ...

The second instance, still within the limits of the abject soliloquy, is a reference, by verbal suggestion, to the star which he has forgotten:

> I never glanced behind to know   (183)
> If I had kept my primal light from wane,
> And thus insensibly am—what I am.

The "primal light" to which Paracelsus refers may be interpreted as a combination of the three stars of Part I: the star representing Paracelsus' human love for his friends, Festus and Michal, and their love for each other; the "star to men"; and the "speck" that "expands into a star." In his disillusionment these three have become indistinguishably merged, as the temper of the soliloquy requires. Paracelsus has set out upon the single course of *knowing;* he has attained *knowing,* but lost the capacity for human love. He has also lost the ardor of his original ambition. It is appropriate that in recalling these images from Part I, Browning should have chosen a phrase of suggestion, "primal light," rather than the actual word, "star," in a context which could not artistically accommodate the direct symbolic force of the very stars to which the "primal light" refers. Furthermore, the phrase is just vague enough not to point to any one of the three definitely, but only to recall them all dimly. Then Paracelsus' depression is relieved by the approach of Aprile

One of the most interesting examples of variation in the quality of symbolic suggestion possible in Browning's use of the star-image is the next instance:

> Or sapphirine spirit of a twilight star, (425)

which occurs in one of the speeches of Aprile, who becomes a dominant "character" in Part II. It is significant that this star is drawn from the realm of mythological fancy, for it is representative of the expansive and uncontrolled enthusiasm of Aprile, the image of one of the ardors for which he lacks the power of expression. The stars of Part I are full of imaginative import, but they are drawn quite frankly from nature itself; we can see them in the heavens. But it is altogether compatible with the nature of Paracelsus' development that, in the particular stage of his history that is set forth in Part II, he should mistake the star of fancy for the light of reality. He has set himself a goal of impossible and unreal accomplishment towards which he progresses with increasing fervor, only to discover later his impetuous blunder. Images of fancy belong to the state of mind thus represented in Paracelsus' unrestrained ambition.

So thoroughly hypnotized does he become, by the over-radiant presence of Aprile, that he forgets his momentary discouragement in the excitement of his illusion. He plunges deeper into the swirling fascination of Aprile's enthusiasm, overwhelmed by the too-ardent *Love* of this new-found spirit whose reality he was at first inclined to doubt. He even accepts Aprile as his guide.

> Even as a luminous haze links star to star, (476)

is a line drawn from Aprile's famous reply to Paracelsus' request: "Tell me what thou would'st be, and what I am." As it proceeds, Aprile's answer turns into a discourse upon the element of fancy in art. As the lines begin to center specifically upon the art of poetry, a more favorable conception of the value of fancy emerges in the part of the passage that contains the line quoted above:

> I would throw down the pencil as the chisel, (464)
> And I would speak; no thought which ever stirred
> A human breast should be untold; . . . . .
> . . . .
> And this in language as the need should be,
> Now poured at once forth in a burning flow,
> Now piled up in grand array of words.
> This done, to perfect and consummate all,
> Even as a luminous haze links star to star,
> I would supply all chasms with music, breathing
> Mysterious motions of the soul, no way
> To be defined save in strange melodies.

In the line that contains the image of the star, it is important to note that the "luminous haze" linking "star to star" is the more significant image in the simile, since its mistiness is sufficiently vague to suggest the "strange melodies" of which Aprile fondly dreams. Fancy can never be defined accurately, nor can its clearly limned image be found. Its meaning and quality can be known best through its associations with sharply drawn images, or through the pointed logic of critical discourse *about* it. Fancy is the "luminous haze" which Browning here associates with the specific star. In the process of achieving his effect he has produced another blend of images, in this instance recalling the association of light and music that we have noted previously in *Pauline.*

Anticipating the hopes of Browning's Sordello, Aprile continues to advance his artistic proposals; he imagines the ecstasy of his followers over the beauties he can assure them, for he would speed to the land whence he came, load his bark with the treasures of that wondrous realm:

> I would dispart the waves, and stand once more   (538)
> .At home, and load my bark, and hasten back,
> And fling my gains to them, worthless or true.
> "Friends," I would say, "I went far, far for them,
>
> . . . .
> "Till, by a mighty moon, I tremblingly
> "Gathered these magic herbs, berry and bud,
> "In haste, not pausing to reject the weeds,
>
> . . . .
> "They are scarce lovely: plait and wear them, you!
> "And guess, from what they are, the springs that fed them,
> "The stars that sparkled o'er them night by night,
> "The snakes that traveled far to sip their dew!"

In this instance the star is one of a rapid succession of images, metonymic in their suggestion of the realm of the marvelous, which at times, in Aprile's imagination at least, seems to be heaven itself. But the dominant image of the passage is the voyage and return from the enchanted region; the "bark," the "waves," and the picturesque landscape.

Paracelsus, Part III, is a book of revelation or of self-realization. It represents Paracelsus' supreme effort to distinguish between the truth and the illusion in his mind; it is his confession, his struggle to cleanse his soul of misconception that he may accomplish his regeneration. Aprile's fascination has led him to imitative extremes; the sheer ignorance of fools, his followers, has set his brains awhirl with ironical disgust. He has condemned the stupidity of men for being incapable of distinguishing between Paracelsus the clown and Paracelsus the superior intellect, and the confusion has entered his own mind. The first image of the star in Part III:

> Saw in the stars mere garnishry of heaven,   (183)

marks one of the important aspects of his regeneration: a return to sympathy for the lives of simple men. While the passage in which this image occurs is in part a condemnation of the uninformed innocence of natural man, it is also a recognition of Paracelsus' wistful discovery that he can no longer understand mankind, and that simple human nature possesses something that he has lost: the impulse to adore Nature's beauty. He has forgotten the star of peace which he promised himself to remember; he can no longer take comfort in human love, for he has been blinded by the over-radiant Love of Aprile.

An interesting double force of imagery may be felt in this passage. Here Browning has so combined plot and methods of presentation that, before this image, we ourselves must choose to be simple men (praising only the "garnishry" of poetry), knowing men (who, like Paracelsus, have stifled an inborn delight in natural beauty), or perceiving men (in whom both knowing and loving have been brought into luminous harmony).

> True, laughter like my own must echo strangely   (176)
> To thinking men; a smile were better far;
> So, make me smile! If the exulting look
> You wore but now be smiling, 'tis so long
> Since I have smiled! Alas, such smiles are born
> Alone of hearts like yours, or herdsmen's souls
> Of ancient time, whose eyes, calm as their flocks,
> Saw in the stars mere garnishry of heaven,
> And in earth a stage for altars only.
> Never change, Festus: I say, never change!

Here the star regains its reality; it is again in heaven, even though simple men cannot imagine its marvelous truth. But Paracelsus in his superior knowledge cannot wonder at the star's beauty with the calm eyes of natural man.

Following the lines quoted above a number of verbal connotations sustain the image of the star: "Dazzled by your resplendent course" (195) reveals Festus' fond opinion that Paracelsus has actually become "a star to men"; "the false glare that confounds A weaker vision" (206) is Paracelsus' opinion of himself; "the fallen prince of morning some short space Remained unchanged in semblance" (222) compares Paracelsus' fall to the fall of Satan; "rush upon a mad And ruinous course" (239) again suggesting the fall of Satan, is otherwise self-explanatory of Paracelsus' career; "this one man Could never lose the light thus from the first His portion" (247) declares Paracelsus' belief in Festus. The specific return of the star-image does not take place, however, until the moment of its most interesting triple appearance in the passage that concludes Part III. I shall take the liberty of quoting this passage at length, since it will show in its entirety many of the characteristics of Browning's use of the star-image, which, the reader will agree, could not be demonstrated as well in shorter pieces drawn from this context:

> *Festus.* . . . . . Best ope the casement: see,
> The night, late strewn with clouds and flying stars,
> Is blank and motionless: how peaceful sleep
> The tree-tops altogether! Like an asp,
> The wind slips whispering from bough to bough.
> *Paracelsus.* Ay, you would gaze on a wind-shaken tree
> By the hour, nor count time lost.

Festus.   So you shall gaze:
Those happy times will come again.
Paracelsus.   Gone, gone,
Those pleasant times! Does not the moaning wind
Seem to bewail that we have gained such gains
And bartered sleep for them?
Festus.   It is our trust
That there is yet another world to mend
All error and mischance.
Paracelsus.   Another world!
And why this world, this common world, to be
A make-shift, a mere foil, how fair soever,
To some fine life to come? Man must be fed
With angels' food, forsooth; and some few traces
Of a diviner nature which look out
Through his corporeal baseness, warrant him
In a supreme contempt of all provision
For his inferior tastes—some straggling marks
Which constitute his essence, just as truly
As here and there a gem would constitute
The rock, their barren bed, one diamond.
But were it so—were man all mind—he gains
A station little enviable. From God
Down to the lowest spirit ministrant,
Intelligence exists which casts our mind
Into immeasurable shade. No, no:
Love, hope, fear, faith—these make humanity;
These are its sign and note and character,
And these I have lost!—gone, shut from me forever,
Like a dead friend safe from unkindness more!
See, morn at length. The heavy darkness seems
Diluted, grey and clear without the stars;
The shrubs bestir and rouse themselves as if
Some snake, that weighed them down all night, let go
His hold; and from the East, fuller and fuller,
Day, like a mighty river, flowing in;
But clouded, wintry, desolate and cold.
Yet see how that broad prickly star-shaped plant,
Half-down in the crevice, spreads its woolly leaves
All thick and glistening with diamond dew.
And you depart for Einsiedeln this day,
And we have spent all night in talk like this!
If you would have me better for your love,
Revert no more to these sad themes.
Festus.   One favour,
And I have done. I leave you deeply moved;
Unwilling to have fared so well, the while
My friend has changed so sorely. If this mood
Shall pass away, if light once more arise
Where all is darkness now, if you see fit
To hope and trust again, and strive again,

You will remember—not our love alone—
But that my faith in God's desire that man
Should trust on his support, (as I must think
You trusted) is obscured and dim through you:
For you are thus, and this is no reward.
Will you not call me to your side, dear Aureole?

These lines conclude Part III of Browning's *Paracelsus*. They follow the long conversation with Festus in which Paracelsus laments the distress of soul that he has brought upon himself. He condemns himself, admits his failure, belittles the honors that have come to him, longs for God's help, but bitterly doubts there is such a thing, tells of his attempt to live as Aprile did, for *love*. His brow is hot, his eye languid, the "plague" has touched him. Festus meanwhile has tried to comfort him, but without success. He tells Paracelsus he has been brave; that his misgivings are shadows:

The weakness you reveal endears you more,   (865)

But Paracelsus will not be comforted. He says:

Come, I will show you where my merit lies.   (870)
'Tis in the advance of individual minds
That the slow crowd should ground their expectation
Eventually to follow; as the sea
Waits ages in its bed till some one wave
Out of the multitudinous mass, extends
The empire of the whole, some feet perhaps
Over the strip of sand which could confine
Its fellows so long time: . . . .
. . . .
. . . . The old dull question   (921)
In a new form; no more. Thus: I possess
Two sorts of knowledge, one—vast, shadowy,
Hints of the unbounded aim I once pursued:
The other consists of many secrets, caught
While bent on nobler prize,—perhaps a few
Prime principles which may conduct to much:

Thus Paracelsus and Festus have worn out the night. The setting of Part III is: "Basil; a chamber in the house of Paracelsus, 1526," and the first line, spoken by Paracelsus, is:

Heap logs and let the blaze laugh out!

It is his blazing soul which has laughed out during the night. Now it has spent itself in talk:

Paracelsus.   'Tis the melancholy wind astir   (997)
Within the trees; the embers too are grey:
Morn must be near.

Then follows the long passage quoted above, lines 999-1057.

Preliminary to a detailed discussion of this passage I have thought it well to recall its position in the poem by means of additional quotations and explanations. If it were not inconsiderate of the reader, it would be appropriate, at this point, to summarize the content of Parts I, II, and III. It is not possible to estimate the importance of the images of the star here displayed without observing their relation to the structure of the poem as a whole, certainly not without reference to the design of the particular division of the poem in which they occur.

It is true that such lines as:

> The night, late strewn with clouds and flying stars,   (1000)
> Is blank and motionless:

possess, intrinsically, the quality of picturesque description, but it is only when they are structurally related to other parts of the poem that they may be regarded as an image of Paracelsus' state of mind at a particular stage in the history which Robert Browning has imagined. In a passage preceding these lines, Paracelsus has described the results of his audacious quest as the discovery of two kinds of knowledge: one, "vast and shadowy"—"strewn with clouds"—; the other, "secrets, caught while bent on nobler prize"— "flying stars." Now both kinds have been reduced through his sheer mental exhaustion to something "blank and motionless." Paracelsus approaches a new dawn with a mind "Diluted, grey," but "clear without the stars." His new day flows in, "clouded, wintry, desolate, and cold," but with enough light to enable him to see himself again as a creature of earth:

> Yet see how that broad prickly star-shaped plant,   (1039)
> Half-down in the crevice, spreads its woolly leaves
> All thick and glistering with diamond dew.

Of greatest significance is the shape of the plant; "star-shaped." The iteration of the star-image in *Paracelsus* has, by the end of Part III, signaled its importance. The "star-shaped plant" therefore becomes more than an ornamental detail in the description of a wintry dawn. It is a symbolic image; a weed wearing the shape of aspiration (Paracelsus would become "a star to men"). It is a creature of earth, bound in a crevice, but spreading its leaves which glister "with diamond dew." It is Paracelsus himself, and at the same time a symbol of hope that light once more may shine "Where all is darkness now, ..." Consequently, we have been prepared by this image for the subtitle of Part IV, "Paracelsus Aspires," and for its opening phrase:

> *Sic itur ad astra!*   (1)

It is obviously not the image of the "star-shaped plant" alone that makes this preparation effective, for other images and "meanings" in the passage have had their share. In point of fact, another of the characteristics of the plant-image is that it combines within itself at least three of the prominent images of the passage: the star, which occurs specifically three times; the gem ("diamond dew"), which occurs twice; the plant, which occurs four times ("tree-tops," "wind-shaken tree," "shrubs," "star-shaped plant"). By association it may even suggest the "asp," which describes the wind slipping from bough to bough, and the "snake" that has let go his hold upon the shrubs.

For the purposes of the present discussion, however, I think it would be better to draw the line of association short of the last suggestion (the "asp" and the "snake"). I mention it here as evidence of the more subtle implications that Browning's imagery produces for the reader who becomes even partially aware of its structural and symbolic import. The more clearly specified relationships, such as those with the star, the gem, and the plant, are sufficient proof that Browning has here woven his images into a complicated pattern representing the complexities of his thought. A certain notable passage, beginning at line 433 of *Paracelsus,* Part I, assures us that Browning was quite conscious of the advantages of this method to his artistic purpose. In poetry its effect is, ideally, to increase the force of various images by causing their powers and their meanings to unite cumulatively at one point in the poem. When Browning over-indulges his pleasure in this practice, the result is obscurity.

Another sort of artistic relationship is implicit in the image of the "star-shaped plant," if our interpretation of its symbolic meaning be correct: a creature of earth wearing the shape of aspiration, for this interpretation coincides with the literal meaning of the following quotation:

> Man must be fed   (1014)
> With angels' food, forsooth; and some few traces
> Of a diviner nature which look out
> Through his corporeal baseness, warrant him
> In a supreme contempt of all provision
> For his inferior tastes—some straggling marks
> Which constitute his essence,

Indeed it is possible to use these lines as an authority for the correctness of our interpretation of the plant's symbolic force. The relationship produced is therefore not only one of image with image, but also one of image with intellectual content. The example represents new evidence in support of the idea that Browning's use of imagery is both structurally and symbolically significant.

One of the most characteristic details of this fusion or blending of images in *Paracelsus* is the combination, water and light. Perhaps the clearest example of it is the comparison, in the passage we have been discussing, in which "day" is represented as flowing in "like a mighty river." This example naturally recalls others, especially the passage in Part I on the nature of truth, in which the light of the star is fused with the flowing of water. An examination of all of the images in *Paracelsus* would reveal a great number of such combinations and the recurrence of their similar patterns. The total effect of this artistic practice is to produce a structural unity that complements the logical and narrative unity of plot, with the result that various divisions of the poem not only draw closer together, but actually blend or fuse in the reader's mind. The characteristics of the imagery in the passage that includes the next appearance of the star-image suggest the probable correctness of these rather general observations. The likelihood of one passage's recalling another is more clearly demonstrated in this example than in the one last noted. Not only the blending or fusion of images, but also other modifications in Browning's use of imagery, such as the cluster and the swift succession of images, are responsible for making the recall possible.

The passage to which I refer is a song in *Paracelsus,* Part IV:

> Over the sea our galleys went,   (450)
> With cleaving prows in order brave
> To a speeding wind and a bounding wave,
>   A gallant armament:
> Each bark built out of a forest-tree

continuing to a conclusion that contrasts sharply with the bounding enthusiasm of the opening lines, a finale of hopeless disillusionment. The mariners, who had set out so hopefully, discover they have delivered the treasures of their barks to those who cannot appreciate or enjoy them:

> O then we awoke with a sudden start   (515)
> From our deep dream, and knew, too late,
> How bare the rock, how desolate
> Which had received our precious freight:

Three star-images have been set into the song. The discussion of their more particular values may be withheld for the moment to permit our observing the association of this song with a passage that has been mentioned previously and which we may call The Voyage of Aprile, as the song before us may be called The Voyage of Paracelsus. Star-images in both voyages first suggest the comparison. It may be convenient to set down a few of their similarities side by side.

Part II, 534-553	Part IV, 450-522
The Voyage of Aprile	— The Voyage of Paracelsus
The stars that sparkled o'er them, night by night,	— starshine—twilight star So the stars wheeled round
bark	— bark
When nights were still, and still the moaning sea,	— the night-wind blew like breath,
And far away I could descry the land	— Now, one morn, land appeared— a speck
dispart the waves	— With cleaving prows
Till, by a mighty moon, I tremblingly Gathered these magic herbs,	— moonlight, cold which maketh mad,
my gains	— precious freight:

Thus, having followed the suggestion of the star-image to examine the relationship that might exist between similar passages in which the star occurs, we find that not only this image, but that several others join the two voyages unmistakably. As a result, the structural function of Browning's imagery becomes clearer. When the reader joins them in his mind, each voyage makes the meaning of the other more significant; the intellectual content of the poem becomes more emphatic, the force of the imagery more insistent, the image-pattern more stimulating. The Voyage of Aprile is a projection of the mind never fully realized; it is what Aprile *would* do if he *could,* "I *would* dispart the waves." It is an image of the personality of Aprile. The Voyage of Paracelsus is the image of Paracelsus' accomplishment ("Over the seas our galleys *went*") and failure. Both voyages end in failure: the second, because the treasure of the barks has been placed where it can do no good. Thus *Love* (or ardor) without knowledge is powerless to act, and *Knowing* without love lacks direction for its energy. These are the failures of Love without power and of Knowledge without beauty. The distinction between Aprile and Paracelsus becomes clear, the unity of the poem is strengthened; the reader becomes more fully aware that Browning "thinks in images."[2]

The three star-images in the Voyage of Paracelsus hold significant positions. The care with which they have been placed in these stanzas moves the reader to join them in his imagination to the general company of stars in whose symbolic force he has begun to see something quite superior to "mere garnishry" of poetry. At first sight, however, the three star-images before us merely delight with their descriptive beauty:

> That neither noontide nor starshine   (467)

simply specifies a quality of light;

> Each helm made sure by the twilight star,   (477)

is an appropriately nautical explanation and description;

> So the stars wheeled round, and the darkness passed,   (484)

picturesquely denotes the passing of night. Considered thus, individually, these star-images seem hardly to possess anything more than ornamental values; but, when associated with the cluster of images that inform the Song, the heightened poetical effect that the star-images assist in producing is clearly recognizable. They not only emphasize the nautical nature of the adventure, because of their inevitable relationship to the life of the mariner, but they assist in giving a general tone of buoyancy and joy to the spirit in which the voyage is undertaken. That this opinion is correct may be inferred by

---

[2] Paul de Reul, p. 126, "Ce tempérament realiste a horreur de l'expression vague, terne, abstraite. Les images lui sont aussi nécessaires que les mots et complètent son vocabulaire comme de nouveaux synonymes. Browning pense en images et tient moins à leur grâce qu'à leur vérité." *Ibid.,* p. 130, "Précisément parce qu'il pense par images, comme l'artiste pense par formes plastique, l'image et le sens, la forme et l'idée sont chez lui unies et non juxtaposées."

observing that, as the voyage approaches its desolate conclusion, the stars no longer appear. Browning has set them in the first half of the Song in which the hearty exuberance of the mariners is dominant. Again his star-images have been composed according to the laws of artistic design.

In Part V Paracelsus' regeneration is finally achieved; he "attains," once and for all time. The first star-image in this division of the poem marks the beginning of a sequence of four that occur in the first two hundred and eleven lines. When it is observed that the other three star-images of Part V occur in the last one hundred and sixty-two lines, with a passage of more than five hundred lines separating the two sequences, we are curious to know the structural considerations that may have determined the poet's having so disposed them.

An examination of the logical structure of the first division of Part V shows the artistic coincidence of the meaning of the star-images and intellectual thesis of this part of the poem. A brief outline of lines 1-211 should help to clarify this remark:

> Festus speaks:
> A. Paracelsus fought for his life (his ideal) to the last, but now he is ruined and dying.   (1-11)
> B. Paracelsus is forgotten; even his innumerable "little" enemies forget to gloat over his defeat.   (12-17)
> C. His struggle has been intense, but he has resigned himself to defeat and death.   (18-35)
> *D. Had God helped him, he who was earth's noblest might have become a "star to men."   (36-65)
> E. But I (Festus) am foolish to doubt God's love and God's way. Save him, dear God!   (66-79)
> F. Now that he wakens from his troubled sleep, I must force him to recognize me, his friend; but, no, it shall be as God directs.   (80-106)
>
> Paracelsus speaks:
> *G. I still have hope that in death, I may become a star, freighted with light, as Aprile was filled with magical music.   (107-109)
> H. I curse my fate and Aprile's that we were both struck down when about to crown our labors.   (120-128)
> I. You mocking fiends of Hell! my very failure is your defeat, for men have learned not to be like me; you will not find another like me to torment.   (129-157)
> J. To be sure I *have* achieved; I have shaken men's reverence for those Arabs, Jews, Latins, and Greeks who joined dead hands against me. I have topped Galen's crown.   (158-185)
> *K. "Oh, emptiness of fame! Oh Persic Zoroaster, lord of stars!"   (186-204)
>
> Festus speaks:
> *L. Paracelsus will yet see the light; he will penetrate the gloom as "A soft star trembles through the drifting clouds."   (205-211)

In the light of the context these images become eloquent expressions of the thoughts of Festus and Paracelsus on the threshold of spiritual triumph:

> Festus. . . . .   (62)
> How could he stop at every step to set
> Thy glory forth? Hadst thou but granted him
> Success, thy honour would have crowned success,
> A halo round a star. Or, say he erred;—
> Save him, dear God; it will be like thee: bathe him
> In light and life!

This is the image of what Paracelsus might have been: "a star to men" crowned with God's halo. This interpretation may be proved reliable, I think, by referring to the image in Part I in which Paracelsus' ambition is first imaginatively recognized:

> Know, not for knowing's sake,   (Part I, 527)
> But to become a star to men forever;

but Paracelsus has not given up hope completely; in his dying confession he sees and "hears" visions. He dreams of Aprile:

> Paracelsus.   Festus! Where's   (109)
> Aprile, then? Has he not chanted softly
> The melodies I hear all night? I could not
> Get to him for a cold hand on my breast,
> But I made out his music well enough,
> O well enough! If they have filled him full
> With magical music, as they freight a star
> With light, and have remitted all his sin,
> They will forgive me too, I too shall know.

Music and light have been symbolically related, the music of Aprile's Love and the light of Paracelsus' Knowing. The lines recall the blending of light and melody in Pauline (lines 201-229) with the essential difference, however, that this instance is an attempt to bring the two ideas together without losing the distinction between them, rather than a deliberate confusion of music and light. It would be symbolically incorrect to allow the distinction between the personalities of Aprile and Paracelsus to be lost in the temptation to produce even the harmonious blending which would result from the fusion of these images. In his extremity Paracelsus longs for a glory similar to, but not identical with that which he imagines Aprile to have attained, for he continues to recognize the fundamental differences between his and Aprile's character. The first image in the sequence was a symbol of what might have been; this, the second, is the image of what may still be.

The third image in the sequence may be interpreted as the sign of what has been, as we shall note that the fourth clearly represents what is still to be. Certain difficulties nevertheless attend the analysis and the interpretation of the third image, for it points not only to achievement, but also to states of mind and character often associated with attainment; a consciousness of fame and a feeling of pride. These meanings in the image, which come principally from the particular context in which it appears, are then confused with associations that are bound to attach themselves to the image itself:

> Oh Persic Zoroaster, lord of stars!   (187)

Thus, by the use of the name "Zoroaster" the idea of legendary celebrity at once rises in the reader's mind, but the apparent definiteness of the image gives rise shortly to the confusion of attempting to decide which one, or how many, of the attributes of Zoroaster Browning means to suggest. For it will be seen quickly that Zoroaster himself, rather than the stars that he rules, usurps the symbolic majesty of the line. In the light of the context preceding the image, one of the achievements of Zoroaster stands as the most appropriate meaning. It is Zoroaster's victory over falsehood. For him Ormazd, lord of Light, was, by the same token, lord of Truth, opposed to the forces of darkness and falsehood, the essence of evil. The old religion which Zoroaster reformed recognized two forms of divinity, the Asuradaiva: Asura, the sublime divinity; Daiva, the anthropomorphic deity. For Zoroaster the daevas, or popular gods, had sunk to the level of the true enemies of mankind. He unmasked their falsehood, declared their worshipers idolators and heretics. Thus he destroyed a popular conception of belief, just as Paracelsus prides himself upon having annihilated the idols of "science." "Where, now, is their fame!"

In order to confirm this interpretation, I have drawn several passages from the context that leads to the image of Zoroaster. While Festus patiently regards his friend's delirium, Paracelsus wrenches the words from his weakened body. With the lustre of Aprile's over-radiance once more firing his senses, Paracelsus' brain burns with pride and arrogant self-pity. In such a state of mind he turns his humiliation into an ironical boast which is to resolve finally into the comparison of himself with Zoroaster:

> Listen: there's shame and hissing and contempt   (139)
> And none but laughs who names me, none but spits
> Measureless scorn upon me, me alone,
> The quack, the cheat, the liar,—all on me!

To the fiends of hell who have accomplished his ruin he cries,

> Try now, persuade some other to slave for you,   (154)
> To ruin body and soul to work your ends!
> No, No; I am the first and last, I think—

Turning to his more positive achievements he claims victory over the tribe of Galen:

> Just think, Aprile, all these leering dotards   (177)
> Were bent on nothing less than to be crowned
> As we! That yellow blear-eyed wretch in chief
> To whom the rest cringe low with feigned respect,
> Galen of Pergamos and hell—nay speak

> The tale, old man! We met there face to face;
> I said the crown should fall from thee. Once more
> We meet as in that ghastly vestibule:
> Look to my brow! Have I redeemed my pledge?
> *Festus.* Peace, peace; ah, see!
> *Paracelsus.* Oh emptiness of fame!
> Oh Persic Zoroaster, lord of stars!
> —Who said these old renowns, dead long ago,
> Could make me overlook the living world
> To gaze through gloom at where they stood indeed,
> But stand no longer?

The rage passes; Festus hopes once more. The fourth image of light reveals what is to be:

> *Festus.* A light (205)
> Will struggle through these thronging words at last,
> As in the angry and tumultuous West
> A soft star trembles through the drifting clouds.

There can be no doubt in our minds as to the interpretation of this symbolic image. It is simple, clear, direct. Its position near the apostrophe to Zoroaster throws into sharp relief the distinctions between the simple image and the image of complicated significance. The contrast in the reader's reactions is similar. The image of a "soft star" at once illuminates its context, while the image of "Zoroaster, lord of stars!" must be illuminated, either by its context or by a note commenting upon the meaning of "Zoroaster." The descriptive qualities of the "soft star" are excellent, while it is doubtful whether the "lord of stars" presents any very definite picture.

In the paragraphs above I have suggested the difficulty of selecting from a number of possible interpretations the one which seemed most plausible for "Oh Persic Zoroaster"; for the "soft star" image I find without difficulty several meanings all of equal and illuminating importance: it signifies Festus' hope that out of the confused ravings of a dying man peace will come at last; it promises final power to Paracelsus to shine through the clouds that have shrouded his life in gloom; it signals that the words Paracelsus is about to speak will be worth attention, that his thoughts are becoming clear, his mind alert. Finally, this fourth star of the sequence in the first division of Part V prepares the way for the noble "lecture" which is to follow, Paracelsus' magnificent spiritual triumph; it recalls the calm luminescence of Paracelsus' original ambition, to become a "star to men." It assures us that his final acts will be illuminated with its steady ray, freed from the influence of Aprile's over-radiance. In structural importance it transcends its immediate context to become one of the great unifying elements of the poem as a whole. It is an organic image.

It will be unnecessary to outline the last division of Part V as we did the first, for the images of light it contains are, when interpreted, a sufficient indication of its content.

> While only here and there a star dispels   (746)

represents the final sober judgment of Paracelsus at the conclusion of his "lecture" to Festus. He maintains that man progresses towards the realization of Man, though the way is long, the task laborious. The hope of mankind is clear in the rise of certain individuals, "stars to men," who increasingly dispel the darkness:

> With apprehension of his passing worth,   (739)
> Desire to work his proper nature out
> And ascertain his rank and final place,
> For these things tend still upward, progress is
> The law of life, man is not Man as yet.
> Nor shall I deem his object served, his end
> Attained, his genuine strength put fairly forth,
> While only here and there a star dispels
> The darkness, here and there a towering mind
> O'erlooks its prostrate fellows: when the host
> Is out at once to the despair of night,
> When all mankind alike is perfected,
> Equal in full-blown powers,—then, not till then,
> I say, begins man's general infancy.

The sustaining force of verbal connotations of the star may be noted in the diction of lines within and beyond the above quotation:

> . . . . a towering mind   (747)
> O'erlooks its prostrate fellows: when the host
> Is out at once to the despair of night,

> . . . . Prognostics told   (773)
> Man's near approach; so in man's self arise
> August anticipations, symbols, types
> Of a dim splendour ever on before
> In that eternal circle life pursues.

> . . . truth avails not wholly to disperse   (792)
> The flitting mimic called up by itself,
> And so remains perplexed and nigh put out
> By its fantastic fellow's wavering gleam.

Nor should the effect of verbal connotations preparatory to the appearance of the star-image go unmentioned. Several of them are of a texture so delicate as to forbid extraction from the text, but one at least is clear in its self-contained brilliance:

> *Paracelsus.* . . . . thus I entered on my course.   (627)
> You may be sure I was not all exempt
> From human trouble; just so much of doubt
> As bade me plant a surer foot upon
> The sun-road, kept my eye unruined 'mid
> The fierce and flashing splendour,

the image of the "sun-treader."

In the last literal designation of the star-image:

As from the over-radiant star too mad   (889)

stands the symbol of Paracelsus' recognition of himself and Aprile. He declares he has mistaken Aprile's extreme ardor for love, and that he has mistaken his own impetuous learning for knowledge. Truth he saw but dimly. Such truth as he now possesses he declares in the last lines of the poem:

Let men   (885)

> Regard me, and the poet dead long ago
> Who loved too rashly; and shape forth a third
> And better-tempered spirit, warned by both:
> As from the over-radiant star too mad
> To drink the life-springs, beamless thence itself—
> And the dark orb which borders the abyss
> Ingulfed in icy night,—might have its course
> A temperate and equidistant world.
> Meanwhile, I have done well, though not all well.
> As yet men cannot do without contempt;
> 'T is for their good, and therefore fit awhile
> That they reject the weak, and scorn the false,
> Rather than praise the strong and true in me:
> But after, they will know me. If I stoop
> Into a dark tremendous sea of cloud,
> It is but for a time; I press God's lamp
> Close to my breast; its splendour, soon or late,
> Will pierce the gloom: I shall emerge one day.
> You understand me? I have said enough?
> *Festus.*   Now die, dear Aureole!
> *Paracelsus.*   Festus, let my hand—
> This hand lie in your own, my own true friend!
> Aprile! hand in hand with you Aprile!
> *Festus.*   And this was Paracelsus!

The observer will be attracted at once to what is probably the final image of the star in *Paracelsus*: "I press God's lamp Close to my breast" as quoted above. In its context, and because of its association with the "dark tremendous sea of cloud," this image instantly unifies the poem by hurling the reader's enchanted mind back through the clouds of Paracelsus' aspirations, strivings, and partial attainments. The vision is one of the past, the present, and the future of Paracelsus' life suddenly becoming one. Considered somewhat more narrowly these lines are a fulfillment of the words of Festus (lines 205-211, Part V):

> *Festus.*   A light
> Will struggle through these thronging words at last.
> As in the angry and tumultuous West
> A soft star trembles through the drifting clouds.
> These are the strivings of a spirit which hates
> So sad a vault should coop it, and calls up
> The past to stand between it and its fate.

The absolute coincidence of imagery and logical division, which the evidence before us shows to be a characteristic of the design of *Paracelsus,* throws into sharp relief our conclusions regarding the imagistic pattern of *Pauline.* However, during the process of analyzing the functions and the qualities of the star-images in *Paracelsus* our observations have led us again and again to note similarities in design between the imagistic patterns of *Pauline* and *Paracelsus.* Admitting, of course, the particular differences of effect toward which the two poems aim, we have been aware, nevertheless, of conformations in pattern and technique. The method of preparing the way for the appearance of the star, or for holding it in the reader's attention after it has appeared, by means of a careful selection of suggestive or connotative words, is employed in both poems. Similarly, the star-images assume, in both poems, a high degree of structural and symbolic importance, through their frequent iteration. But in spite of these similarities we have been conscious, also, of a distinct difference, in the controlling literary forms of the two poems, which has undoubtedly affected a change in the poet's uses of, and the reader's reactions to the imagery of *Pauline,* a confessional poem, and the imagery of *Paracelsus,* a dramatic poem.

A discussion of the star-images in *Strafford,* the next work which will require analysis, presents the occasion for a somewhat more pointed conclusion regarding the relationship of the star-image to the dramatic form of *Paracelsus.* A comparison of *Paracelsus* and *Strafford* points to a contrast in dramatic form. In *Strafford,* the work of lesser distinction, we behold the type of play that fulfills perfectly the mid-nineteenth century requirements for the more "noble" form of drama, in everything except the theatrical success of a profitable run. It was a play whose form corresponded well enough to the current imitative convention of Shakespearean drama. In *Paracelsus* we recognize a work of art which refuses classification except in the terms of its author. However, if the phrase "closet drama" should be applied to either of these works, it would suit *Paracelsus* better than *Strafford.* For *Strafford* the phrase would merely imply, euphemistically, that a play intended for the stage was unfit for the stage.

There is an interesting difference between *Strafford* and *Paracelsus* that Browning has mentioned in his preface to the original edition of *Strafford* in 1837:

> I had for some time been engaged in a Poem [presumably *Sordello*] of a very different nature, when induced to make the present attempt; and am not without apprehension that my eagerness to freshen a jaded mind by diverting it to the healthy natures of a grand epoch, may have operated unfavorably on the represented play, which is one of Action in Character, rather than Character in Action.

For the purpose of making a sharp critical distinction between the two kinds of dramatic writing, represented, respectively, by *Paracelsus* and *Strafford,* the phrases Browning has used are of almost no assistance. The point to be noted is that he did wish to recognize the difference critically, however unsatisfactory the phrases "Action in Character" and "Character in Action" may be. Indeed, the phrase "Action in Character," which I interpret to mean action *within* character, suits better the type of drama represented in *Paracelsus;* it implies a course of action marked by the episodes occurring within the theatre of an individual soul, in contradistinction to a course of action represented by the conflict of many characters on the physical stage. It is a phrase, therefore, that explains why Browning should have declared of *Pauline* in 1867: "The thing was my earliest attempt at 'poetry always dramatic in principle, and so many utterances of so many imaginary persons not mine,' which I have since written according to a scheme less extravagant and scale less impracticable than were adventured in this crude preliminary sketch."[3] By its focus of attention upon the conflicts within a single personality *Paracelsus* may be distinguished from modern "psychological drama" which often depends for its effects upon the interaction of many psychological types, or "characters," and even upon an abundance of physical movement.

To an author familiar with the Greek language the essential meaning of the word "drama" would be "action"; from the poet capable of the supreme literary novelty of a *Sordello* an unusual conception of drama is to be expected. The objection, therefore, that since so much of the character of Robert Browning is revealed in *Paracelsus* the poem cannot be dramatic at all, is not really an objection but a recognition of one of the qualities which marks the difference between Browning's earlier and some of his later compositions "dramatic in principle." If *Paracelsus* were nothing but Browning, as it certainly is not, conflict and action would remain in full vigor, for there is abundant drama of this sort within the personality of the young poet.

Browning's artistic problem in writing *Paracelsus* was therefore one of devising the means of expression, rather than of deciding upon the nature of the content which should fill a ready-made form. The "characters" of the conventional drama, who, by their action on the stage, produce the image of dramatic conflict, could not be well adapted to a kind of drama that concentrated upon the inner conflict of one character. Imagery of another sort, poetical rather than conventionally theatrical, would better supply the want of vivid and concrete projection. The result is a new form of dramatic poetry. To confirm this opinion we have only to turn to *Strafford,* the conventional play, to find so complete a repression of poetical imagery as to suggest, by comparison with the imagery of *Paracelsus,* a virtual elimination of that mode of expression.

With these observations in mind we may well conclude our examination of the star-image in *Paracelsus* with Browning's very interesting preface to the

---

[3] *Pauline,* Author's Preface to the Edition of 1868.

first edition of the poem. Both for its illuminating suggestions, and because of its infrequent accessibility in complete form, I shall quote the preface in full from the edition: *Paracelsus. By Robert Browning.* London: Published by Effingham Wilson, Royal Exchange. MDCCCXXXV.

"I am anxious that the reader should not, at the very outset,—mistaking my performance for one of a class with which it has nothing in common,— judge it by principles on which it was never moulded, and subject it to a standard to which it was never meant to conform. I therefore anticipate his discovery, that it is an attempt, probably more novel than happy, to reverse the method usually adopted by writers whose aim it is to set forth any phenomenon of the mind or the passions, by the operation of persons and events; and that, instead of having recourse to an external machinery of incidents to create and evolve the crisis I desire to produce, I have ventured to display somewhat minutely the mood itself in its rise and progress, and have suffered the agency by which it is influenced and determined, to be generally discernible in its effects alone, and subordinate throughout, if not altogether excluded: and this for a reason. I have endeavored to write a poem, not a drama; the canons of drama are well known, and I cannot but think that, inasmuch as they have immediate regard to stage representation, the peculiar advantages they hold out are really such only so long as the purpose for which they were at first instituted is kept in view. I do not very well understand what is called a Dramatic Poem, wherein all those restrictions only submitted to on account of compensating good in the original scheme are scrupulously retained, as though for some special fitness in themselves— and all new facilities placed at an author's disposal by the vehicle he selects, as pertinaciously rejected. It is certain, however, that a work like mine depends more immediately on the intelligence and sympathy of the reader for its success—indeed were my scenes stars it must be his co-operating fancy which, supplying all chasms, shall collect the scattered lights into one constellation— a Lyre or a Crown. I trust for his indulgence toward a poem which had not been imagined six months ago; and that even should he think slightingly of the present (an experiment I am in no case likely to repeat) he will not be prejudiced against other productions which may follow in a more popular, and perhaps less difficult form."   "15th March, 1835"

STRAFFORD, 1837

Browning's play, *Strafford,* was one of the "incidents" that interrupted his work on *Sordello*,[4] for in March, 1836, Browning was hailed by John Forster,

[4] Probably, not only *Strafford* but *Paracelsus* as well, interrupted the composition of *Sordello*. In the Griffin and Minchin *The Life of Robert Browning,* New York, Macmillan Company, 1910, p. 89, the following statement occurs: "In April, 1835, in writing to Fox about the publication of *Paracelsus*, Browning remarked, 'I have another affair on hand rather of a more popular nature, I conceive; but not so decisive and explicit on a point or two, so I decide on trying the question with this.' "

in the *New Monthly Magazine,* in these words: "Mr. Browning has the powers of a great dramatic poet." Forster's enthusiasm was founded upon his interest in *Paracelsus,* and his desire to encourage the young poet was seconded by William Macready, the actor, who, in May of the same year, asked Browning to write him "a tragedy to save him from going to America."[5] The "tragedy" turned out to be *Strafford,* published three years before *Sordello.* Because it is related in this way, through a number of circumstances, to the success of *Paracelsus,* I have chosen to discuss the star-imagery of *Strafford* here, rather than in Chapter IV, "Browning's Plays." Furthermore, I should like to suggest that the observations I am about to present may be regarded as an extension of the discussion of *Paracelsus,* for *Strafford,* as a play and as an example of the poet's use of imagery, is an interesting contrast to *Paracelsus. Paracelsus* is the drama of "Action in Character" and *Strafford* is intended to be the drama of "Character in Action."

For the profuse poetical imagery of *Paracelsus* Browning has proposed to introduce into *Strafford* a more conventional and much less effective imagery that he evidently considered to be appropriate to compositions for the stage. That in making this change Browning was not following the natural course of his literary development may be seen as soon as one turns to the book of *Sordello,* or, indeed, to the pages of a hundred other poems composed after he had written *Strafford* and his other plays for the London theatre. A contrasting of the imagistic weakness of the three star-images in *Strafford* with the structural and symbolic force of the star-imagery of *Paracelsus* shows the result of this change clearly. The same opinion would hold, I think, were we to compare the effects of other images besides the star in these two works. Browning had come to a conclusion, it seems, perhaps more hastily than need be, that in a play of "Character in Action" the effects of poetical imagery should of necessity be ruled out, or at least diminished, to give full play to the dramatic imagery of scenes, characters, and the interaction of characters produced by the episodes of a plot suited to physical performance. It did not occur to him, as it did to Shakespeare, to use both. In a poetical drama of "Action in Character," such as *Paracelsus,* he had decided that the effects of poetical imagery were of utmost importance; for by means of the clear and concrete forms of poetical images he could represent the conflict of forces *within* his principal character and their impact upon each other.

But if the opinions held by the young poet are considered from a slightly different point of view, it will be seen that they are the expression of an aesthetic theory and of a consciousness of form in the mind of one who has been accused of having, particularly in his youth, no sense of form and little notion of the responsibility of an artist to produce form. That he may have been mistaken or uninformed in regard to his conceptions of form is an

---

[5] These and other facts related to the composition of *Strafford* are recorded in the Griffin and Minchin *The Life of Robert Browning,* 1910 edition, pp. 107-108.

opinion we may still be at liberty to hold, but that he was aesthetically irresponsible is, it seems to me, a mistaken idea. *Pauline,* as we have seen, is a poem with a design, unfamiliar and aesthetically odd to be sure, but not in every sense formless.

In the story of the composition of *Strafford,* could all the facts be known, there is a clear suggestion that we are dealing with a poet who had a lively sense of the importance of form. He is at least not only conscious of the demands of expression within a single form, but he is also aware of distinctions among kinds of form, as he understands them. He does not make the mistake of indulging his enthusiasm for poetic imagery when the task calls for something else. The three stars of *Strafford* are as significant in demonstrating Browning's aesthetic conscience, as they are insignificant to the play in which they occur.

For the sake of emphasis, I have suggested that the star-images of *Strafford* are in no sense important in their symbolic or structural function. It must be admitted, however, that the three star-images of the play are not without implications of both symbolic and structural significance. The discovery of these implications should be possible for the sensitive reader or playgoer, for it is not only by analysis that such effects of style become manifest. At any rate, my analysis of the nature of these images reveals symbolic effects of slightly more than incidental importance, and structural effects that qualify the poet's use of these images in the body of the play. They are ancillary rather than formative; they assist our understanding of human relationships, but they do not provoke our discovery of character, as the images of *Paracelsus* do.

Two of these images occur, most appropriately, in Act II, Scene ii, where they illuminate the sentiment of Lady Carlisle and Strafford. The third appears in a scene between Strafford and his children, Act V, Scene ii, "The Tower." In each instance they have been reserved for a particular use, a use which accords well with the conception which one is likely to form, through one's study of *Pauline* and *Paracelsus,* regarding the functions of the star-image.

> *Strafford, Act II, Scene ii*
> *Strafford.*   Child, your hair   (369)
> Is glossier than the Queen's!
> *Lady Carlisle.*   Is that to ask
> A curl of me?
> *Strafford.*   Scotland—the weary way!
> *Lady Carlisle.*   Stay, let me fasten it.
>   —A rival's, Strafford?
> *Strafford. (showing the George).*   He hung it there:
>   twine yours around it, child!
> *Lady Carlisle.*   No—no—another time—I trifle so!
> And there's a masque on foot. Farewell. The Court
> Is dull; do something to enliven us

In Scotland: we expect it at your hands.
   Strafford.   I shall not fail in Scotland.
   Lady Carlisle.   Prosper—if
You'll think of me sometimes!
   Strafford.   How think of him
And not of you? of you, the lingering streak
(A golden one) in my good fortune's eve.
   Lady Carlisle. Strafford . . . Well, when the eve
     has its last streak
The night has its first star.   (*She goes out.*)
   Strafford.   That voice of hers—
You'd think she had a heart sometimes! . . . .
   Curse nothing tonight! Only one name   (402)
They'll curse in all those streets to-night. Whose fault?
Did I make kings? Set up, the first, a man
To represent the multitude, receive
All love in right of them—supplant them so,
Until you love the man and not the king—
The man with the mild voice and mournful eyes
Which send me forth.
           —To breast the bloody sea
That sweeps before me: with one star for guide.
Night has its first, supreme, forsaken star.

She is the "lingering streak (A golden one)" in the evening of his life; her voice makes him "think she had a heart sometimes!" but she is not identified in his thoughts, nor in his heart, as a presence distinguishable from his regard for the King. He is night's first star; for her a specific entity, separable from all other stars in her affection. He accepts her designation of himself, as the final lines of the quotation disclose, but he is too thoroughly preoccupied with his loyalty to monarchy, and his conception of personal responsibility, to allow the tone of her language to entreat his affection. Consequently, a certain lyric quality accompanies the dramatic soliloquy spoken by Strafford after Lady Carlisle leaves him, her character having become the more charming through a delicacy of affection that restrains her from making an obvious declaration of her feelings.

Like Strafford, Browning accepts the star as a designation of his hero. He significantly causes it to appear in the second scene of Act V, in a setting whose dramatic and poetic qualities are strikingly similar to those of the scene from Act II. The dramatic situation ("The Tower. Strafford *sitting with his* Children. They sing.") at once inspires a flow of sentiment and an apprehension of approaching doom. The poetical manner in this scene is lyric; it begins with a song:

        O bell' andare   (V, 42)
        Per barca in mare,
        Verso la sera
        Di Primavera!

William.　The boat's in the broad moonlight all this while—
　　　　　Verso la sera
　　　　　Di Primavera!
And the boat shoots from underneath the moon
Into the shadowy distance; only still
You hear the dipping oar—
　　　　　Verso la sera,
And faint, and fainter, and then all's quite gone,
Music and light and all, like a lost star.

Here is the familiar association or blending of music and light reminiscent of the fusion of similar themes in *Pauline* and *Paracelsus;* here, also, is the image of twilight and evening star explicit in its recall of "fortune's eve" and night's "first, supreme, forsaken star," in the second scene of Act II. According to the demands of the plot, the star has changed: then it was rising; now it is lost! It is thus impossible not to see the structural and symbolic necessity that prescribes the use of these images. It is the privilege of the analyst to wrench two widely separated scenes from their natural positions, to place them side by side, in order to show the quality of their imagery; but it is doubtful whether an audience in the theatre could be expected to respond to the effects of imagery in a manner approximating the experience of one who is especially concerned to see these effects. On the other hand, it is the privilege of the playwright, especially if he be Robert Browning writing drama in blank verse, to introduce a lyric quality into the action, as he has done in these scenes, which, if capably expressed by the actor, would enhance the importance of everything that is done and said. Under the spell of action and dialogue that are both lyrically and dramatically moving, an audience would be inspired to see beyond, above, and around the literal meanings of the dialogue; so that it is quite possible to claim for the star-images of these two scenes a meaning that transcends the ordinary powers of descriptive imagery. So, at any rate, would our experience with *Pauline* and *Paracelsus* prompt us to imagine; but, even without such preparation, so would the charm of the barcarolle in the latter scene, with its repetition of the picture of twilight, mesmerize our sensibilities, for this song belongs to a scene that for a moment strangely suggests the symbolic style of the plays of Maeterlinck.

Even a casual consideration of these opinions must awaken our admiration for the care with which Robert Browning has deftly inserted the star-image where, in his belief, it will prove most effective, and where its situation is well suited to enhance its significance. The same control of artistic method is revealed in his selection and use of other images in the play. For his Puritans he evokes comparisons with Biblical characters: David, Jonathan, Ezekiel, Judas, and enlivens their speeches with the imagery of scriptural allusion. Above all, however, and in strict accord with the demands of our present analysis, the most noteworthy evidence of *Strafford* is its sharply diminished quantity of poetical imagery, a phenomenon which, when it is contrasted with the profuse imagery of *Pauline* and *Paracelsus,* looks like the poet's virtual abandonment of the poetical image as an artistic form. Here is the poet, whose earlier works sometimes give us the impression that he creates images for imagery's sake, abruptly checking his headlong course, suddenly restraining one of his most cherished delights in consistent agreement with the requirements of a form of expression that he attempts for the first time, proving himself, therefore, at least a technical master of the new form's limitations and possibilities, as he understands them. In *Sordello* his poetic imagery returns with a rush.

CHAPTER II

SORDELLO, BOOKS I, II, AND III

SINCE the time of its publication in 1840, Browning's *Sordello* has been the subject of many critical reviews, analyses, anecdotes, and jests. To one who in the present day would add to the body of commentary thus established comes the notion that the attitude with which one approaches the task is as important as the labor. Tradition has seemed to suggest that the critic shall be either excessively profound or wittily merry when he speaks of *Sordello*. Neither of these attitudes, it seems to me, can be suited to the form of the present investigation without strain and discomfort. If one decides to be profound, one must arrive solemnly at the conclusion that those who consider *Sordello* in any sense obscure are simply confessing their inability to read; if the critic chooses to be merry, he must somehow equal the witty observations of a Tennyson, a Lowell, or a Chesterton, the vitality of Mrs. Carlyle, the oppressed humor of Douglas Jerrold, or the urbanity of Professor Lounsbury. The amount of explanation and annotation that has been supplied *Sordello* (including the running commentary of Browning himself in the page-headings of the edition of 1863) is sufficient testimony to the essential complexity of the poem, even though such explanations have succeeded in removing much of the original obscurity. But so many difficulties remain, which must stand permanently in the way of the unqualified acceptance of *Sordello* as a supreme artistic achievement, that no real excuse may be offered for pretending their non-existence.

The complexities of *Sordello* must lead to difficulties in the analysis of its star-images. When these difficulties arise, they must be acknowledged, even though the course of the analysis may thus run into confusing complications. The poem must be faced as it is; its complexities regarded frankly as part of that which the poet has made. Consequently, while we may expect a degree of uncertainty to attend the formulation of some of the conclusions we shall want to draw, it will be necessary to follow the course clearly marked by the objectives before us.

The first general problem is one of form. No literary tradition guides us, as the dramatic tradition does in the instance of *Strafford*, to the discovery of the specific literary form of *Sordello*, unless it be a combination of forms such as those represented by *Aucassin et Nicolette*, Scott's *Marmion*, Carlyle's *History of the French Revolution*, and Dante's *Divine Comedy*, presumably reduced to unity through the instrument of the pentameter couplet. Within this enveloping form, or formlessness, three modes of discourse compete for supremacy: the narrative, the dramatic, and the mode of direct commentary. It is not only the novelty of Browning's invention that increases our perplexity, for we have seen a new form in his *Paracelsus* become acceptable through the clarity of its structural design, but it is also Browning's apparent disregard for the customary standards of organization, both in the general plan of the work and in the detail of organizing the single sentence, that often leads us into confusion. Furthermore, the narrative mode presents two kinds of content, which Browning has distinguished as the "historical decoration," and "incidents in the development of a soul"; the dramatic mode often enters either the historical or the spiritual narrative, and the direct commentary of the author interrupts both, in passages that range in length from a single line to half a book. In addition to these complications come such chronological rearrangements as the long address of Palma to Sordello in Book III, which, in point of time, precedes the action beginning at line 328 of Book I. Since one of the objects of the present analysis is to study the structural and organic functions of the star-image, it will be seen at once what difficulties may be expected to beset the work of investigation.

The second complication, to some degree explanatory of the first, is the history of the poem's composition. In my discussion of *Strafford* (pp. 42-43) a few of the details of this history have been introduced: the point, for example, that Browning's labors on *Strafford* interrupted his work on *Sordello,* and the note, which gives the opinion of Griffin and Minchin, that *Sordello* was actually begun before Browning composed *Paracelsus*. These and other items of a similar nature would be unimportant to the present study were it not that they help to explain the use of certain star-images whose irregularities seem to suggest they have no place in the poem.[1]

Among the singular incidents that interrupted Browning's progress with *Sordello* was another literary work on the same subject, the *Sordello* of Mrs. Busk, a poem of two thousand lines, which appeared in 1837. There were also the adverse criticisms of *Paracelsus* that, Kenyon suggests, Browning answered with his "rigid repression,—not of ideas nor of imagery, but of words, thus replying to the implications that his style in that poem [*Paracelsus*] was too diffuse."[2] An incident of great importance for its effect upon the poem was Browning's visit to Italy in the summer of 1838, the results of which are especially noticeable in the digression in the third book of *Sordello*.[3]

---

[1] In his *A Browning Handbook* Professor William Clyde DeVane writes (p. 68): "It is probable that *Sordello* cost Browning more time and pains than any other poem or volume of poems, even more, perhaps, than *The Ring and the Book*. He was occupied seven years in its composition, from the publication of *Pauline* in March, 1833, to the appearance of *Sordello* in March, 1840. We may well believe Browning's word in his letter to Miss Barrett on December 22, 1845, that 'There were many singular incidents attending my work on that subject.' During these seven years there were four distinct periods of composition, and four different *Sordellos* were written. The final result may be said to be a conglomeration of all these conceptions."

[2] F. G. Kenyon, editor, *The Works of Robert Browning,* Centenary Edition, I, xvi. A similar comment is made by C. Porter and H. A. Clarke, editors, *The Works of Robert Browning,* Camberwell Edition, II, xix.

[3] The clearest accounts of the history of the composition of *Sordello* are those to be found in

A third complication, perhaps not so important as the others in its effect upon the present analysis, is the difference between the first edition of the poem and its later forms, one of which appeared, in 1863, with certain revisions and a running commentary of page-headings supplied by the author. In the edition of 1888, and in subsequent editions, the "elucidatory page-headings" were dropped and but few other changes made. It is this final form of the poem that provides the text for the analysis of its star-images.

The manner in which these several complications affect this study may be seen in the difficulty that attends the formulation of the first general observation regarding the use of the star-image in *Sordello*. One of the conclusions suggested by the study of *Pauline* was the assumption that the star-images of that poem show a close connection between imagery and structural design, implying, in fact, that the basic design in Browning's mind was one of images, rather than one of logical divisions. The analysis of *Paracelsus* tends to support this opinion, and, like the evidence drawn from the examination of the poetical imagery of *Strafford,* to show that in *Paracelsus* the union of two kinds of structural organization, logical and imagistic, were fundamental to the design of the poem. It is my belief, that in spite of the complications enumerated above, a similar intention existed in the poet's mind for *Sordello*. But in composing *Sordello* Browning's sense of imagistic design must have been strained severely by his efforts to construct a new literary form and to deal with the problems arising out of the "singular incidents" that interrupted his labors. It is nevertheless difficult to demonstrate the belief that I hold. I cannot plot a briefly interpreted sequence of star-images, as I did in discussing *Paracelsus,* and expect it to give a fair synopsis of Sordello's story. I resort therefore to another method, the illustrative chart.

Having reduced the size of this chart to its present proportions, I have lost the opportunity to indicate the exact position in which the selected images occur. My intention, however, is to show merely the general distribution of these images within the poem, not, primarily, to indicate the specific lines that contain them. I have selected nine. The first, "death," is unlike the others in the list, since, strictly speaking, it is not always the image, but often the abstraction, "death," that Browning has indicated through his use of the word. It acquires its imagistic effect largely through implied personifications. I have included it for its implied rather than for its close similarity to the others. For the "star," the "osprey," and the "font" I have marked both specific instances of their occurrence and verbal associations of these images. The verbal associations have been indicated on the chart with broken lines. Only the specific appearances of the other images on the list have been noted, although, naturally, verbal associations are to be found for them, particularly

Griffin-Minchin, pp. 89-103, and in W. C. DeVane's *Handbook,* pp. 68-80. Another interesting study of these problems of composition is DeVane's "Sordello's Story Retold," *Studies in Philology,* XXVII (Jan., 1930), pp. 1-24.

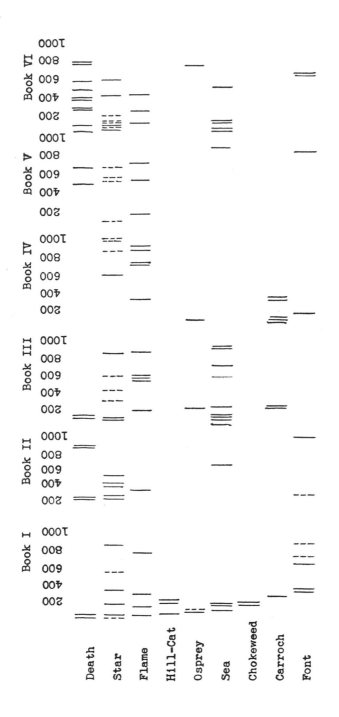

for the image of the sea, in such words as "billow," "wave," and "surge." Otherwise the chart should be self-explanatory.

Interesting variations in the functions and values of Browning's imagery might be demonstrated by carefully tracing each of the images here represented through the poem. The iteration of the "flame," for example, suggests for it an importance equal to that of the star-image. On the other hand, images like the "hill-cat" and "chokeweed" appear in the chart to have little significance. The chart, however, merely indicates their lack of frequent repetition, rather than their non-importance. The symbolic force of the "hill-cat" is at once consistent, specific, and lasting, even though it is also quite obvious. Of the chokeweed image it is fair to say that, because of its consistent meaning, it is more apt than the star to produce certain and immediate effects for the reader. Likewise, the font-image may be depended upon to imply always a particular phase in the life, and a particular quality in the character of Sordello, while the star-image represents a variety of meanings that, at first glance, seem to indicate its symbolic ineffectualness. Certainly the effects of the star-image are less obvious than those of the "hill-cat," "chokeweed," and "font," but that they are really less significant is doubtful. Its iteration and its difference from these other images nevertheless suggest the star's importance as an object of analysis.

For expository purposes the differences noted above may be simplified by letting one image, the "font," stand for the group that represents symbolic consistency, and another, the "star," for those images that suggest symbolic variation. The "sea," for example, is an image of this second classification. Omitting, for the moment, the consideration of the count of the repeated occurrences of these images, one might be tempted to suppose axiomatically that the structural importance of the font-image is greater than that of the star-image, because the differences between consistency and variation appear to be identical with the differences between order and disorder. But, for reasons that should become clearer in the course of this discussion, it is the star-image that is structurally the more consequential of the two. The differences between the "font" and the "star" may be more surely known by recognizing that they represent generally the basic differences between symbolism and symbolic imagery.

By its very nature a symbol must be consistent in its meaning in life or in art. In poetry the affinity of the symbol for the allegorical *genre* at once suggests the necessity of fixed meanings; for allegory is essentially systematic, planned, arbitrary, and insistent upon its preliminary artistic assumptions; it is an extended metaphor that would cease to be a metaphor if its original comparisons were allowed to change. Symbolic imagery, on the other hand, may be subject to variation.

We have observed in *Paracelsus,* for example, a number of variations in the meaning of the star-image. Some of these meanings, either through iteration, or the singular vitality of a unique occurrence, acquire artistic effects that equal those of the symbols in allegory. We have observed also in *Paracelsus* that these variations in the symbolic effect of the star-image were determined by structural necessity; they represented states of mind and moments of action in the history of the leading character. They not only signaled the importance of "incidents in the development of a soul," but, in turn, acquired much of their own emphasis from the incidents that they symbolized. They may be said, perhaps, to possess a structural importance that is both active and passive.

In *Sordello* the star-image, both in function and value, assumes characteristics similar to those of the stars in *Paracelsus*. It is the star-image, rather than the font-image, that holds the course, and, at the same time, is held to the course of the narrative. It often marks incidents and ideas of great consequence to Sordello's development, and just as often receives symbolical emphasis from its textual environment. The font, on the other hand, stands upon its symbolic integrity, refusing variation in meaning, an allegorical symbol in a poem that plainly lacks the systematic scheme essential to allegory. The font is not without structural significance, but it belongs to a particular period in Sordello's development and a particular quality in his character, both of which it suggests in every one of its actual or verbally suggested appearances.

These remarks, which attempt to distinguish the fundamental differences between the star- and font-images (and the two varieties of imagery for which they stand), should be regarded merely as an arbitrary simplification of a somewhat puzzling element of design. There is a certain value in recognizing these basic differences between the star- and font-images, but it must not be forgotten that, in the process, other differences *and similarities* have been ignored. The advantage gained is, paradoxically, a further demonstration of the presence of obscurities in the style of *Sordello*. The characteristics of the font-image, for instance, suggest that, in addition to the forms and modes of discourse previously enumerated, Browning has injected elements of allegory into a poem already stuffed to the point of artistic congestion. Observations such as these can do nothing to save *Sordello* from perpetual failure to become recognized among the great poems in English literature, but for the student of Browning they should increase interest in this, the poet's most remarkable artistic adventure. Browning's oft repeated belief in the revealing powers of imperfection, both in life and in art, can find no better proof than this work whose flaws are, in a sense, the "images" of his artistic growth. A question, which I shall not try to answer save by implication, arises inevitably: why did the poet who shows a command of his technique in *Paracelsus* and *Strafford* (the poems whose composition interrupted his labors on *Sordello*) fail signally in his attempt to tell the story of Sordello?

To increase the difficulty, not to bring it to solution, appears another aspect of the comparison of the star and font: the immediate clarity of meaning of the font-image as compared to the hidden subtleties of the star-image. The suggestion, for example, that the star-image is to the poem the more important structural element, is the product of a rather painstaking analysis; it is not the natural by-product of a reader's impressions. The font-image strikes the reader forcefully, for it comes into the poem under the auspices of an accurate and sustained description; the star enters casually, unobtrusively; it never attains the descriptive prominence of the font or, indeed, of the chokeweed-image of Book I. Thus apparent contradictions follow any attempt to simplify the problem, but when the substance to be analyzed is obscurity itself, one should expect to find the contradictory elements that compose obscurity. Furthermore, there is good reason in this instance not only to admit, but even to preserve the confusion, for it is only by adopting this attitude that we can see more clearly what Robert Browning has produced in *Sordello*.

Without Browning's elucidatory page-heading in the edition of 1863, "Shelley departing, Verona appears," the first instance of the star's appearance in *Sordello* would probably go unnoticed. Even so, it cannot be insisted upon as a clear example, for its effect depends entirely upon verbal connotation, and also upon the association of the star and Shelley in an earlier poem, *Pauline*:

> . . stay—thou, spirit, come not near   (I, 60)
> Now—not this time desert thy cloudy place
> To scare me, thus employed, with that pure face!

The suggestion of the home among the clouds and the light of the "pure face," since we know that the "spirit" *is* Shelley, recalls former flashing appearances of the "sun-treader." Furthermore, the frequent association of the stars in *Sordello* with poets and poetry requires our notice of this instance.

In the second instance an actual occurrence of the image makes the example clear. Browning proclaims that the presence of Shelley in his company of listeners would make even

> the silver speech   (I, 68)
> Of Sidney's self, the starry paladin,
> Turn intense as a trumpet sounding in
> The knights to tilt, ...

There is, of course, an obvious meaning in the poetic name of Sir Philip Sidney, "Astrophel," that may explain the choice of the adjective "starry," but such a comment does not explain why Sidney, rather than some other poet, should have been chosen as the shining image of silver speech. If the image is further examined with this question in mind, it becomes clear that Sidney himself, rather than the adjective "starry," is the real star-image of the passage, and that the answer to the question is, possibly, that Sidney, being an accomplished poet, a valiant warrior, and, by his own designation, a lover of the star, would be the perfect image to introduce his Italian prototype, Sordello, to an English public. Sordello is to appear first as the "herald-star," knight and poet. Such an interpretation of the "starry paladin," however, does not accord very well with the conception of Sordello that emerges from the poem as a whole. There is good reason why it should not. It is a reason to be found by considering again the changes in content and form that evidently followed the "singular incidents" of interrupted composition.

In point of fact, the next instance of the star's occurrence continues to focus attention upon the conjectures just presented. In its significance for Sordello, the character, it amounts to a contrast rather than a comparison. It is an image of Count Richard St. Boniface, Sordello's rival for the hand of Palma:

> . . . "let the Count wind up the war!" (I, 174)
> "Richard, light-hearted as a plunging star,"

According to historical accounts it was not Palma, but her half-sister, Cunizza, daughter of Adelaide the Tuscan, who became first the wife of Richard, later the wife of Sordello. But the substitution of Palma, demanded by Browning's conception of the story, does not diminish the force of rivalry between the two knights. The lines quoted above are drawn from a passage of "historical decoration" from which the star-image is, as a rule, eliminated. Our recognition of the care with which Browning has used the star-image in his earlier poems at once raises the question as to why he used it in this instance, attached, as it is, to a figure in the "historical decoration," when practically all its other appearances belong to "the incidents in the development of a soul." Generally it is asssociated with Sordello, or with poets and poetry; only in this instance, with a purely "historical" and military character.

Were it not true that the careful reading of both *Pauline* and *Paracelsus,* and even *Strafford,* has taught us to regard the star-image as significant in its function, and that it is likely to possess either one or more of the symbolic or structural values of imagery, there would be no reason for pausing before this apparently irregular example. The "plunging star's" power of contrast, however, may give it a reason for artistic existence. Not many lines further on in Book I, heavy-hearted Sordello is to be introduced formally as the "herald-star" of his race; here, "light-hearted" Richard appears as the "plunging star" of thoughtless military prowess, already betrothed to Palma, who is about to confess her love for Sordello. But such an interpretation, while plausible, does not explain why Browning should have dropped the force of the contrast, which he has thus introduced, from the succeeding divisions of the poem. The rivalry between Sordello and Richard is replaced in later books, insofar as leading motives are concerned, by the rivalry of conflicting forces within Sordello's own soul, and by the contrast between the characters of Sordello and Taurello Salinguerra. For the poem as a whole, then, this instance of the star-image seems to have been unintentionally inserted, but for another conception of the poem, a story of Sordello that followed historical legend more closely, it would be in perfect accord.

In other words, the star-images associated with both Sidney and Richard point strongly to Browning's having at one time conceived of the personality of Sordello more nearly in terms of traditional legend, a source of information that emphasized the military achievements of the hero as well as his success as a troubadour. At just what time in the period of composition the military aspects of the story asserted their claims to the author's interest it is difficult to say. The evidence of this analysis would support the opinion of Professor DeVane in his "Sordello's Story Retold,"[4] that it was later rather than earlier in the period of composition.[5] That this theme at no time became a dominant motif in Browning's mind may be understood by observing that by no stretch of the imagination can the courtly Astrophel be compared with the Sordello who finally emerges from the complexities of the poem. Certainly the rivalry of Sordello and Count Richard is not sustained as a theme important to an understanding of the development of Sordello's soul.

The next passage containing the star-image may be regarded as sufficiently organic, in its relationship to the poem as a whole, to qualify, with its image, as an effectively structural and symbolic element. To be sure, it announces the advent of Sordello in an auspicious tone that does not harmonize perfectly with the heaviness of physical and spiritual agony that is to dominate so much of his life; but its subject, Poetry, is a dominant theme throughout the poem. The style of this passage is inconsistent with the "rigid repression" (which to most readers seems anything *but* repression) of the greater portion of *Sordello*. It is a style familiar to readers of *Pauline* and *Paracelsus*; diffuse, rather than repressed. In content it presents simultaneously the story of Sordello proper, and the direct commentary of Robert Browning upon the nature of his hero and the nature of poetry, compact in the address to Dante. To paraphrase:

> You, Dante, absorbed the herald-star of Italian poetry, Sordello, into the orb of your consummate power. The star was thus withheld from its natural course. I, Robert Browning, will set it in motion once more; "If I should falter now!"

For he—for he,   (I, 345)

> Gate-vein of this heart's blood of Lombardy,
> (If I should falter now)—for he is thine!
> Sordello, thy forerunner, Florentine!
> A herald-star I know thou didst absorb
> Relentless into the consummate orb
> That scared it from its right to roll along
> A sempiternal path with dance and song
> Fulfilling its allotted period,

---

[4] *Studies in Philology*, XXVII (Jan., 1930), pp. 1-24.   [5] See below, p. 93.

Serenest of the progeny of God—
Who yet resigns it not! His darling stoops
With no quenched lights, desponds with no blank troops
Of disenfranchised brilliances, for, blent
Utterly with thee, its shy element
Like thine upburneth prosperous and clear.
Still what if I approach the august sphere
Named now with only one name, disentwine
That under-current soft and argentine
From its fierce mate in the majestic mass
Leavened as the sea whose fire was mixt with glass
In John's transcendent vision, launch once more
That lustre? Dante, pacer of the shore
Where glutted hell disgorgeth filthiest gloom,
Unbitten by its whirring sulphur-spume—
Or whence the grieved and obscure waters slope
Into a darkness quieted by hope;
Plucker of amaranths grown beneath God's eye
In gracious twilights where his chosen lie,—
I would do this! If I should falter now!

Of all the star-images in *Sordello* it is only this one that is sustained through the effects of verbal connotation or association in the lines that immediately follow the specific appearance of the image. It is this characteristic of style that recalls the earlier poems, for it is a method of expression often used in *Pauline* and *Paracelsus*. There are only twelve lines, in this passage of twenty-nine, that do not carry at least one element of diction whose connotation is clearly one of stars. These are the first three and the last nine lines of the quotation. Even among these last lines, six of which borrow their imagery from the *Divine Comedy,* there are suggestions of the star in such phrases as, "transcendent vision" and "lustre," and in the implications of the lines:

> Plucker of amaranths grown beneath God's eye
> In gracious twilights where his chosen lie,—

where the star and the amaranth may be said to blend in a manner characteristic of the work of a poet whose associations of light and music and light and flowing water have modified several of the star-images in *Pauline* and *Paracelsus*. The logical content of the passage remains intact in spite of this fusion of images. By absorbing a star into his "consummate orb," Dante has plucked an everlasting flower of beauty. It is not necessary to list the words, in the other lines of this passage, that demonstrate the explicit association of Browning's diction with astrological lore.

With the appearance of the next image of the star in Book I,

> Compress the starriest into one star,   (I, 854)

an interesting relationship, both logical and imagistic, may be observed to exist between the image we have last examined (the "herald-star") and the image that for the moment becomes our chief concern. Approximately five hundred lines separate the passages in which these images occur, a fact which rather obscures their relationship. In order to set forth the details of this association it will be well, I think, to locate the new passage by referring to its position in the story with something more than the number of a line.

Since it has been necessary to locate similarly a number of passages in the poem, I shall take the liberty of inserting a brief explanation of the method I have used. To state it as simply as possible, I have sought in each instance to supply only those details of content and form that will recall the positions of various passages to a reader who is already familiar with the general plan of the poem. I have sometimes presented brief synopses of narrative drawn principally from the story of Sordello, rather than from the "historical decoration"; I have mentioned literary *genres* and the modes of discourse, narrative and dramatic, or the mode of direct commentary, when that seemed important to the interpretation of a star-image; I have attempted to suggest, or diagnose the condition of Sordello's spiritual health when occasion seemed to demand it. I have combined these practices and employed them separately, in each instance allowing the peculiarities of the occasion to decide the particular method. In no sense have I attempted to present an outline of the poem.[6]

To return from the digression to the instance at hand—"the starriest into one star." This image occurs in a passage that, in spite of its allusions to characters and cities important in the historical background of the poem, lies wholly within the narrative of Sordello's personal development. He has reached the point of confessing some of his lamentable weaknesses; he has begun to turn from the absorbed contemplation of himself to the "out-world." As yet it is not the real "out-world" that he faces, but simply the personages of chronicle and romance who, nevertheless, entice his interest. He will read himself into them, as he has been accustomed to read himself into Nature and the sculptured figures of his beloved "font." Consequently he does not really turn to the "out-world" at all, but sees men only as he thinks they should be. When he tries to imitate practically the manly arts of his new-found world, he is appalled with a sense of his physical weakness. He returns sensitively to the world of dreams, vaguely promising himself he will "one day" accomplish his conquest of reality. Such is the state of mind he has attained when the passage to which I have referred begins:

> ". . . . . though I must abide   (I, 832)
> "With dreams now, I may find a thorough vent
> "For all myself, acquire an instrument
> "For acting what these people act; my soul

[6] An excellent analytical outline of *Sordello* may be found in the Camberwell Edition of Browning's Works, II, pp. 309-351. The explanatory outline, consisting of separate introductions to each of the six books, in A. J. Whyte's edition of *Sordello,* is also interesting, especially for its commentary on Books V and VI.

"Hunting a body out may gain its whole
"Desire some day!" How else express chagrin
And resignation, show the hope steal in
With which he let sink from an aching wrist
The rough-hewn ash bow? [for]⁷ Straight, a gold
      shaft [of fancy] hissed
Into the Syrian air, struck Malek down
Superbly! "Crosses to the breach! God's Town
"Is gained him back!" Why bend [the] rough ash-
      bows [of reality] more?
Thus lives he: if not careless as before,
Comforted: for one may anticipate,
Rehearse the future, be prepared when fate
Shall have prepared in turn real men whose names
Startle, real places of enormous fames,
Este abroad and Ecelin at home
To worship him,—Mantua, Verona, Rome
To witness it. Who grudges time so spent?
Rather test qualities to heart's content—
Summon them thrice selected, near and far—
Compress the starriest into one star,
And grasp the whole at once!

Having resigned himself once more to the dream-world, Sordello easily replaces the "ash-bow" of reality with the "gold shaft" of fancied activity. He rehearses the future. His energy will be spent upon the discovery of "qualities," not upon participation in real events. He is confident, however, that real men will finally adore him; for they will be amazed at his genius, overcome by his power to "compress the starriest" of discovered qualities "into one star"—one "consummate orb."

The force of the image is obviously two-fold: its design relates it immediately to the "herald-star" passage, the "consummate orb" of Dante; its symbolic force suggests that Sordello, in spite of his ineffectualness, realizes the secret power of poetic genius, the power to "compress the starriest into one star." It is this realization that makes him one with Dante, the difference between them being one of degree and not of kind; the difference, in other words, between a "star" and a "consummate orb." Both images have been carefully chosen. The relationship between the passages that contain them is specific, for both in thought and in imagery the compression of the "starriest into one star" is imitative of the absorption of the "herald-star" into the "consummate orb"—the act of creating unity out of unrelated particles of beauty. Such, at least, seems to have been the passionate conviction of the young author of *Sordello*.

However well chosen these images may be for the story of Sordello, they are expressive also of the development of a poet who had not as yet given up entirely the confessional manner of his *Pauline* and *Paracelsus*. Whatever

⁷ The explanatory parentheses have been added to suggest grammatical clarity.

our opinions may be regarding the appropriateness of these star-images for Dante and Sordello, we can be sure that Robert Browning paid for them with a struggle that in turn makes them eloquent symbols of his own experience. It was he who knew only too well the task of realizing the poetic principle that they represent, for his *Sordello* became the insuperable labor of compressing unrelated particles of truth into one star. It was Robert Browning, rather than Sordello, who was sure he had discovered the essential quality of poetic genius: a creative power that would transform the unrelated particles of chaos into the unity of a single personality. It is therefore impossible to overlook the double significance of these images; they have been carefully chosen, but not, as the phrase might imply, because of their ornamental virtues; they are the inevitable images of a strong conviction in the mind of Robert Browning.

Corollary to this hypothesis is a passage in *Paracelsus* in which Browning proclaims the belief that the supreme development of a poet and a man is the acquisition of an increasing power that most resembles the creative energy of God:

> Thus he [God] dwells in all,
> From life's minute beginnings, up at last
> To man—the consummation of this scheme
> Of being, the completion of this sphere
> Of life: whose attributes had here and there
> Been scattered o'er the visible world before
> Asking to be combined, dim fragments meant
> To be united in some wondrous whole,
> Imperfect qualities throughout creation
> Suggesting some one creature yet to make
> Some point where all those scattered rays should meet
> Convergent in the faculties of man.
> (*Paracelsus*, V, 681-692)

If additional confirmation be necessary to support the opinions just presented, it may be found readily within the first book of *Sordello*. Midway between the passages that have been the objects of the comparison above is a group of lines whose verbal connotations suggest the star-image, and whose meaning parallels the quotation from *Paracelsus*:

> So runs   (I, 515)
> A legend: light had birth ere moons and suns,
> Flowing through space a river and alone,
> Till chaos burst and blank the spheres were strown
> Hither and thither, foundering and blind:
> When into each of them rushed light—to find
> Itself no place, foiled of its radiant chance.

This legend of light constitutes an important illustration in a passage of approximately one hundred lines in which Browning is again speaking of poets and poetry. Here he has joined the mode of direct commentary to the narrative of Sordello's development and produced, incidentally, a blending of the images of light and of flowing water. His analysis of Sordello's youthful nature leads him to comment upon what he considers to be the two chief classes of poets. In Sordello's face Browning sees "a soul fit to receive Delight at every sense; you can believe Sordello foremost in the regal class Nature has broadly severed from her mass of men." Sordello has been born with the instincts of the poet; but to which of the two general classes of poets does he belong?

The nature of the first class of poets, whom "One character" denotes, may be observed in the following quotation to which I have supplied my own italics and explanatory parentheses. The distinguishing characteristic of these poets is

> *A need to blend with each external charm,*   (I, 507)
> *Bury themselves,* the whole heart wide and warm,—
> *In something not themselves; they would belong*
> *To what they worship*—stronger and more strong
> Thus prodigally fed—[to a thing] which gathers shape
> And feature, [and which] soon imprisons past escape
> The votary [who is] framed to love and to submit
> Nor ask, as passionate[ly] he kneels to it [the thing
>   he worships],
> Whence grew the idol's empery. So runs
> A legend; light had birth ere moons and suns, . . .

From this point the passage continues with the lines already quoted. These lines declare that Light first enjoyed an independent existence. Light flowed like a great river, until "chaos burst and blank the spheres were strown Hither and thither, foundering and blind." Light, suddenly deprived of its independent course of existence, rushed impulsively into the darkened spheres, which thence became its abiding place. With its energies scattered, its power was limited by the spheres that then contained it. So the poets of the first class lose their independent existence, become slaves to the objects that they adore, find themselves powerless within the limitations of the "spheres" that have absorbed their energies. "Let such forego their just inheritance."

But there is a second class of poets whose genius demands independence. If they *will,* it is they who can reestablish the ancient empery of Light, who, to the degree in which they are capable, may recreate the river of truth and beauty. They accomplish their objectives not by disregarding the beauty that they see around them, but by restraining themselves from a complete loss of individuality. They never lose themselves in emotional contemplation, for they recognize the light within their own souls as part of the beauty of the world. For every beauty in Nature they discover the counterpart in their own personalities. Their contemplation of Nature completes the expansion of their individualities. It is these poets of the second class who compress "the starriest into one star," who absorb the particles of light into one "consummate orb" of personality.

> For there's a class that eagerly looks, too,   (I, 523)
> On beauty, but, unlike the gentler crew,
> Proclaims each new revealment born a twin
> With a distinctest consciousness within,
> Referring still the quality, now first
> Revealed, to their own soul—its instinct nursed
> In silence now remembered better, shown
> More thoroughly, but not the less their own;
> A dream come true, the special exercise
> Of any special function that implies
> The being fair, or good, or wise, or strong,
> Dormant within their nature all along—

In *Paracelsus,* upon the same general theme, Browning has written:

> Truth is within ourselves; it takes no rise
> From outward things . . . .
> . . . . and to know
> Rather consists in opening out a way
> Whence the imprisoned splendour may escape,
> (*Paracelsus,* I, 726 ff.)

But alas! they too, poets of the second class, may be guilty of excesses. Their insistence upon preserving their independence turns too often into a desire for personal acclaim. They forget the ancient stream of light, as if the only beauty that ever existed were their own self-contained brilliance. They become over-anxious to impress their individualities upon the world, exchanging a sense of worship for the exhilarating experience of becoming objects of popular adoration.

The essential distinctions, then, between the two classes of poets are: that the first class adores Beauty, and in excess of adoration may be enslaved by Beauty, with a total loss of individuality; that the second class commands Beauty to the preservation of the individual soul, and in excess becomes so self-centered as to ignore Beauty.[8] It is the *excesses* of both these classes of poets that Browning condemns in his treatment of Sordello's earlier development. Sordello's Goito-life produces the excesses of the first class of poets; his Mantua-life, the excesses of the second.

With the primary objectives of both classes of poets Browning is inevitably sympathetic. He cannot forget, nor allow his reader to forget that Sordello is a poet born, that his spiritual problem is to find a way to subdue his impulses toward poetic disaster. He describes Sordello as a youth:

---

[8] A more conventional distinction between these two classes of poets is the one employed in several commentaries upon this passage: poets of the first class are called *objective*; those of the second, *subjective*. For the interpretation I have given these terms hardly apply. Furthermore, even though Browning has used them in his *Essay on Shelley,* they are terms which, for many reasons, I wish to avoid using.

Yourselves shall trace   (I, 462)
(The delicate nostril swerving wide and fine,
A sharp and restless lip, so well combine
With that calm brow) a soul fit to receive
Delight at every sense; you can believe
Sordello foremost in the regal class
Nature has broadly severed from her mass
Of men, and framed for pleasure, as she frames
Some happy lands, that have luxurious names,
For loose fertility; a footfall there
Suffices to upturn to the warm air
Half-germinating spices; mere decay
Produces richer life; and day by day
New pollen on the lily-petal grows,
And still more làbyrinthine buds the rose.
You recognize at once the finer dress
Of flesh that amply lets in loveliness
At eye and ear, while round the rest is furled
(As though she would not trust them with her world)
A veil that shows the sky not near so blue,
And lets but half the sun look fervid through.

It is to the "regal class" that Sordello belongs; he must be saved from its excesses. In my opinion, the poem as a whole turns upon this fundamental problem, as truly for Robert Browning as for Sordello. It is the problem of finding the means of giving direction to the poet's genius, the discovery of a discipline against pleasurable but pointless extremes. The problem has been solved, for Browning finally leads his Sordello to the realization of social responsibility, a cause, a way of life, an orb that will unify his energies. For Robert Browning, living optimistically in the nineteenth century, such a realization might find practical expression; for Sordello it was a tragic victory,

A task indeed, but for a clearer clime
Than the murk lodgment of his building-time.[9]

It is inevitable that our regard for the importance of the star-image in *Sordello* should increase when we see the course of our analysis leading to the very center of the poem and unquestionably clarifying the obscure motives of the poet. The organic, structural, and symbolic qualities of the image impress their claims upon our attention. The very act of gathering together these instances of the star-image's occurrence becomes for us a practical compression of "the starriest into one star." Nowhere in his works is Browning's demand that the reader himself become the poet so strenuously urged as it is in *Sordello*. (Too strenuously to be fair, we are bound to confess.) Consequently, the temptation to redirect the course of our investigation to an examination of Browning's theories of poetry accompanies our discovery of

[9] Book III: lines 853-854,
A task indeed, but with a clearer clime
Than the murk lodgment of our building-time.

the star-image's heightened significance, especially when it redirects our attention to images and ideas in other poems that are illuminating to our understanding of Browning's genius.

With the last star-image in Book I we have left Sordello in contemplation of the best and the worst aspects of poetry of the second class. He has realized not only the principle of compressing the "starriest into one star," but his thoughts of the future include also the anticipation of men's adoration of his personal brilliance. The first star-image in Book II offers no difficulties of interpretation, if the meaning of the images in Book I are kept in mind. The star continues to refer, generally, to poets and poetry. The example now before us represents a distinction between poetry and a kind of polished verse that Browning refuses to accept as poetry. It occurs in a digression from the principal theme, which is the story of Sordello. Sordello has at last come into contact with real men; upon impulse he has challenged and defeated Eglamor, the most accomplished troubadour of the age. Eglamor's defeat is Eglamor's death. Browning digresses to tell the story of Eglamor (Book II, 195-295) while Sordello's story waits. This star-image occurs within a passage in which Browning comments upon the character of Eglamor and the quality of his art:

> He, no genius rare,   (II, 213)
> Transfiguring in fire or wave or air
> At will, but a poor gnome that, cloistered up
> In some rock-chamber with his agate cup,
> His topaz rod, his seed pearl, in these few
> And their arrangement finds enough to do
> For his best art. Then, how he loved that art!
> The calling marking him a man apart
> From men—one not to care, take counsel for
> Cold hearts, comfortless faces—(Eglamor
> Was neediest of his tribe)—since verse, the gift,
> Was his, and men, the whole of them, must shift
> Without it, e'en content themselves with wealth
> And pomp and power, snatching a life by stealth.
> So, Eglamor was not without his pride!
> The sorriest bat which cowers throughout noontide
> While other birds are jocund, has one time
> When moon and stars are blinded, and the prime
> Of earth is his to claim, nor find a peer;
> And Eglamor was noblest poet here—

The condemnation is severe. The "poor gnome," the maker of verses arranging his little patterns of "seed-pearl," is glorious only in an age when poetry is dead, when the "moon and stars are blinded." The direct commentary of Robert Browning is unmistakable in these lines. "So much for Eglamor."

Returning to the story of Sordello, we become involved once more in the forward-backward motion of his development. His defeat of Eglamor was a victory of genuine poetry over verse-making, but Sordello was incapable of recognizing the meaning of his sudden achievement. For him the prize song was a burst of passionate frenzy, unconscious in its art, spontaneous, and more perfect than he realized. It was not a product of the will; it happened. Such an experience could not be repeated, for it represented no artistic control in Sordello's soul; at its end he had fallen into a senseless swoon. The effect of his victory was to assert once more the necessity of his coming to a conclusion that would recognize the true nature of poetry and reveal the function of the poet's will. Characteristically Sordello fails to make the effort.

When we next see him, he has decided to become another Eglamor. An easy-going sophistry has set such an interpretation upon his triumph. He has surrounded himself with the emblems of his new profession, assumed the purposeless attitudes of tapestried minstrelsy, the negligent pose, with lute, amid the "flowering laurel," the abstracted gaze over a romantically arranged landscape. Beneath the sheer beauty of the description lies a meaning doubly pathetic; the picture of Sordello's lassitude, and ours in similar situations. From the cold stars of heaven he turns to the intoxicating loveliness of the stars of earth, whose imitative beauty is, in the eyes of the critic Naddo, a most acceptable substitute for the genuine light of poetry:

> 'T was a sunrise of blossoming and May.   (II, 297)
> Beneath a flowering laurel thicket lay
> Sordello; each new sprinkle of white stars
> That smell fainter of wine than Massic jars
> Dug up at Baiae, when the south wind shed
> The ripest, made him happier; filleted
> And robed the same, only a lute beside
> Lay on the turf. Before him far and wide
> The country stretched.

He does not see, as Paracelsus did, the fragile image of himself in the "star-shaped plant." He is seduced by the delicate fragrance of "each new sprinkle of white stars."

His romantic posture collapses when some of its supports are removed suddenly. Sordello hears a legend of his birth which declares him to be the son of the archer, Elcorte. Having never discovered the value of his own character, having never realized his Will, he naturally crumples before a blow that deprives him of his self-esteem and his respectable nobility. He accepts the false legend without question, and thoughtlessly concludes that all his other dreams have been quite as illusory. Cynically, he resolves that all of his former hopes and beliefs have had no foundation. Henceforth he will not make the mistake of giving his allegiance to any suspicious ideal, to any cause. Other men may follow their stars; he will live independently and allow perfect freedom to his soul. He will dwell a man apart:

> —the seal was set; never again   (II, 367)
> Sordello could in his own sight remain

> One of the many, one with hopes and cares
> And interest nowise distinct from theirs,
> Only peculiar in a thriveless store
> Of fancies, which were fancies and no more,
> Never again for him and for the crowd
> A common law was challenged and allowed
> If calmly reasoned of, howe'er denied
> By a mad impulse nothing justified
> Short of Apollo's presence. The divorce
> Is clear; why needs Sordello square his course
> By any known example? Men no more
> Compete with him than tree and flower before.
> Himself, inactive, yet is greater far
> Than such as act, each stooping to his star,
> Acquiring thence his function; he has gained
> The same result with meaner mortals trained
> To strength or beauty, moulded to express
> Each the idea that rules him; since no less
> He comprehends that function, but can still
> Embrace the others, take of might his fill
> With Richard as of grace with Palma, mix
> Their qualities, or for a moment fix
> On one; abiding free meantime, uncramped
> By any partial organ, never stamped
> Strong, and to strength turning all energies—
> Wise, and restricted to becoming wise—
> That is, he loves not, nor possesses One
> Idea that, star-like over, lures him on
> To its exclusive purpose.

The symbolic emphasis of the star-image has changed. In "each new sprinkle of white stars" the meaning, poetry and poets, was still apparent, though changed from a designation of the true, to a suggestion of the imitative kinds of verse. In the two star-images of the above quotation no such connotation remains, except that which may cling to the image from its former associations (and then only for the analyst who has been more painstaking in his examination than a reader would expect to be). The significance that the image *now* assumes is of a meaning well-known to the reader of *Pauline*: the repeated symbolic significance, in that poem, of the "lode-star." The poet in *Pauline* declares:

> But I have always had one lode-star; now,   (*Pauline,* 292)
> As I look back, I see that I have halted
> Or hastened as I looked towards that star—

but Sordello has resolved to free himself from any such attachment.

Because the "lode-star" of *Pauline* held a definite relationship to the idea of poetical achievement, one may advance the argument that the star-images before us suggest a similar meaning. But the necessity of going to an earlier poem for the interpretation of an image in *Sordello* rather defeats the most skillful argument. It is better to accept this change in the symbolic emphasis of the star-image, and attempt to discover what it signifies for the present analysis.

Our first impulse is to say that, whatever qualities of Browning's imagery may be involved in this instance, the star-image has lost much of the force that it had acquired through cumulative iteration. We might conclude, naturally, that both in structural and symbolic significance the image has been weakened. But such a conclusion is the result of assuming that the star-image must always mean the same thing in a given poem. So it would, if Browning's imagery were governed always by the law of a systematic symbolism. We have already seen in *Paracelsus,* however, a poem in which the star-image acquires dominant importance, that the symbolic force of the image may shift, let us say, from a suggestion of truth, to a suggestion of fancy and unreality, and still retain its structural significance. In other words, the idea in the poet's mind requires the subservience of his means of effect. If he allows a new symbolic meaning to replace the dissolution of another, it is because, for the moment, he is very much more concerned with the development of Sordello's soul than he is with the preservation of the symbolic consistency of all his images. He, not they, is master.

It is true, however, that the change in meaning that we note here is not accomplished with the finesse that marks similar changes in *Paracelsus.* In that poem we were aware, from the beginning, of the diversity in Paracelsus' character, and we therefore accepted his fluctuating regard for the star as an inevitable consequence of his spiritual confusion. The excellent organization of *Paracelsus,* together with its expository clarity, kept us *en rapport* with the development of the principal character; so that we accepted changes in the significance of images, as it were, automatically. The difficulties that we confront in reading *Sordello,* especially those that have been mentioned pointedly, preclude our following the turns of Sordello's story with similar ease and success.

To prepare for the discussion of the next star-image, in which we shall notice a further shifting in symbolic effect, let us return for a moment to a few details in that story. Sordello has abjured the star, refused obedience to a consuming ideal, ignored the necessity of love. That in spite of his pretensions to freedom he is nevertheless the slave of ill-begotten vanity becomes clear in the lines that immediately follow the last quotation. His own words expose him:

> "So range free soul!—who by self consciousness   (II, 405)
> "The last drop of all beauty dost express—
>
> . . . .
> . . . . . . the world that counts men strong or wise,
> "Who, themselves, court strength, wisdom—it shall bow
> "Surely in unexampled worship now,
> "Discerning me!"—

He must give his allegiance to something, having scorned the "lode-star," and he turns out of sheer bravado to his own person, assuming the while an immaculate aloofness from the common strivings of mankind. At this point in his development the poet, Robert Browning, interrupts with his direct comment:

> (Dear monarch, I beseech,   (II, 415)
> Notice how lamentably wide a breach
> Is here: discovering this, discover too
> What our poor world has possibly to do
> With it! . . . .
> . . . . why want us
> To know that you yourself know thus and thus?)

We are not surprised, therefore, that the next star-image should carry the symbolic meaning of fame. Sordello, indeed, has turned himself over to the professional propagandist, Naddo, whose chief business, in spite of his literary pretensions, is the promotion of his own and, if possible, his client's fame.

> He [Sordello] thoroughly read o'er   (II, 473)
> His truchman Naddo's missive six times more,
> Praying him visit Mantua and supply
> A famished world.
>   The evening star was high
> When he reached Mantua, but his fame arrived
> Before him: friends applauded, foes connived,
> And Naddo looked an angel, and the rest
> Angels, and all these angels would be blest
> Supremely by a song—

The image therefore continues to keep pace with the narrative and, in this instance, even to foreshadow coming developments. Is not an evening star, for all its beauty, less reassuring of lasting fame than a morning star or noonday sun? It is interesting to recall, furthermore, that it was the "first, supreme, forsaken star" of night that pointed to the fall of Strafford. We may therefore claim for this image, and those that have immediately preceded it in our analysis, a structural and a symbolic importance. We cannot claim that it dominates the passage in which it occurs, for its symbolic meaning is manifestly dependent upon the context and the development of the narrative. If it were dominant, we should expect an opposite effect to be realized: an illumination of the context by the image, such as the star-images of preceding divisions of the poem often produce. Our conclusion for the present is that Browning has allowed the significance of the star-image to change in meaning and in importance according to the necessities of his theme and his narrative technique.

The evening star high over Mantua is the last appearance of the image in Book II. Between this and its next appearance, at line 69 in Book III, significant incidents occur in Sordello's development that may be very briefly summarized to prepare the way for the discussion of the first star-image in Book III. Under the tutelage of Naddo, Sordello surrenders himself to the life of the professional troubadour. "Casting about to satisfy the crowd," he gives his talents to the making of songs; "it was song's effect He cared for, scarce the song itself"; and Browning comments:

> I am loth   (II, 492)
> To say the rhymes at last were Eglamor's;
> But Naddo, chuckling, bade competitors
> Go pine; "the master certes meant to waste
> "No effort, cautiously had probed the taste
> "He'd please anon: true bard, in short, . ."

The commonplace mind of Naddo was satisfied; Sordello had become an undeniable success. But there was a quality within the real Sordello that Naddo could never understand, the soul of a poet. Sordello therefore grew dissatisfied with success; he realized vaguely, as Andrea del Sarto did clearly, the fatal error of mere technical perfection.

Sordello then attempts to face the dilemma. He succeeds in giving new life to his songs by adapting the language of the people to the uses of poetry; his songs quicken with dramatic intensity. But his enthusiasm smothers beneath the first wave of opposition to the newness of his style. He goes back to the easy, perfect way; to the biddings of Naddo. The world praises his verses— but the world does not praise him. He is tempted, nevertheless, to enjoy his success as a verse-maker, to withstrain the vague impulses in his soul, which insist upon his groping for a truth that he cannot understand. But try as he will to deny his soul, the spiritual conflict between the world's way and the poet's way becomes more and more intense. His reputation as a successful bard continues to mount, in direct contradiction to his sinking spirit. Finally, on the occasion when most is expected of his craft, he fails utterly, his perfect technique refuses to work; the song to celebrate Salinguerra's triumph is never written. For Sordello was no Eglamor, content with topaz rod and seed pearl. He returns to the seclusion of his Goito where a transformation reassures his spirit:

> One declining autumn day—   (III, 69)
> Few birds about the heaven chill and grey,
> No wind that cared trouble the tacit woods—
> He sauntered home complacently, their moods
> According, his and nature's. Every spark
> Of Mantua life was trodden out; so dark
> The embers, that the Troubadour, who sung
> Hundreds of songs, forgot, its trick his tongue,
> Its craft his brain, how either brought to pass
> Singing at all; that faculty might class
> With any of Apollo's now. The year
> Began to find its early promise sere
> As well. Thus beauty vanishes; thus stone

> Outlingers flesh; nature's and his youth gone,
> They left the world to you, and wished you joy.
> When, stopping his benevolent employ,
> A presage shuddered through the welkin; harsh
> The earth's remonstrance followed. 'T was the marsh
> Gone of a sudden. Mincio, in its place,
> Laughed, a broad water, in next morning's face,
> And, where the mists broke up immense and white
> I' the steady wind, burned like a spilth of light
> Out of the crashing of a myriad stars.
> And here was nature, bound by the same bars
> Of fate with him!
>   "No! youth once gone is gone:
> "Deeds, let escape, are never to be done.
> "Leaf-fall and grass-spring for the year; for us—
> "Oh forfeit I unalterably thus
> "My chance? nor two lives wait me, this to spend,
> "Learning save that? Nature has time, may mend
> "Mistake, she knows occasion will recur;
> "Landslip or seabreach, how affects it her
> "With her magnificent resources?—I
> "Must perish once and perish utterly."

A stagnant mind has been transformed for the moment into a flowing energy. The marsh gives way to the movement of flowing water; "Mincio, in its place, Laughed a broad water." Imagery thus produces a harmonious accompaniment to Browning's narrative theme. Of particular interest is the return of a symbolic meaning that has been denied the star during the interlude of Sordello's capitulation to Naddo. Here the force of both narrative and imagery signifies the rebirth of the poet-soul. The reader is convinced immediately that the "spilth of light," which so amazed Sordello, is of a quality quite different from the light of fame; that it is, indeed, the light of truth and poetry. Robert Browning's conception of his hero's present attitude of mind shows clearly in this imagistic detail. Sordello is not prepared to see truth itself, for its dazzling light would blind him; he must be stimulated, therefore, by a reflection that he instinctively recognizes as having originated

> Out of the crashing of a myriad stars.

The examination of this detail in Browning's technique leaves no question as to Sordello's state of mind at this critical moment in his development. He does not see "plain," but he has realized the full effect of those intimations, which, in spite of everything, continue to inform his poet-soul, bringing him ever nearer to the point of full realization.

By comparison with the star-images of Books I and II, in which the symbolic meaning is clearly poetry, it will be noted that this is the first that shows Sordello himself to be in close contact with the meaning of poetry. The others have been, principally, attempts on the part of Robert Browning to demonstrate the nature of poetry and poets; they have represented the possibilities of Sordello's personality, but they have not shown his direct contact with or knowledge of the nature of poetry. Indeed, even in this instance of the "myriad stars" Sordello's nearness to the ideal that must ultimately fill his being does not take the form of complete realization. Sordello stands on the threshold of discovery, but his mind is unprepared to enter. His self-conscious egoism swerves him aside. His thoughts turn inward upon himself, his exhilaration melts into a confounded comparison of himself and Nature, *but with a notable difference* that marks a distinct change in his attitude. He finds himself no longer able to regard Nature with the romantic ardor expressed in the opening lines of the above quotation.

Further considerations of this passage involve us in exceedingly complicated problems of analysis, especially in the study of relationships between the images just referred to and certain images in Book I. The task becomes, paradoxically, an attempt to understand the obscurity of images of light. For example, the flowing "spilth of light Out of the crashing of a myriad stars" must certainly remind us of

So runs   (I, 515)

> A legend; light had birth ere moons and suns,
> Flowing through space a river and alone
> Till chaos burst—

When we recall that the legend of light was used to illustrate the loss of original individuality by the extremists of the "first class of poets," we are prompted to go further in our present interpretation. In the image before us light rushes back from the stars, out of their crashing, into a flowing river. Therefore, while we cannot insist, we can at least offer the conjecture that in this sudden flash of light Sordello has become intuitively aware of the dangerous excesses of poets of the "first class." He has beheld the reflected vision of the independent existence of light that, according to Browning, it is the poet's task to recreate to the degree his genius will permit. The question then arises: If Sordello has seen the vision, why, then, does he hesitate to act at once in the full light of his discovery? The answer is two-fold: (1) His vision has been intuitive, rather than intellectually certain; reflected, rather than real. (2) He is still a victim of the excesses of the "second class of poets" who, in their desire to preserve their personalities, become slaves to their own self-importance. But even a reflection of the truth produces a change, though it be merely partial, in Sordello's activity.

We already have noted his changed attitude towards Nature, a negative rather than a positive change: Nature is *not* as he formerly imagined it to be. Similarly, his conception of new activities is at first negative. As the next passage containing the star-image will show, there are certain things he resolves *not* to do:

> ". . . . Tush! No mad mixing with the rout   (III, 117)
> "Of haggard ribalds wandering about

"The hot torchlit wine scented island house
"Where Friedrich holds his wickedest carouse,
"Parading,—to the gay Palermitans,
"Soft Messinese, dusk Saracenic clans
"Nuocera holds,—those tall grave dazzling Norse
"High-cheeked, lank-haired, toothed whiter than
          the morse,
"Queens of the caves of jet stalactites,
"He sent his barks to fetch through icy seas,
"The blind night seas without a saving star
"And here in snowy birdskin robes they are,
"Sordello!"

But a negative course of action may spring from the desire for a new and positive form of existence. Sordello's transformation is therefore manifest in renunciation. He must give up his "strollings now at even-close Down the field-path" to delight in the pleasant pastimes of idle and idyllic love. He must renounce the pointless round of worldly pleasure.

It is the *pointlessness* of courtly society that is his most significant discovery, and it is this quality, or lack of quality, that Browning has marked with the star-image. He causes Sordello to see in Friedrich's court the image of beauties that have been assembled to no purpose, beauties gathered together from the far corners of the earth, but in the "blind night" without the aid of a guiding star. Sordello confronts the spectacle of *collected* beauties, the artistic antithesis of unified beauty, or of the compression of "the starriest into one star," and realizes its meaninglessness. As yet he cannot think of the positive values that must replace the objects of his renunciation. As yet he accepts no "lode-star" for himself, but at least he has seen the results of actions that have been undertaken in

The blind night seas without a saving star . . .

A portion of Book III, approximately seven hundred lines in length, separates this from the next literal occurrence of the star-image. Between these two points in the poem, however, three verbal connotations or associations with the star appear at regularly spaced intervals. Sordello's development in this division of the poem is influenced particularly by his contact with Palma, whose disquisition on the importance of the "out-soul" to life's fulfillment impels Sordello to make the positive resolution from which he formerly shrank.

Our position may be quickly charted. We have observed Sordello's renunciation of idleness and pointless pleasure, which amounts to his renunciation of the way of the world. He recognizes the fruitlessness of the professional troubadour's existence, for such a life holds success to be nothing more than his becoming the darling of a senseless society; it withholds any possibility of genuine achievement. The beauty of this ribald world is a collection of sensual delights. It is beauty without unity, without purpose; empty. It holds no happiness for a growing soul. It is the end of mind and body, complete annihilation.

> "Happiness must be,   (III, 162)
> "To feed the first by gleanings from the last,
> "Attain its qualities, and slow or fast
> "Become what they behold; . . . ."

One who accompanies this development attentively becomes hopeful that the change which Sordello has experienced may lead him at last to a positive resolve concerning which he can be intellectually conscious. He cannot, as yet, make the resolution himself; so that a suggestion from another mind must provide the impetus to decision.

Naddo interrupts with news from Mantua:—Ecelin has entered a monastery, divided his dukedom between his sons; Count Richard plans an immediate marriage to Palma. Sordello impulsively rushes to Verona; he must see Palma. "Appears Verona," and, incidentally, the point in the story of Sordello that, chronologically speaking, the reader has already reached in Book I, line 85.

> I' the palace, each by each,   (III, 273)
> Sordello sat and Palma: little speech
> At first in that dim closet, face with face,
> (Despite the tumult in the market-place)
> Exchanging quick low laughters: now would rush
> Word upon word to meet in sudden flush,
> A look left off, a shifting lip's surmise—
> But for the most part their two histories
> Ran best thro' the locked fingers and linked arms.

Then Palma speaks at length—. Her subject is the "out-soul." Her remarks include at least three instances of verbal association with the star-image:

> "How dared I let expand the force   (III, 319)
> "Within me, till some out-soul, whose resource
> "It grew for, should direct it? Every law
> "Of life, its every fitness, every flaw,
> "Must one determine whose corporeal shape
> "Would be no other than the prime escape
> "And revelation to me of a Will
> "Orb-like o'er shrouded and inscrutable.
> "Above, save at the point which, I should know
> "Shone that myself, my powers, might overflow
> "So far, so much, ...
> . . . .
>   "Seemed that orb, above
> "The castle-covert and the moutain-close,
> "Slow in appearing? . . . .
> . . . .
> "Was I to have a chance touch spoil me, leave
> "My spirit thence unfitted to receive
> "The consummating spell?"

Palma continues to relate her experiences, and to explain how the events of her life have led finally to the discovery of her "orb":

> "Exiled   (III, 427)
> "Within Goito, still one dream beguiled
> "My days and nights; 't was found, the orb I sought
> "To serve, those glimpses came of Fomalhaut
> "No other: but how serve it?—authorize
> "You and Romano mingle destinies?"

She has determined that her destiny, her "orb," is to serve the house of Romano, whose policy and fortunes depend upon her guidance. Furthermore, she has identified the "orb" with the star, Fomalhaut,[10] a fact which may argue the acceptance of this instance as a literal star-image. But since the "orb" is the more vividly emphasized image in the context of Palma's address to Sordello, I have regarded Browning's preference for the *name* of a star, rather than for the *word* "star," as a mark of his intention to suggest, rather than to *specify* the star-image in a passage whose subject is largely "historical."

Her half-brothers, Ecelin III and Alberic, have refused the burden of their inheritance, but she, Palma, will assume the task, advance the cause of the Emperor Friedrich with all the resources of ancient Romano. At the conclusion of her address she asks for Sordello's assistance; she proposes, therefore, to absorb him into her "orb":

> ". . . Then say if I have misconceived   (III, 549)
> "Your destiny, too readily believed
> "The Kaiser's cause your own!"

These are the words Sordello has heard, when, in Book I, lines 328-332, the same scene is referred to:

> . . . . . . does that one man sleep whose brow
> The dying lamp-flame sinks and rises o'er?
> What woman stood beside him? not the more
> Is he unfastened from the earnest eyes
> Because that arras fell between!

The lines in Book III repeat and complete the picture with another suggestion of the star-image:

> And Palma's fled.   (III, 551)
> Though no affirmative disturbs the head

---

[10] I have transcribed a note from *The Works of Robert Browning*, Camberwell Edition, II, 372: "Fomalhaut: a star of the first magnitude in the Southern Fish, evidently associated here (as in Dante's astronomy in 'Purgatory' i. 19-21 foll.: 'The fair planet which incites to love was making all the Orient to smile, veiling the fishes that were in her train') with Venus, who was a fish-goddess, and whose glance is dominant over Dante's Cunizza and Browning's Palma. The planet Venus is in the sign of the Fishes at the Spring equinox, the season when Dante arrived on the shores of Purgatory." Another note, in the edition of *Sordello* prepared by the Rev. Arthur J. Whyte, reads: " 'A star of the first magnitude in the mouth of the South Fish in the second degree of Pisces of the nature of Venus and Mercury' (Wilson, *Dict. of Astrology*). I can find no clue to its particular use here."

> A dying lamp-flame sinks and rises o'er
> Like the alighted planet Pollux wore,
> Until morn breaking he resolves to be
> Gate-vein of this heart's blood of Lombardy
> Soul of this body—to wield this aggregate[11]
> Of souls and bodies, and so conquer fate
> Though he should live—a center of disgust
> Even—apart, core of the outward crust
> He vivifies, assimilates.

The suggestions of the star-image before us, then, are the instances of the "orb" and the "lamp-flame" that resembles "the alighted planet Pollux wore." The passage in which these images occur is directly concerned with Sordello's development, but its content is largely that of the "historical decoration" of the poem. It is obvious, therefore, that the course of analysis here leads again to complications; not only the complications of form and composition, which affect the literary reputation of the poem, but also those complications that rightly belong to the complex development of Sordello's character.

The "orb," however, has been identified with the star, Fomalhaut; further-more, it cannot fail to suggest the passage in Book I in which Browning speaks of Dante's having absorbed the "herald-star," Sordello, into his "con-summate orb," especially when the details of the narrative here represent Palma as wishing to do the same thing. The symbolical force of Palma's "orb" is political, or possibly romantic, rather than poetical, but the action that she contemplates follows a pattern similar to that of the poetical activity imputed to Dante. For Sordello, indeed, the "orb" signifies a pattern of psychological activity that is of utmost importance to his development. He will discover later that he has given himself to an "out-soul" that does not suit his nature, but for the moment it is enough that he should have the experience of a positive resolution that involves his allegiance to a cause.

Stated somewhat differently, Sordello has admitted the value of the "lode-star," which he so arrogantly disavowed at an earlier stage in his experience. However, in what seems to me a most subtle act of controlling the complexi-ties of his narrative with the means of his artistic method, Browning has produced the image:

> A dying lamp-flame sinks and rises o'er
> Like the alighted planet Pollux wore,

that instantly reveals the positive value of Sordello's latest psychological experience without obscuring the negative condition of his intellect. Emo-tionally, Sordello turns to the "lode-star," but the star to which he turns is not real for him; it is a lamp-flame that looks like a mythological planet, a star of fancy, reminiscent of the ardent visions of Aprile. In other words, Sordello, overcome by his love for Palma, fancies himself competent to follow

[11] See also *Sordello,* I, 829-837.

the star of political action, when his real star is poetry. Whether or not this interesting effect is the, result of conscious artistry on the part of Robert Browning we cannot state or prove. The "facts" upon which we discuss it are admittedly tenuous. They arise from our general observations of the care with which Browning has used the star-image. They are supported by the particular observation that Browning has allowed only verbal associations with the star-image to appear in a section of the poem whose content is largely political, and in which the poet-hero is attempting to see himself actively engaged in an unpoetic enterprise, an act that would involve him in the affairs of the very world he has lately renounced,—the court of Friedrich. The real star does not belong to such a context.

In the light of these observations it may be appropriate to restate the opinion that the poem as a whole turns upon the problem of finding the means of giving direction to the poet's genius, the discovery of a discipline against pleasurable but pointless extremes. In the end, Sordello must solve this problem by the realization of his social responsibility. His present attitude (in the middle of Book III) is a sign that the first important move towards the goal has been accomplished. He has turned his attention positively to the "out-soul," with certain egocentric reservations, to be sure, but with sufficient emotional vigor to convince himself that he has at last seen the vision of his destiny. The intellectual error in his decision has already been stated; he has still to discover how poetic genius may serve society. Robert Browning himself leaves us in no doubt as to the significance of the transformed Sordello:

For thus [says Browning]   (III, 561)
I bring Sordello to the rapturous
Exclaim at the crowd's cry, because one round
Of life was quite accomplished.

As further proof of his intention that this is to be regarded as the turning point in Sordello's development, and in the poem itself, Browning continues with a long digression in his own character. The lines quoted above introduce the direct commentary that continues to the end of Book III. This division of the poem is perhaps one of the most puzzling for the reader as well as one of the most interesting for the student who is interested in Browning's artistic development. This digression is concerned incidentally with theories of poetry, but principally with the question of the poet's responsibility to society. It marks a transformation in Browning's conception of the "consummate orb," or the poem, that he was composing, and it foreshadows the events, or "incidents in the development of a soul," that were to occur as Sordello's story continued. It reveals, pertinently, the results of two of the most important of those "singular incidents" that interrupted the course of Browning's composition of the poem—the voyage to Italy in 1838, and the composition of *Strafford* in 1837—for both of these experiences led to his discovery of the "warped souls" of suffering humanity.

A star-image occurs within this digression. It is related by its context to the image of the machine, which is a symbol of the instrument of civilization. This machine, or "wheelwork," is the important image of the passage, so that the "stars" at the end of the following quotation are significant mainly because of what they imply for the "wheelwork" (that is, for civilization) and, to some degree, because of the nature of their association with other star-images in the poem:

> What do we here? simply experiment (III, 837)
> Each on the other's power and its intent
> When elsewhere tasked,—if this of mine were trucked
> For yours to either's good,—we watch construct,
> In short, an engine: with a finished one,
> What it can do, is all,—nought, how 'tis done.
> But this of ours yet in probation, dusk
> A kernel of strange wheelwork through its husk
> Grows into shape by quarters and by halves;
> Remark this tooth's spring, wonder what that valve's
> Fall bodes, presume each faculty's device,
> Make out each other more or less precise—
> The scope of the whole engine's to be proved;
> We die; which means to say, the whole's removed,
> Dismounted wheel by wheel, this complex gin,—
> To be set up anew elsewhere, begin
> A task indeed, but with a clearer clime
> Than the murk lodgment of our building time.
> And then, I grant you, it behoves forget
> How 't is done—all that must amuse us yet
> So long: and, while you turn upon your heel,
> Pray that I be not busy slitting steel
> Or shredding brass, camped on some virgin shore
> Under a cluster of fresh stars, before
> I name a tithe o' the wheels I trust to do!

Man forever moves towards the perfection of the "strange wheelwork" of civilization. Each individual, according to his capacity, adds "spring" or "valve" to the construction of the whole. Much depends, however, upon the nature of the "building time." In an age when the world in general is unconscious of the accomplishments of its able minds, progress is precarious. The death of creative individuals leaves no one to continue the work of construction, and no one, in fact, to operate that which already has been constructed; the machine falls to pieces to await the invention of better times and a "clearer clime." In addition to its suggestion of an afterlife, it is as a qualification of the "clearer clime" that the "cluster of fresh stars" seems to have been introduced into the picture of the "virgin shore," the direct contrast of the "murk lodgment" of an unsympathetic time and place. A poetical age, as contrasted to an age of ignorance.

Perhaps a poet may realize his social responsibility best by reassuring his age against the murky confusion of its ignorance. If he can produce a "cluster of fresh stars" to guide and to encourage the labors of statesmen, engineers, and scientists, are not his abilities thus better employed than they would be if he supposed himself to be destined to enter the purely political activities of men without vision? Such, at any rate, are the conclusions of Sordello, as we shall see upon following his adventure through the fourth main division of the poem. Such were the convictions of Robert Browning as he expressed them briefly in a letter to Elizabeth Barrett, February 11, 1845:

> I shall live always—that is for me—I am living here in this 1845, that is for London. I write from a thorough conviction that it is the duty of me, and with the belief that after every draw-back and shortcoming, I do my best, ... But of course I must, if for merely scientific purposes, know all about this 1845, its ways and doings, ...

CHAPTER III

SORDELLO, BOOKS IV, V, AND VI

THE problem of analysis becomes even more complex when one turns to the fourth, fifth, and sixth books of *Sordello*. In some respects the task becomes an analysis of confusion. It has seemed best, however, to recognize this confusion as a significant element in that which the poet has made. Consequently, there has been no attempt to explain away the existing irregularities of Browning's style, but an effort, rather, to bring them to light as important details of evidence.

In Book IV the star-image itself is hardly important. We have noted previously that it is an image that suits best a context that treats of the nature of poetry and poets, rather than the question of the poet's function in society. Book IV, however, deals principally with this question of social function. Sordello is here represented as ambitious to adjust his faculties to the performance of his social duties, and as hopeful that he may learn how to construct a "spring" that will be as useful to mankind as, let us say, the engineer's "valve."

It is appropriate, therefore, that "historical decoration," that is to say, the social background of the story, should fill the greater portion of Book IV. The representation of a man of action, Taurello Salinguerra, is a central theme. The characters of Taurello and Sordello are thrown into sharp contrast. Sordello's devotion to Palma now leads him to conclude that the life-pattern of a Taurello, although it may seem otherwise, is after all a design for the promotion of the welfare of mankind. But Sordello's first attempt to act in accord with his "conclusion" suggests its speciousness. When he tries to see the essential differences between Guelf and Ghibellin, he can find none:

> "Two parties take the world up, and allow   (IV, 939)
> "No third, yet have one principle, subsist
> "By the same injustice; whoso shall enlist
> "With either, ranks with man's inveterate foes. . ."

But some way, he thinks, must remain to serve the people:

> ". . . . . . . What if there remained   (IV, 940)
> "A cause, intact, distinct from these, ordained
> "For me its true discoverer?"

Sordello decides upon a course of action:

> Rome's the Cause!   (IV, 1012)
>
> . . . .
>
> . . . .
>
> Rome typifies the scheme to put mankind
> Once more in full possession of their rights.
> "Let us have Rome again! On me it lights

"To build up Rome—on me, the first and last:
"For such a future was endured the past!"
And thus, in the grey twilight, forth he sprung
To give his thought consistency among
The very People—

Because his attention is thus focused upon the experience of Sordello's attempt to realize his social function, it is not surprising that Browning has almost excluded the star-image from Book IV. One may pause to wonder, however, why Browning did not continue to chart the course of Sordello's development, even in this part of the poem, with the star-image. It seems as though he might have done so by using appropriate variations of the image, in accord with a method similar to that which produced the *star of fame* and the imitative *flower-stars,* which we have noted previously.[1] In these instances of variation it is nevertheless true that both represented states of mind in a poet's consideration of poetry and poets as such, the general subject of the first half of *Sordello*. In Book IV, however, the general theme has shifted, as we have seen, to the problem of discovering a social function for the poet.

But there are at least three instances of the occurrence of the star-image in Book IV: one of them is specific; the others are merely suggestive of the star. In both symbolic and structural importance it is the two verbal suggestions of the star-image that here outrank the specific instance. Furthermore, the order of their importance, which I have followed in presenting them for discussion, exactly reverses the order in which they appear in Book IV. The instance that most clearly recalls the symbolic force of the star-images in Books I, II, and III is the verbal association or suggestion near the end of Book IV. It is at this point in the narrative that the true poet-soul of Sordello once more asserts itself. It is an image that follows Sordello's query,

". . . . . What if there remained
"A cause, intact, distinct from these . . . . ?"

and that precedes by a few lines his decision to present Rome as a recreated Utopia. The appearance of the image at the moment of poetic resolve gives it added significance:

And Rome, indeed,   (IV, 1000)
Robed at Goito in fantastic weed,
The Mother-City of his Mantuan days,
Looked an established point of light whence rays
Traversed the world; for, all the clustered homes
Beside of men, seemed bent on being Romes
In their degree; the question was how each
Should most resemble Rome, clean out of reach.

[1] See above, p. 68 (the star of fame), and p. 65 (the flower-stars).

Thus Rome itself is represented as a fixed star. The reference to Goito assists in making this imagistic association emphatic by recalling those divisions of the poem in which the analysis of the nature of poetry is prominent.

Next in importance, as an example of the star-image, is the other verbal suggestion that recalls the association of the star and the "consummate orb." Sordello is talking to Palma of his interview with Taurello, whose words have thrown Sordello's efforts to recognize his social function into further confusion:

> " I   (IV, 907)
> "Esteemed myself, yes, in my inmost mind
> "This morn, a recreant to my race—mankind
> "O'er looked till now: why boast my spirit's force,
> "Such force denied its object? why divorce
> "These, then admire my spirit's flight the same
> "As though it bore up, helped some half-orbed flame[2]
> "Else quenched in the dead void, to living space?
> "That orb cast off to chaos and disgrace,
> "Why vaunt so much my unencumbered dance,
> "Making a feat's facilities enhance
> "Its marvel?"

This conception of the "orb," as representative of a cause, or of a unifying, directing entity, is similar to instances that have been noted previously. The *orb's* close association with the *star* is obvious.

The literal appearance of the star, at line 601, is, curiously, the least effective of the three. Its symbolic and structural meanings are insignificant. It does not, like the other star-images which have been analyzed (even those of Sidney and Count Richard in Book I), represent an artistic value of much interest. Its meaning, like its appearance, seems to be quite literal: it records a simple fact, that Taurello, among other accomplishments, did not hesitate to study the astrological lore of the Arabs:

> Carelessly, meanwhile, his life   (IV, 590)
> Suffered its many turns of peace and strife
> In many lands—you hardly could surprise
> The man; who shamed Sordello (recognize!)
> In this as much beside, that, unconcerned
> What qualities were natural or earned,
> With no ideal of graces, as they came
> He took them, singularly well the same—
> Speaking the Greek's own language, just because
> Your Greek eludes you, leave the least of flaws
> In contracts with him; while since Arab lore

[2] It is interesting to note here a change from the first edition that enhances the importance of the orb-image:

> First edition: As though it bore a burden which could tame
>   No pinion, from dead void to living space
>   — That orb consigned to chaos and disgrace,
>   —. . . .

> Holds the stars' secret—take one trouble more
> And master it! 'T is done, and now deter
> Who may the Tuscan, once Jove trined for her,
> From Friedrich's path!

It is interesting to note, furthermore, that the reading of the first edition of *Sordello* confirms the suspicion that a literal designation of the star-image should not appear in this context, even though the astrological connotations, "Arab lore," "Jove," and "trined" are common to both versions. The differences between the two texts suggest on Browning's part a correction to assure logical clarity, rather than a change to improve the effects of imagery.

> *First edition*:
> With no ideal of graces, as they came
> He took them, singularly well the same—
> Speaking a dozen languages because
> Your Greek eludes you, leave the least of flaws
> In contracts, while, through Arab lore, deter
> Who may the Tuscan, once Jove trined for her,
> From Friedrich's path!

This is the only "correction" in the final edition that adds a literal star-image to the text of the poem.

Taurello, who is after all the central figure of Book IV, is essentially practical, an able man of action. His way of life, like his famous garden, is methodical, systematic, orderly. He says, in effect: If the Arabs hold the secret of the stars—learn Arabic; but don't stop to wonder at the stars or the personal accomplishment of mastering another language. Greek may be a noble tongue, but the importance of knowing the Greek language is to assure one's self of protection against the crafty Greek who draws a legal contract. Taurello is like the captain of industry who becomes the advocate of "creative research," so long as it improves his product.

Since the star before us occurs within a part of Book IV that presents a contrast between Sordello and Taurello, there is perhaps one way in which one might argue its artistic necessity. One could say that since contrast is in the poet's mind as he writes, he might thus represent Taurello's thoroughly practical attitude towards an object of beauty, in contrast to the "impractical" and poetical attitude of Sordello towards the same object. It would be ridiculous to suppose, however, that the most competent reader of the poem should be expected to "feel" this effect, as he would be expected to "see" the effects of star-images in a poem like *Paracelsus*.

One remark, of some interest to a consideration of Browning's imagery in general, may be permissible in concluding these observations on *Sordello*, Book IV. It is this: the comparative unimportance of the star-image in Book IV does not signify a general removal of the elements of imagery from the poet's style or content. Actually, one of the most interesting images in the poem, judged by the significance of its symbolic, structural, organic, and even dominant effects, appears in this part of *Sordello*. It is the image of the garden that represents the character of Taurello Salinguerra.

The conclusion to Book IV reveals Sordello's intention to recreate Rome: a Rome poetically resplendent, assured of ascendancy as the fixed-star of social idealism, a Utopia marking the objectives of political progress. The inspiration is short-lived ; it is checked by the painful realization that the first lines of Book V disclose:

> Is it the same Sordello in the dusk   (V, 1)
> As at the dawn?—merely a perished husk
> Now, that arose a power fit to build
> Up Rome again? The proud conception chilled
> So soon? Ay, watch that latest dream of thine
> —A Rome indebted to no Palatine—
> Drop arch by arch, Sordello! Art possessed
> Of thy wish now, rewarded for thy quest
> Today among Ferrara's squalid sons?
> Are this and this the shining ones
> Meet for the Shining City? Sooth to say,
> Your favoured tenantry pursue their way
> After a fashion! This companion slips
> On the smooth causey, t'other blinkard trips
> At his mooned sandal. "Leave to lead the brawls
> "Here i' the atria?" No, friend! He that sprawls
> On aught but a stibadium. . . . What his dues
> Who puts the lustral vase to such an use?
> Oh, huddle up the day's disasters! March,
> Ye runagates, and drop thou, arch by arch,
> Rome![3]

The fixed star vanishes in the presence of "disasters." Sordello understands that a "Shining City" must be inhabited by shining citizens. His vision has been just another dream, true "Goito-manufacture," the product of a poet-nature that is still reluctant to face reality. But a growing intellectual competence warns him against the social impracticability of mere poetic fancy. Unwillingly he accepts his defeat; he is forced to see his *Rome* as the creation of a vainly individual and self-centered mind. He has seen the social fact: he is part of all men, and they part of him. But at the moment when his maturing intelligence should have disciplined his poetic vanity, he has been too weak for the struggle. He expresses his vision, knowing that his newly created star will burn out in confusion.

---

[3] An interesting commentary upon this suggestion of the fixed-star, though possibly not exact, occurs in a letter to Elizabeth Barrett, May 3, 1845: "For never did man, woman or child . . . . like a thing, not to say love it, but I liked and loved it, one liking neutralizing the rebellious stir of its fellow, so that I don't go about now wanting the fixed stars before my time [as Sordello did]; this world has not escaped me, thank God; and—what other people say is the best of it, may not escape me after all, though until so very lately I made up my mind to do without it; . . ."

The "Shining City" and the "shining ones," contrasted with the ugly fact of "disasters," connotatively suggest the star-image. It is only a few such verbal suggestions that permit our associating the star-image with Book V. There are no instances of its specific occurrence. These examples of verbal association may be presented most effectively by relating them to their positions in the narrative of Book V.

Sordello's first attempt to accomplish the fusion of his social and poetical ambitions has been a failure. His reluctant conclusion is that perfection, the dream, can be of no use to imperfect men; *Rome* falls:

<blockquote>

"Thou archtype   (V, 78)
"Last of my dreams and loveliest, depart!"
</blockquote>

It is Sordello speaking, and resolving that, if he is to help men, he must adopt their imperfect ways and use them for the creation of better ways:

<blockquote>

. . . . .   a low voice wound into his heart   (V, 80)
"Sordello!" . . . .
. . . .   "Sordello, wake!
"God has conceded two sights to a man—
"One, of men's whole work, time's completed plan
"The other of the minute's work, man's first
"Step to the plan's completeness: . . . . . .
. . . . the veil rent   (V, 102)
"Read the black writing—that collective man
"Outstrips the individual."
</blockquote>

To supply the "narrative" in very brief synopsis, Sordello has reached the point of greater intellectual firmness. His awakened intelligence, as distinct from his poetic vision, impels him to see the course of social evolution, particularly in its European aspects, down to his own times. The result is his adoption of the Guelf cause, which, though imperfect, he accepts as the better of the two political rivalries of the age. Sordello resolves to convert Taurello Salinguerra to the cause of the Guelfs, but his argument merely evokes Taurello's patronizing smile and pretended interest. The fault is not so much in the argument itself as in the spirit in which it is delivered. Sordello's manner gives the impression of his being more vitally concerned with himself as a champion than with the people whose wrongs he would right. His vanity has not left him. His failure to impress Taurello stirs his anger; whereupon, with heated passion, he makes a second attempt, this time launching the thesis of the poet-king. It is a subject better suited to his nature, for it declares the poet supreme among men. It is his reply to Taurello's indulgent insinuation that the poet can have little knowledge of, and little effect upon political affairs. The poet, declares Sordello, is responsible for all progress; men of action (the Taurellos of the world) are the poet's liegemen, helpless without direction from a creative mind.

It is within the address on the poet-king that suggestions of the star-image appear. Their values may be understood without extending the discussion beyond the limits of quotation:

> ". . . . . the world o'erlaid   (V, 541)
> "Long since with you, shall have in turn *obeyed*
> "*Some orb still prouder,* some *displayer,* still
> "More potent than the last, *of human will,*
> "And some new king depose the old. Of such
> "Am I—whom pride of this elates too much?
> "Safe, rather say, 'mid *troops of peers* again;
> "I, with my words, hailed brother of the train
> "Deeds once sufficed; for, let the world roll back,
> "Who fails, through deeds howe'er diverse, retrack
> "My purpose still, my task? A teeming crust—
> "Air, flame, earth, wave at conflict! Then, *needs must*
> "*Emerge some Calm embodied,* these refer
> "The brawl to—*Yellow-bearded Jupiter?*
> "No! *Saturn;* some existence like *a pact*
> "*And protest against Chaos,* some *first fact*
> "*I' the faint of time.* My deep of life, I know
> "Is unavailing e'en to poorly show" . . . . . .
> (For here the Chief Taurello immeasurably yawned)

I have italicized the words and phrases, in the quotation, which clearly suggest the image of the star, and which also suggest several of its symbolic meanings: poetry, poet, "lode-star," and "consummate orb."

As the address on the poet-king acquires its passionate momentum, Taurello's yawn is replaced by his immeasurable apprehension that Sordello is deadly in earnest. Further suggestions of the star-image mark Sordello's argument:

> ". . . . . : my art intends   (V, 642)
> "New structure from the ancient: as they changed
> "The spoils of every clime at Venice, ranged
> "The horned and snouted Libyan god, upright
> "As in his desert, by some simple bright
> "Clay cinerary pitcher—Thebes as Rome,
> "Athens as Byzant rifled, *till their Dome*
> "*From earth's reputed consummations razed*
> "*A seal, the all-transmuting Triad blazed*
> "*Above.*"

It is at the conclusion of this impassioned declaration that Sordello once more urges Taurello to join the Guelf cause (since it is the poet, rather than the man of action, who can see the end of the strife). Taurello, not in the least overcome by Sordello's argument, is nevertheless alarmed by his vehemence, and fearful lest Sordello's intense seriousness may work real harm to the cause of Romano. After a brief discussion with Palma, who is present, Taurello acts. He throws the badge of the house of Romano upon Sordello, seeming to say, in as complete a misinterpretation of Sordello's argument as possible: "All right, you would be a poet-king; now you *are* a king in fact; Romano's fate is in your kingly hands." To increase the intensity of the action, Palma then reveals the true parentage of Sordello; Taurello Salinguerra is his father. The "act," or "book," closes in a state of feverish emotion for Sordello, who is overwhelmed and completely unprepared for the sudden turn of events; for Palma, who sees Sordello absorbed finally into her "orb," and therein the realization of her ardent ambition; for Taurello, who, in sudden release from great strain, is already furiously busy with extravagant political schemes for the future.

That no literal designation of the star-image appears in Book V, unless the pointed references to Jupiter and Saturn should be so considered, is a fact which may well support the opinion frequently enunciated: that in *Sordello* this image is best suited to a context that discusses poetry and poets, as such, and the incidents peculiar to the development of Sordello's poetical nature. Book V is largely "political," concerned, in so far as it narrates Sordello's progress, with the social function of poetry. It is interesting to note, however, that the verbal associations with the star-image, in Book V, occur where we should reasonably expect them: in the opening lines, which refer to the poetic vision of new Rome, and in the plea for the poet-king.

It is nevertheless important at this point in our discussion to recognize an unmistakable change in the temper of the poem that to some extent contradicts, or at least modifies, the opinion that has just been restated. Since the moment of Browning's extended commentary in Book III, it is possibly a fact that we have been examining a different poem from the one of the first two and a half books. The difference in Browning's "argument," that is to say, the turning from the question, what is the poet? to the question, what is the poet's function in society? is not the cause of this change in temper; for, in our desire to credit *Sordello* with an essential unity of purpose, we have claimed that the poem as a whole turns upon the fundamental problem that is represented in the combination of these two questions. The change in temper is indicative, rather, of a change in Browning's attitude towards his subject with its consequent manifestation in a change in style.

This change in style is hardly apparent in Book IV, except as that portion of the poem may be seen in relationship to Books V and VI. For it is in discussing these final divisions of *Sordello* that we become defenseless in an attempt to claim complete artistic unity for the poem. For the purpose of emphasis, it may be said that for the comparatively detached, or dispassionate interest of the poet in the first half of his poem, these last two books disclose a projection of the author's personality and beliefs upon the materials of his narrative that is almost violent. This is the result of Browning's having "read" his tumultuous and manifold interests in poetry into the character of his hero. To depose the emphatic form for a language less extravagant, let me hasten to add that it is only by comparison that this difference between the first and the latter part of *Sordello* becomes evident. We have been aware repeatedly of the presence of Robert Browning in the first books of the poem, but we have noted that digressive commentary, rather than a too insistent identification of himself with his hero, has been the mode of his personal expression there. In Books V and VI he has either conceived of his hero's having reached a state of development that distinctly resembles himself, or he has become so much interested in the problem of a poet's social responsibility as to cause Sordello to become a Robert Browning. If the explanation lies in either of these suggestions, it is the second which seems to me the more likely. It is as if Browning suddenly realized all the problems that confront the poet who attempts to explain himself as a useful member of society; it is as if he then sought to defend himself against error by making an excited confession of his doubts and fears, in an effort to discover the one true way that could give him a full poetic life and a useful one.

The dramatic intensity of the poem reaches a peak in Book V, with the feverish energy of the "badge scene" and Palma's revelation that Taurello is Sordello's father. It is in these scenes, and in the action that immediately follows them, that Browning represents the triangular conflict among three forms of human activity: methodical and practical intelligence (Taurello), romantic devotion to a cause (Palma), and poetic insight (Sordello), each struggling to absorb the other two into an "orb" of action. The sudden turn of the "badge scene" practically forces the victory upon Sordello. Taurello experiences a sudden release from responsibility, Palma has achieved her ardent wish to unite Sordello to her cause. But Sordello is unprepared for his unexpected "victory." He discovers, instead of the decisive results to be expected of victory (the satisfying solution of former embroilments) that the conflict has been transferred to his own soul, where the struggle of the three forces continues with increased violence (the subject of Book VI) until death releases him. It is the conflict of head (Sordello) and heart (Palma) and hand (Taurello), a theme common to many of Browning's later poems, sometimes represented in the dual form of heart versus brain, spirit versus body, or, as in *Paracelsus,* Loving versus Knowing.

In spite of the allegorical style, which this interpretation of scenes in Book V may suggest, the characters nevertheless retain sufficient human personality to maintain a dramatic impression (the drama of "Action in Character," of course, of a kind represented in *Paracelsus*).[4] Taurello's release sends him off into a sudden whirl of political scheming, which is an interesting revelation of his emotional tension, and a contrast to his normal practicality of conduct; Palma is triumphant; Sordello, overwhelmed. Furthermore, the vigorous presence of Browning's own personality in both Book V

4 See above, pp. 40-43.

and Book VI produces a kind of poetry that we may call "confessional" drama.

The effect of the author's change in temper is to preclude the possibility of his attaining to the profound "consummation" that such a poem on such a theme might well have had. These final books of *Sordello*, we may conjecture, show signs of having been written in the heated mood of introspective analysis by a poet (of his own "second class") who has been impatient for expression, who has not waited to reflect in tranquillity, but who has completed his work in the excitement of self-revelation.

It is only by considering the importance of these changes in the poet's attitude towards his subject that some of the qualities of Browning's imagery in Books V and VI can be explained, and it is for this reason that I have thought it necessary to comment at some length upon aspects of the poem that may seem to have little to do with an examination of the functions of the star-image. The star-images in Book VI do not suggest conclusions quite the same as those drawn from the analysis of the symbolic and structural functions of the star-images in the preceding books, but our interest is, after all, to see what the poet has produced, rather than to plead his perfect consistency.

The star-images in Book VI, of which at least four are specific, again reveal changes in the author's attitude towards his subject. It is significant, also, that they appear in the first half of the book in which the intense internal conflict of Sordello's soul concludes with his death. The "confessional" quality in the action here presented is apparent in a characteristic of imagistic design that has been noted in the "confessional," *Pauline*, and also in the partially "confessional" *Paracelsus*, a pattern that has been identified as the blending and clustering of images. In *Sordello* the star-image of the first four books does not become a part of this artistic pattern to an appreciable degree. There are occasional instances of blending, like those of the *amaranth* and *star*, in the passage on Dante in Book I, and the *laurel blossom* and *star*, in the idyllic "each new sprinkle of white stars" of Book II, but nothing comparable to the design of the opening lines of Book VI.

The first of the specific occurrences of the star-image in Book VI shows the difference:

> The thought of Eglamor's least like a thought,   (VI, 1)
> And yet a false one, was, "Man shrinks to nought
> "If matched with symbols of immensity;
> "Must quail, forsooth, before a quiet sky
> "Or sea, too little for their quietude":
> And, truly, somewhat in Sordello's mood
> Confirmed its speciousness, while eve slow sank
> Down the near terrace to the farther bank,
> And only one spot left from out the night
> Glimmered upon the river opposite—

> A breadth of watery heaven like a bay,
> A sky-like space of water, ray for ray,
> And star for star, one richness where they mixed
> As this and that wing of an angel, fixed,
> Tumultuary splendours folded in
> To die.

The star is here only one of a number of significant images, or "symbols of immensity": the "quiet sky," "eve," "night," "river," "A breadth of watery heaven," "bay," "space of water," "wing of an angel," "Tumultuary splendours." Consequently, the star's former symbolic meaning, *poetry,* while possibly implicit in this instance as an element of "immensity," loses its particular emphasis in a blending with other aspects of "immensity." I have said that this blending and clustering of images is indicative of Browning's "confessional" manner. There is another reason why it is appropriate that these particular images should be gathered together at this particular point in the poem, a reason that exists apart from the consideration of the attitude of the poet towards his subject, and that arises out of the structural necessities of making a literary conclusion. We are thus forced into another complication of analysis, which, it seems to me, it is important to recognize and to preserve as one of the real complexities of the poem. Sordello, whether he be a Robert Browning or a character in his own right, has reached a point in his development where he at last confronts the "immensities" that affect all men, rather than those few that may affect a particular individual. Sordello is at last in the presence of truth:

>   And at last   (VI, 26)
> The main discovery and prime concern,
> All that just now imported him to learn,
> Truth's self, like yonder slow moon to complete
> Heaven, rose again, and naked at his feet,
> Lighted his old life's every shift and change,
> Effort with counter effort; nor the range
> Of each looked wrong except wherein it checked,
> Some other—which of these could he suspect,
> Prying into them by the sudden blaze?
> The real way seemed made up of all the ways—
> Mood after mood of the one mind in him;
> Tokens of the existence, bright or dim,
> Of a transcendent all-embracing sense
> Demanding only outward influence,
> A soul, in Palma's phrase, above his soul,
> Power to uplift his power,—such moon's control
> Over such sea-depths,—and their mass had swept
> Onward from the beginning and still kept
> Its course: but years and years the sky above
> Held none, and so, untasked of any love,
> His sensitiveness idled, now amort,
> Alive now, and, to sullenness or sport

Given wholly up, disposed itself anew
At every passing instigation, grew
And dwindled at caprice, in foam-showers spilt,
Wedge-like insisting, quivered now a gilt
Shield in the sunshine, now a blinding race
Of whitest ripples o'er the reef—found place
For much display; not gathered up and, hurled
Right from its heart, encompassing the world.
So had Sordello been, by consequence,
Without a function; others made pretense
To strength not half his own, yet had some core
Within, submitted to some moon, before
Them still, superior still whate'er their force,—
Were able therefore to fulfil a course,
Nor missed life's crown, authentic attribute.
To each who lives must be a certain fruit
Of having lived in his degree,—a stage,
Earlier or later in men's pilgrimage,
To stop at; and to this the spirits tend
Who, still discovering beauty without end,
Amass the scintillations, make one star
—Something unlike them, self-sustained, afar,—
And meanwhile nurse the dream of being blest
By winning it to notice and invest
Their souls with alien glory, some one day
Whene'er the nucleus, gathering shape alway,
Round to the perfect circle—soon or late,
According as themselves are formed to wait;
Whether mere human beauty will suffice
—The yellow hair and the luxurious eyes,
Or human intellect seem best, or each
Combine in some ideal form past reach
On earth, or else some shade of these, some aim,
Some love, hate even, take their place, the same,
So to be served—all this they do not lose,
Waiting for death to live, nor idly choose
What must be Hell—a progress thus pursued
Through all existence, still above the food
That's offered them, still fain to reach beyond
The widened range, in virtue of their bond
Of sovereignty. Not that a Palma's Love,
A Salinguerra's Hate, would equal prove
To swaying all Sordello: but why doubt
Some love meet for such strength, some moon without
Would match his sea?

While it has seemed proper to recognize the confessional temper of Books V and VI, especially the *first half* of Book VI, it must also occur to the observer of the imagery in the above quotations that the confessional manner by no means implies a complete loss of artistic control, even though it may preclude the poet's attainment to profundity or sublimity of expression. We have noted in the predominantly confessional *Pauline,* and in the partially confessional *Paracelsus,* that Robert Browning is capable of a degree of artistic control that saves even *Pauline* from utter formlessness. That he has sought in this instance to give artistic unity to the whole of his *Sordello* is a fact which both the logic and imagery of the above passage suggest.

Logically, he has returned to the fundamental problem of the poem, declaring,

> So had Sordello been, by consequence,
> Without a function.

This problem has nevertheless undergone a multiplex expansion; from a proposition that at first seemed simply "vocational," it has become the expression of the exhausting conflict within an individual soul seeking divine intelligence, the image of the quest for absolute and humanly unattainable truth. Sordello thus becomes involved in the interminable debate of Good and Evil, Spirit and Body, Man and Society, Beauty and Ugliness, Love and Knowledge, Truth and Fancy, Well and Ill, Virtue and Vice, Eternity and Time, Right and Wrong, Poetry and Politics. Too late does he realize what his *function* might have been (a thing that Robert Browning here proposes to decide for himself early in his own career); he crushes the badge of Romano beneath his foot, and dies.

The imagery in harmonious accompaniment to the logical thesis achieves a similar effect of unification and expansion. The most clear of the blended images in the passages quoted above have appeared in other parts of the poem: "sky," "sea," "eve," "river," "bay," "moon," "blaze" (flame), "foam" (surge), "ripples," "outward influence" (orb), "star." One of them, the moon, is now with a heightened significance that it formerly lacked. In other words, just as he has restated the fundamental thesis of the poem, both in its simple and in its expanded forms, so the poet has marshalled his images that they may assist in recalling the principal episodes of Sordello's story. The quotation imputed to Eglamor designates these images as "symbols of immensity"; so that they are obviously intended to assist in performing the double function of unification and expansion consistent with a literary conclusion; in other words, the *com*pression of "the starriest into one star" and the *ex*pression of one "consummate orb" of Truth.

The star-image therefore appears in its old and its new significance. It is a light of poetry, blended with other "symbols of immensity," in

> A breadth of watery heaven like a bay,   (VI, 11)
> A sky-like space of water, ray for ray,
> And star for star, one richness where they mixed

It is a "lode-star," or "out-soul," now completely fused with the image of the moon:

Of a transcendent all-embracing sense   (VI, 39)
Demanding only outward influence,
A soul, in Palma's phrase, above his soul,
Power to uplift his power,—such moon's control
Over such sea-depths,— . . . .
. . . .
. . .
. . . . such moon without   (VI, 92)
Would match his sea?

It is a "consummate orb" with both a poetical and spiritual significance:

. . . . . . and to this the spirits tend   (VI, 67)
Who, still discovering beauty without end,
Amass the scintillation, make one star
—Something unlike them, self-sustained, afar,—

Less clearly demonstrable, but nevertheless significant, is Browning's intention to relate the star-image to other important images of the poem as the story of Sordello's final struggle unfolds. His method is to suggest, rather than to define this relationship through the device of verbal association. The following quotations are intended to illustrate the method and to specify the nature of these relationships:

(1) The star and the sphere,

External power! If none be adequate   (VI, 111)
And he stand forth ordained (a prouder fate)
Himself a law to his own sphere? "Remove
All in completeness!"

(2) The star and the flame (and volcano),

Must truth be casual truth, elicited   (VI, 185)
In sparks so mean, at intervals dispread
So rarely, that 'tis like at no one time
Of the world's story has not truth the prime
Of truth, the very truth which, loosed, had hurled
The world's course right, been really in the world
—Content the while with some mean spark by dint
Of some chance blow, the solitary hint
Of buried fire, which rip earth's breast, would stream
Sky-ward!
          Sordello's miserable gleam
Was looked for at the moment:

(3) The star and virgin shore, wheelwork, and flame,

". . . . . . . but no mad wings transmute   (VI, 418)
"These limbs of mine—our greensward was so soft!
"Nor camp I on the thunder-cloud aloft:
"We feel the bliss distinctlier, having thus
"Engines subservient, not mixed up with us.
"Better move palpably through heaven; nor, freed
"Of flesh, forsooth, from space to space proceed

"Mid flying synods of worlds! No: in heaven's marge
"Show Titan still, recumbent o'er his targe
"Solid with stars—the Centaur at his game,
"Made tremulously out in hoary flame!"

Browning's comment upon Sordello's dilemma repeats the introductory lines of Book VI:

Must life be ever just escaped, which should   (VI, 561)
Have been enjoyed?—nay, might have been and would,
Each purpose ordered right—the soul's no whit
Beyond the body's purpose under it.
Like yonder breadth of watery heaven, a bay,
And that sky-space of water, ray for ray
And star for star, one richness where they mixed
As this and that wing of an angel, fixed,
Tumultuary splendours folded in
To die—would soul, proportioned thus, begin
Exciting discontent, or surelier quell
The body if, aspiring, it rebel?
But how so order life? still brutalize
The soul, the sad world's way, with muffled eyes
To all that was before, all that shall be
After this sphere—all and each quality
Save some sole and immutable Great, Good
And Beauteous whither fate has loosed its hood
To follow? Never may some soul see All

. . . .

As the poem continues to the conclusion of its sixth and last book, even the images of the *font* and *osprey* reappear. Their symbolic forces remain unchanged, for they belong to that class of images which has been defined as allegorical.[5] They may be regarded, however, as further evidence of the author's intention to complete the artistic pattern which he strove to perfect.

In the light of an examination of these phenomena in the imagery of Book VI, it is possible to suppose that the "irregular" *starry paladin* and *plunging star,* which qualify, respectively, the characters of Sidney and Count Richard in Book I, may have been inserted, with the same unifying intention, *after* Books IV, V, and VI had been written. It is pure conjecture, but nonetheless interesting, to imagine that the new emphasis that Browning gave to social background in the last books of the poem induced not only the heightened importance of Taurello Salinguerra[6] as a foil to Sordello, but also demanded a new Sordello. Accordingly, Browning may have returned (or turned intensively for the first time) to the original legends concerning his hero, to draw from them materials in evidence of Sordello's political and military achievements. It is certainly in Books IV, V, and VI that these accomplish-

---

[5] See above, pp. 52-53.
[6] See W. C. DeVane, "Sordello's Story Retold," *Studies in Philology*, XXVII (Jan., 1930), 1-24.

ments are given most attention, though possibly without convincing the reader of their importance. Having discovered a new Sordello, Browning may have felt the artistic necessity of introducing the theme of the poet-knight into a part of the poem, Book I, where it does not really receive adequate treatment. Such a change, unless it were a complete revision, would have resulted in a merely superficial alteration, in the simple though ineffectual addition of the images of the *starry paladin* and the *plunging star*.[7]

Such is the complex nature of the poem as a whole, that I have thought it unwise to withhold the conclusions to be drawn from various parts of my analysis until the end of the discussion. Accordingly, I have introduced several paragraphs in the nature of conclusion at various points where, it seemed to me, they would be most appropriate. The complications in literary form and in the history of the poem's composition, which we faced immediately in undertaking this analysis, have made the course of investigation uneven, to say the least. The differences between the first edition of the poem and the final "corrected" edition have not affected our analysis materially, for with but one, or possibly two exceptions already noted, the star-images of the first and final editions remain intact. The changes have been chiefly those of word-order and punctuation. All of the passages quoted above have been compared in their original and revised forms.

Very briefly we may recall some of the more significant conclusions. Of real importance to an appreciation of many of Browning's poems is the recognition of the difference we have noted in comparing the characteristics of two types of images that are distinguishable through their functions. These are the allegorical symbol, and the image capable of symbolic variation, represented, for purposes of simplification, by the *font* and the *star*-images, respectively. We have noted, also, the comparative structural effects of these two types of imagery and have attempted to prove that the type represented by the star is the more interesting. The artistic importance of the star-image has been demonstrated further by our having observed how often the study of its functions leads to a consideration of the basic themes of the poem, and how it marks the course of Sordello's development as a theme separable in a way from the "historical" incidents of the poem. Quite often the star-image has revealed not only the struggles of Sordello, but also the strong poetic convictions that were taking form in the mind of Robert Browning as he wrote and worked. It has pointed to similarities and differences between *Sordello* and other poems, principally *Pauline* and *Paracelsus*. The iteration of the star-image implies not only its structural, organic, and symbolic value, but suggests, as well, the possibility of its dominance in Browning's imagistic design. To make certain that it is a dominant image in *Sordello* would nevertheless require a comparative analysis of all the prominent images in the poem. Finally, the imagistic design of *Sordello* shows one of the important

---

[7] See above, pp. 54-56.

differences between the two general modes of discourse; the narrative, which for Browning was essentially the dramatic mode, and the "confessional" mode, which reveals, as it did in *Pauline,* the presence of the poet's own personality.

Certainly the star-images of *Sordello* point to a design for the poem as a whole that it is difficult otherwise to discern. From the moment of Sordello's general introduction as the "herald-star," we may trace the development of his regal nature by following the specific and verbally suggested occurrences of the star-image, a plan of procedure that is more orderly than the criss-cross design of the narrative. We discover him first as a boy, a poet born; then as an adolescent sophist, dallying with the excesses of the "first class" and the "second class" of poets; then as a young man abjuring the "lode-star" to please his vanity, trifling with imitative verses, which look so much like the real thing, and which promise worldly fame. As he approaches intellectual maturity, he realizes the pointlessness of a purposeless art, and a *starless* society that is about to make him its darling. His renunciation of this vain activity prompts his quest for the "lode-star" and his understanding of society as "collective man." He struggles to know his function. Palma absorbs him into her "orb," which for a time he conceives to be his proper sphere. His assurance leads to the vision of the fixed star of re-created Rome, only to be followed by the final shock to his vanity. This is the ultimate disillusionment that makes his vision of "immensity" possible. There is something eminently satisfying in this scheme of development, and it is not any the less logical because it has been pointedly emphasized by the image of the star.

Professor Paul de Reul in his *L'Art et la Pensée de Robert Browning,* p. 33, referring to the poet's preface to *Paracelsus,* makes the following significant observation regarding *Sordello*: "Dans *Sordello,* l'auteur pousse aux dernières limites le principe énoncé dans la préface de *Paracelse,* datée du 15 mars 1835 qui compte sur la collaboration du lecteur: Supposé que ma scène représente des étoiles, la fantaisie complaisante suppléera aux vides et unira les lumières éparses en une seule constellation, Lyre ou Couronne,—*Indeed, were my scenes stars, it must be his* [the reader's] *cooperating fancy which, supplying all chasms, shall connect the scattered lights into one constellation,—Lyre or Crown."*

It is possible, therefore, to see in *Sordello* an imagistic design that attempts to give unity to a complex narrative. It is a pattern similar in many respects to the design of imagery in *Pauline,* where the same complications, to a lesser degree, tend to obscure the "logical" plan of composition. Of the many stories told about *Sordello* the most interesting is the one relating Rossetti's discovery of the authorship of the anonymously published *Pauline* on the basis of his belief that it had been written by the author of *Sordello.* It is comforting to think that Rossetti, an artist and a poet, may have observed some of the same similarities in the design of images that the present analysis seeks to recognize.

Browning continues to work at least as much in the manner of painter and musician as in the traditional style of the writer. In a peculiar and perhaps unreal sense, his *Sordello* succeeds as painting and music; his color patterns have been repeated with skill, his musical themes echo according to a symphonic design. But his powers of logical exposition weaken beneath the conflict of mixed *genres* and rival modes of discourse.

Browning has here proposed to write a *story* of a kind that calls for diffuse rather than "repressed" expression. In other words, he has attempted to write a psychological novel in rhymed couplets. Of all the forms common to our literary heritage it is the novel which by its artistic "formlessness" best accommodates the dramatic and the narrative modes of discourse, and the mode of direct commentary. The analysis of character, and the effects of social environment upon character are familiar themes of the novelist. Description in the novel often becomes symbolic in an Egdon Heath, or in the *bull, wasp,* and *cypress tree* of a novel like Galsworthy's *Patrician,* to cite only two well-known examples.

That Browning was thoroughly conscious of the advantages of the novel form, in spite of his pretended disparagement of all novelists, may be observed in his *Sordello* and also in a portion of one of the famous letters to Elizabeth Barrett; August 11, 1845:

> Do you know, "Consuelo" wearies me—oh, wearies—and the fourth volume I have all but stopped at—there lie the three following, but who cares about Consuelo after that horrible evening with the Venetian scamp, (where he bullies her, and it does answer, after all she says) as we say? And Albert wearies too—it seems all false, all writing—not the first part, though. And what easy work these novelists have of it! a Dramatic poet has to *make* you love or admire his men and women,—they must *do* and *say* all that you are to see and hear, really do it in your face, say it in your ears, and it is wholly for *you,* in *your* power, to *name,* characterize and so praise or blame, *what* is so said and done . . . if you don't perceive yourself, there is no standing by, for the Author, and telling you. But with these novelists, a scrape of the pen—out blurting of a phrase, and the miracle is achieved— "Consuelo possessed to perfection this and the other gift"—what would you more? Or, to leave dear George Sand, pray think of Bulwer's beginning a "character" by informing you that Ione, or somebody in "Pompeii," "was endowed with *perfect* genius"—"genius!" What though the obliging informer might write his fingers off before he gave the pitifullest proof that the poorest spark of that same, that genius, had ever visited *him? Ione* has it *"perfectly"*—and that is enough! Zeus with the scales? With the false weights!

In *Sordello* the poet and the novelist, the artist and the psychologist are at war with each other. The result is what Professor Santayana has called "The Poetry of Barbarism," if by that phrase we are to understand the deliberate refusal of the poet to accept the forms of poetic art that already had been perfected for the uses of English poets. It does not follow, however, that

Sordello was written by a barbarian, but rather by a young artist who stood upon the threshold of an age which, for better or worse, demanded new forms of expression. He *could* wave the "topaz rod," as he did over *Strafford,* but he evidently felt utterly uncomfortable doing so. The overpowering conviction that he must discover his own age was stronger than his ambition to become one of the greatest of English poets; his passionate desire to recreate the ancient river of Light broke the partitions of traditional literary forms, so that, like his *Sordello,* he sought a social function that would provide the discipline which, as an artist, he knew he lacked, and which he could not find in imitating even the best models of poetical tradition. The struggle thus became a conflict of compression and expansion: the compression of his art, "the starriest into one star"; the expansion of his soul into "one consummate orb" of Truth.

CHAPTER IV

BROWNING'S PLAYS, 1835-1855

THE years during which Browning was occupied chiefly with the composition of *Sordello* were made even more strenuous by several "interruptions" which mark the beginning, or approximately the first third of the period which these years enclose. Among these "interruptions" were his plays. In point of time, the period of Browning's specifically dramatic interests extends from the date of *Paracelsus*, 1835, to the publication of *In a Balcony* in "Men and Women," 1855. However, the most productive years in this period closed with the publication of *Luria* and *A Soul's Tragedy*, 1846, only six years after *Sordello* had astonished the poet's reading public.

It is significant that the themes of practically all of Browning's plays show a direct relationship to the intellectual opinions and the philosophical speculations of *Sordello*. Perhaps this relationship shows most clearly in the earlier plays, *Paracelsus*, *Strafford*, *Pippa Passes*, and *King Victor and King Charles*, although the theme of love-caught-in-the-web-of-political-policy of *In a Balcony* is interestingly reminiscent of scenes between Sordello and Palma. Similarly, the plots of *The Return of the Druses*, *A Blot in the 'Scutcheon*, *Colombe's Birthday*, *Luria*, and *A Soul's Tragedy* show, if they are judged solely on the basis of intellectual content, that the close thematic connection with *Sordello* holds for the ten works here enumerated.

If it is true, as his own statements imply, that the course of Browning's poetical development was interrupted by the composition of plays for the stage, it is also true that the course of his intellectual progress is regular throughout this period of composition. Consequently, it will be well in undertaking an examination of these plays to observe the distinction between intellectual or philosophical development, on the one hand, and poetic or artistic development on the other. Beyond the thematic association mentioned above, for example, there is much less evidence to point the relationship between the plays and *Sordello*. Of necessity there are differences in form between his plays and his poems corresponding to Browning's conception of the differences between drama and poetry.

Furthermore, it will be accepted, I trust, on the basis of previous analyses of *Paracelsus* and *Strafford*, that among the plays themselves there are sharp variations in artistic design that, undoubtedly, have been made as the result of Browning's intention to write in some instances dramatic poems; and in others, plays for the stage. The analysis of the functions of the star-image in Browning's plays therefore becomes part of the many-sided problem of observing differences in artistic design, of attempting to understand Browning's attitude towards the theatre, and of explaining why the author of excel-lent dramatic monologues never became a first-rate dramatist.

It seems to me quite appropriate, therefore, to consider all of Browning's plays in a single section of this study and, for the sake of contrast, to include among them three important dramatic poems. *Paracelsus, Pippa Passes,* and *In a Balcony* were not intended for production in a theatre; the other plays, from *Strafford* to *Luria,* were, although Browning insisted that *A Soul's Tragedy*[1] was unfit for the stage. I include *Paracelsus* for reasons that have been stated in my discussion of the dramatic qualities of that work as com-pared with *Strafford;* I include *Pippa* because it is designated by Browning as a "drama," and because it contains some of his most effective dramatic poetry. *In a Balcony,* if for no other reason, claims a place in this list because of its successful performance on several occasions both in England and America.[2] Obviously, although I may refer to them in the course of discussion, I shall attempt no further analysis here of *Paracelsus* and *Strafford.*

The method that I have employed in analyzing the function of the star-image in these plays has been identical with that which I have used previously. The results of analysis have been different. In the first place, they point to a distinction between the general effects of the star-image in the stage plays and the non-stage plays. It is the distinction that already has been noted in the comparison of imagistic effects in *Paracelsus* and *Strafford:* that the *genre* of *Paracelsus* is original, and the *genre* of *Strafford* is imitative. These differences between originality and imitation may be accepted, I think, as indicating, respectively, the principal difference between Browning's non-stage plays and his stage plays.

In the analysis of *Strafford* I have made certain statements that, in the light of an examination of Browning's plays as a whole, may seem to call for retraction. I have commented there upon the young artist's command of form, upon his restraint, and upon his apparent technical mastery of the *genre* in which he was working for the first time. It seems to me unnecessary to retract the purport of these remarks. *Strafford* is after all a first play, written by a very young man. The youth of the playwright and the novelty of his undertaking warrant a certain critical indulgence. But when the playwright tries again and again without noticeably improving his dramatic technique, or appreciably increasing his knowledge of the theatre as a unique form of expression, when it is noted that the style of *Strafford* is essentially typical

---

[1] Browning thought ill of this play, probably, as Professor Lounsbury ironically suggests in discussing it in his *The Early Literary Career of Robert Browning,* because of all his plays it was the best qualified for dramatic presentation. Elizabeth Barrett thought well of it, as her letter to Browning, March 30, 1846, shows. *A Soul's Tragedy* was performed by the London Stage Society, March 13, 14, 1904. (See DeVane, *Handbook,* p. 174.)

[2] W. C. DeVane, *Handbook,* p. 225. Sir Frederick G. Kenyon in the Centenary Edition, *The Works of Robert Browning,* IV, xxii, adds this detail: "In the *Poetical Works* of 1863, . . . *In a Balcony* was removed from *Men and Women,* and placed among the 'Tragedies and other Plays' which occupied vol. II; and in 1868 it received its present position, which chronologically is the most suitable, between *Men and Women* and *Dramatis Personae.*"

of all the plays Browning wrote for the stage, with the possible exception of *A Soul's Tragedy*, then, one can only record one's critical disappointment. In no sense do Browning's plays, with the exception of those that I have classified as his original, or non-stage plays, suggest an artistic development comparable to the pattern of development otherwise manifest from *Pauline* through the dramatic lyrics and romances to *The Ring and the Book*. In a very real sense the stage plays are a digression from the main line of the poet's development.

Except for its multiple appearance in *Paracelsus*, the star-image is restricted in all of Browning's plays to an approximate average of three literal instances. In *Pippa Passes* it occurs nine times; in two of the plays, *The Return of the Druses* and *A Soul's Tragedy*, it does not appear at all. As the direct result of my examination of the star-images, and, unavoidably, of many of the effects in these plays of imagery in general, I have assumed that the essential difference between the "stage" and the "non-stage" plays is, respectively, the difference between *imitation* and *originality*. Instead of calling *Paracelsus, Pippa,* and *In a Balcony* "non-stage plays," it will be better to call them Browning's *original* plays, and to call the "stage plays" his *imitative* plays. This definition is useful, I think, because it coincides with another opinion that many readers of Browning have held either frankly or in innocent disguise: the opinion that the poetic vitality of these original plays is superior to the intended or hoped-for dramatic vitality of the imitative plays.

Of the difference in the results of analysis, which I have mentioned, the opinions stated in the last several paragraphs are typical. In other words, my investigation has led to the formulation of opinions that have more to do with Robert Browning's general artistic development than with the detail of occurrences of the star-image. While the functional characteristics of the image continue to form the basis of discussion, the noticeable change in these functional characteristics, which is to be observed by comparison with the imagistic phenomena of earlier poems, requires a change in the mode and in the matter of discussion. The natural consequence of having observed the comparatively limited appearance of the star-image in this group of plays was to begin a search for causes that would explain this change in the poet's method of expression.

In searching for these causes, I have been brought to the task of attempting to realize the artistic struggle that was going on in Browning's mind as he wrote. I have been unable to ignore, for example, the comparatively diminished force of the star, and other images, in his imitative plays. Furthermore, I have decided that this weakening in the force of his imagery cannot be explained satisfactorily on the basis of the "count" of images, or merely by reference to *genre*, although both of these phenomena explain some things. Reference to *genre*, as we have seen in our analysis of *Strafford*, may explain the diminished number of poetical images, but from such an explanation it does not follow, necessarily, that fewer images should mean less forceful images. Poetical imagery in the plays of William Shakespeare is forceful, in spite of its dramatic application, whether abundant or limited. The explanation lies elsewhere. It is to be sought for, with a minimum of success, perhaps, and with much greater difficulty, through an attempt to understand the attitude of the artist toward his subject and toward his form. After all, we are not concerned primarily with the question of whether or not Browning should have used poetical imagery in his plays, but with why, apart from dramatic considerations, he did not use it more effectively.

One fact we should not forget in any consideration of Browning's plays, imitative or original: when he began to write them he was a very young man, intensely striving, as we have seen him revealed in *Sordello,* for spiritual and artistic control. Towards the end of the period in which he was working so hard over his plays, he confessed to Elizabeth Barrett that all he ever wanted or intended to do was to write *R. B. a poem.*[3] It was this that he was aiming to do in his original plays and in *Pauline* and *Sordello.* It was this that he may have thought he was doing when he wrote his *imitative* plays, in which the subjects, but not the forms, were his own. Another fact, which is implicit in his personality, and which seems often to be ignored, or at least not emphasized, by his biographers, is that he was very ambitious for literary success. Writing was his job, and he wanted to make it a profitable one. What more natural than that an enthusiastic young man, such as he was, should become rationally convinced that the invitation from Macready to write a play was the way to success, as, in a measure, it really was? But it was this invitation, and others like it, that interrupted the composition of not only *Sordello,* but of *R. B. a poem.* The imitative plays, in spite of their many evidences of genius, never rise to the artistic level of the poems for which Browning became famous, nor to the intensity of those for which he became infamous.

The examination of an artist's motives, interesting though it is always, leads to pitfalls of interpretation that one can only do one's best to avoid. One does not go far in one's examination of these plays before becoming aware of paradoxical complications; such as, that in writing his plays Browning emerges almost at once from the obscurity of *Sordello* into the comparative clarity of *Strafford* and *King Victor and King Charles,* a fact which cannot be denied as a great improvement in his art. Furthermore, it is a real question whether the great poems to come would have been written as well without the technical discipline that a course in playwriting would and did provide. In a certain sense Browning was "going to school" for the first time in his life, beginning to discover the values of a formal, as distinct from a "natural" education. Was it not *discipline* for which he confessed a consuming need in telling the story of *Sordello?*

[3] Letter to Elizabeth Barrett, February 11, 1845.

Paradoxical collision, such as these observations produce, is likely to lead to confusion, except that, in the instance of the present analysis, one has only to return to the star and other images in the imitative plays to rediscover the comparative ineffectiveness of these images in the light of the great effect of imagery in other works by the same poet. It is possible to know these plays rather well without giving much attention to their imagery. Analysis of the functions of the star-image, and, I am partially convinced, of other images in Browning's imitative plays, does not reveal the imaginative power of the poet as does the analysis of imagery in an original play like *Paracelsus*. Examination of the imagery of *Macbeth* reveals a greater Shakespeare; examination of the imagery in Browning's imitative plays shows a young artist in the process of submitting for the first time to the dictates of pre-scribed form. A study of the star-image, at any rate, does not disclose the greater or hidden beauties of his plays in the same sense that it illuminates the darkness of *Sordello*.

One of the conclusions we should be inclined to draw in regard to the nature of the star-image in Browning's imitative plays is that its presence seems to have been skillfully *arranged for,* rather than artistically demanded; that the star-image in these plays is part of a well modeled *organization,* rather than an inevitable detail in the creation of *organic unity.* We cannot remove it from its context without damage to a well-made pattern, but, on the other hand, we cannot think of it as wholly essential to our understanding of these plays. Looking for the cause which will explain these facts, we reach the con-clusion that the task before the dramatist was one of organization according to pre-established pattern, as he understood that pattern, rather than the search for the form that was inevitable for his dramatic energy.

The less effective use of the star-image in the imitative plays must be ex-plained, I think, by giving some attention to Browning's attitude towards the drama of his age and to the pre-established pattern of dramatic form that he sought to follow, for it cannot be explained fully by our observing its relationship to the structure and meaning of the plays in which it occurs. Such an explanation is effective only when total form and imagistic pattern are so closely bound together as to become virtually one. In *Pauline, Paracelsus,* and *Sordello* this unity exists, for the imagery in these works is not only one with the total design, but, in *Pauline* and *Sordello,* it *is* the design.

For readers of his dramatic monologues a most natural query is: why did Robert Browning never become a great dramatist? or, to state it otherwise, why did he, of all poets in the nineteenth century who seemingly might have done so, fail to produce one dramatic masterpiece? In a large measure Browning has answered this question himself by omitting to "confess" any such ambition. In his works he has given us nothing comparable to Hamlet's speech to the players, nor has he written any letters or diaries that would remove all doubt as to his genuine interest in, and real knowledge of the theatre. He wrote magnificently of painters, musicians, and poets, and his *The Bishop Orders His Tomb* alone shows his detailed interest in sculpture. His fondness for historically obscure and long-forgotten personages might have found a Paracelsus among the minor Elizabethan dramatists (several of whom were to be exhumed during the early nineteenth century), had his interest in the theatre equalled his enthusiasm for other art forms.

None of the details of Browning's relations with the theatre of his time explains his attitude more clearly than the circumstances under which he began to write plays for the stage, for these circumstances disclose the pertinent fact that his career as a dramatist did not begin at his own suggestion.

> *Paracelsus* seemed to herald a change. In March 1836, there appeared in the *New Monthly Magazine* an article by John Forster headed "Evidences of a new genius for dramatic poetry," which boldly proclaimed that "Mr. Browning has the powers of a great dramatic poet," and that his genius waits only the proper opportunity to redeem the drama and elevate the literary repute of England. "Mr. Browning" was without doubt a precocious youth, but the task which was thus proposed him must have seemed a bit terrifying to a young man who was just about to complete his twenty-fourth year.
>
> Such an opportunity was offered to Browning by Macready on the evening of 26 May, 1836, after the first representation of Talfourd's classical *Ion.* . . . After the excitement of the theatre [a great success for Macready] came the supper at 56 Russell Square, with the toasts to Macready the actor, to Ellen Tree the actress, to Talfourd the host and dramatist, and . . . to the youthful poet, Robert Browning. As the guests were dispersing, Macready turned to the young poet of twenty-four and said, "with an affectionate gesture, 'Will you write me a tragedy, and save me from going to America?'" Browning was willing enough, but he was already so deep in *Sordello,* that two months elapsed before Forster, Macready's neighbour in Lincoln's Inn Fields, called to say that the subject decided upon was *Strafford.*[4]

The scene is an exhilarating one: Macready in the best of spirits, and the young poet ebullient, we may be sure, over the compliment he has received; but perhaps neither of them aware of what had been asked and promised. Browning's feelings may have been well expressed in his own lyric lines:

> My own month came;
> 'Twas a sunrise of blossoming and May.
> Beneath a flowering laurel thicket lay
> Sordello; each new sprinkle of white stars
> That smell fainter of wine than Massic jars
> Dug up at Baiae, when the south wind shed
> The ripest, made him happier; filleted
> And robed the same, only a lute beside

---

[4] Griffin-Minchin, pp. 107-108.

Lay on the turf. Before him far and wide
The country stretched:

(*Sordello,* II, 296-305)

But there was this important distinction in the artistic positions of the two young poets: no Eglamor had shown the perfect dramatic form to the nineteenth century; no Naddo, save in the blurred composite of a number of contemporary critics, stood at Robert Browning's side to direct his craftsmanship.

The circumstance suggests an analogy in which the facts are essentially the same, though the details and the degree of their importance are different. I have in mind a young artist who had exhibited to his friends a genuine though uninstructed talent for pen-and-ink drawing. In a moment of unguarded enthusiasm one of his cordial admirers, who was writing a book of stories from the *New Testament,* asked the artist if he would not prepare a set of suitable illustrations. The compliment, of course, evoked an immediate acceptance. For models the young illustrator selected copies of famous religious paintings; the results of his labor were meant to please, but they were, of course, unfortunately dismal. The venture thus became the occasion of awkward constraint for both author and illustrator. Something of the same nature was to embarrass the friendship of Browning and Macready as time went on. In other words, a young artist, who as yet knew nothing critically of the linear medium in which he had begun to work, attempted to imitate the pre-established design of another artistic *genre,* which depended for its effects not upon line, but upon the harmonious distribution of areas of color. Something of this kind happened to Robert Browning when he accepted Macready's invitation, and went on with it to produce *Strafford,* even though he was aware of many of the external differences that separated poetry and drama. Of his many intellectual gifts the power of criticism of his own and other men's work was not among those most noticeable. It is possible, I think, that Browning never properly understood the essential differences between his *original* and his *imitative* plays. But he was ambitious for the *literary* success that Macready's invitation promised. His attitude towards the drama remained, therefore, essentially uncritical; he was animated by the desire for success, hopeful of hitting upon a play that would please, but he never settled down to the real work of injecting life and beauty into the theatre of his age, a theatre in which, Professor Nicoll and other scholars assure us, there was room for both life and beauty. Had he determined of his own accord to become a dramatist, rather than to write *R. B. a poem,* the results might have been different.

Typical of Browning's attitude toward the stage, and, likewise, of the attitude of the stage towards Browning, is a letter he wrote urging the production of his *A Blot in the 'Scutcheon:*

Hanover Cottage,
Southampton,
Monday morning

My dear Macready,

"The luck of the third adventure" is proverbial. I have written a spick and span new Tragedy (a sort of compromise between my own notion [*King Victor and King Charles, The Return of the Druses*] and yours—as I understand it at least) and will send it to you if you care to be bothered so far. There is *action* in it, drabbing, stabbing et autres gentillesses, who knows but the Gods may make me good even yet? Only make no scruple of saying flatly that you cannot spare the time, if engagements of which I know nothing, but fancy a great deal, should claim every couple of hours in the course of this week.

Yours ever truly,
Robert Browning.[5]

The important phrase in this note to Macready is the parenthetical enclosure stating that Browning considered *A Blot in the 'Scutcheon* "a sort of compromise" between his and an actor-manager's notions of what a tragedy should be. He is not certain however; "a sort of compromise . . . as I understand it at least." Nor was Macready in any sense critically certain of the kind of dramatic literature he wanted. He was certain merely of his desire for a star's rôle, a fat part, which would swell the number and applause of his audience. He was an actor-manager attempting to demonstrate the practicality of the star-system.[6] Macready was not really concerned with the artistic distinctions between Browning's dramatic efforts and the kind of play for which he was instinctively seeking. Macready wanted *action,* which Browning interprets to mean "drabbing, stabbing et autres gentillesses." It seems to me that this fragment of intercourse between the poet and the stage of his time is a touchstone to an appreciation of a deep rooted misunderstanding that from the first held Browning and Macready apart, and that finally broke their friendship. It represents the impact of conventional theatrical opinion (an opinion far from being at all times critically conscious of the art of the theatre) upon native poetical genius in the act of attempting to pour its energy into a mould that no one concerned really understood.[7] Macready wanted plays that would fill the theatre, a fact which a self-centered poet in the process of discovering his "orb" could not be troubled to understand. Macready, on the other hand, could not be expected to appre-

---

[5] T. L. Hood (ed.), p. 5. Hood dates this letter "*ca.* 1840," under the heading, "To John Macready." I have assumed that the substance of the letter is nevertheless pertinent to the point which I wish to establish.

[6] Allardyce Nicoll, p. 47, "Above all we may look at the actor-manager star system and see there elements of danger for the theatre."

[7] *Ibid.,* p. 63, "Yet there were some poets who entered into the lists. Coleridge and Byron in the earlier years, aided by Talfourd, Sheridan Knowles, and Browning towards the end of the half century, tried hard to win popular applause for their efforts. None of them, however, really gripped the imagination of the age."

ciate that the man with whom he was dealing was to declare in his *Sordello* that the function of the poet (dramatic or lyric) was to reveal Man to men. It was an actor-manager's business to think of the box office, too. Both Browning and Macready were in a measure right in their objectives, but there was no common ground upon which they could discuss their objectives critically.

Another obstacle to Browning's success as a dramatist, and, at the same time, an indication that his mind was not focused upon the real objectives of the dramatist, was his ardor for publication. The evidence of letters, diaries, and literary anecdotes points unmistakably to the poet's ambition to succeed as a man of letters. Elizabeth Barrett comments upon his delight at seeing *Luria* in print.[8] Another item of more certain implications is the affair of *Colombe's Birthday* which, after his quarrel with Macready over *A Blot in the 'Scutcheon,* Browning had written at the request of Charles Kean.[9] In a letter to his friend Dowson he reveals his impatience:

New Cross, March 10, 1844.

My dear Dowson,

You remember I told you my appointment with C. Kean *had* been for that morning (Monday). . . . Yesterday I read my play to him and his charming wife (who is to take the principal part) . . . but he wants to keep it till "Easter next Year"—and unpublished all the time! . . . my play will take him two months at least to study, he being a special slow head. . . . Of all which notable pieces of information I was apprised for the first time *after* the play was read and approved of . . . for, it certainly never entered into my mind that anybody, even an actor, could need a couple of months to study a part, only, in a piece, which I could match with such another in less time by a good deal.

But, though I *could* do such a thing, I have a head,—that aches oftener now than of old,—to take care of; and, therefore, *will* do no such thing as let this new work lie stifled for a year and odd, . . . for something I *must* print, or risk the hold, such as it is, I have at present on *my* public. . . . You will not wonder if I have determined to print it directly. . . . The poorest man of letters (if *really* of letters) I ever knew is of far higher talent than the best actor I ever expect to know: . . . can't study a speech in a month! God help them, and bless you, my dear Dowson, says and prays,

Yours,

R. Browning.[10]

It is customary in defending Browning's reputation as a dramatist to blame his admitted failures upon the condition of the stage in the first half of the nineteenth century. We are informed upon Professor Nicoll's reliable authority[11] that there were conditions in the theatre of that time that certainly

---

[8] Letter to R. B. from Miss Barrett, March 30, 1846.

[9] See W. C. DeVane, *Handbook,* p. 133. DeVane also quotes from the letter to Dowson.

[10] T. L. Hood (ed.), p. 9, letter to Christopher Dowson, Jr.

[11] A. Nicoll, p. 57, "As is perfectly obvious a whole series of hindrances were operative cal-

wrought havoc upon the life of the drama. Professor Nicoll suggests, however, that the conditions in the Elizabethan theatre at the time of Shakespeare's arrival in London were perhaps as bad in their way as those that overcame ambitious playwrights of the early nineteenth century. If we could imagine the Elizabethan theatre without a Shakespeare, we might come closer to knowing the action Robert Browning should have taken to become a great dramatist. If we blame the age for his lack of dramatic success, we must also remind ourselves again that Browning did not attempt to understand the art of the theatre as he had the arts of painting, music, and poetry.

In the letter to Dowson quoted above, we may observe Browning's opinion of actors and the histrionic art. There is no suggestion that he ever paid much attention to the possibilities and limitations of dramatic as distinct from poetic projection. The dramatist works in a complex medium; for he must think not only of the literary quality of his work, but also in terms of the physical projection of his play in the theatre. The instrument of projection is, of course, the stage in one of its various forms, Greek, Roman, Mediaeval, Elizabethan, or Modern, involving such matters of concern as the relation, physical and mental, of the audience to the actors, the architecture of the theatre, the size of the theatre, the projecting platform, the "picture frame," the "fourth wall," and the importance or non-importance of scenery, lighting, costume, properties, and make-up. Browning's disdain for the art of acting is equalled by his apparent disregard of all the other means of dramatic projection, and, as in the instance of at least one of his plays, *A Blot in the 'Scutcheon,* by his demanding, from stage lighting, effects that the theatre of his time had no means of producing. He writes in a form that externally resembles the stage-pattern of his contemporaries, but that inwardly resembles theatre-design of poetic vision. He fails, or, let us say, he does not attempt to see the anatomy of the physical stage and the flexibility or rigidity of its several means of expression, a discovery that every great dramatist has made, before and since the early nineteenth century. He had been preceded by poetic dramatists who paid as little attention to the real stage as he. Two of them he admired in his youth, Shelley and Byron. For Byron the stage was "little more than a toy";[12] for the author of *Prometheus Unbound,* the physical stage hardly existed.

Browning did not regard the stage as a toy, and he was certainly aware of the physical reality of actor-managers. He attempted, however, to realize his success as a dramatist by following a pattern that was distinctly literary. The pattern itself is a difficult thing to understand, for it was a confused combination of "Beauties," which were thought vaguely to be Elizabethan.

culated to retard the development of higher drama. The coarseness of the audience, the vagaries of the actor-manager, the pruriency of the censor, the activities of the 'pirate' and the niggardliness of the publisher, all these cast their clouds over the playwriting profession. . . ."

[12] A. Nicoll, p. 168.

Even though the tradition of Shakespeare *had* survived in its original form, the theatre of the early nineteenth century could hardly have accommodated it physically. It had undergone several changes, however, in which the criticism and the dramatic technique of John Dryden, the editors and actors of the eighteenth century, and finally the romantic criticisms of the early nineteenth century had all had their share.[13] Added to this were the anthologies of "beauties" and "specimens," such as: *The Beauties of the English Stage,* London, 1737; William Dodd's *Beauties of Shakespeare,* 1752, significantly republished in 1821; Charles Lamb's *Specimens of English Dramatic Poets Who Lived About the Time of Shakespeare,* 1808, and republished, with the addition of the "Extracts from the Garrick Plays," the year after Lamb's death, 1835.

Confronted with reminders of his heritage such as these, a nineteenth century dramatist could but do his best to bring them all together in his work. Browning's imitative plays show several of these influences: his respect for the dramatic "unities," particularly the unity of time, in the morning-noon-afternoon-evening-night arrangement of acts and scenes, his imitations from Shakespeare's *Romeo and Juliet* and *Othello,* and, as we have seen, his willingness to accept a confused dramatic tradition rather than to invent a new one.[14]

But his imitative labors were partial rather than complete; so that while he achieved an external approximation of "Elizabethan" form, his internal form belonged very much to the tradition of *Sordello,* as the social theses of his plays disclose. He remained very much himself in the subjects he selected, and insisted upon driving his investigations of society ever farther into the question of social responsibility. Consequently, he does not escape the complications of artistic confusion that had made the composition of *Sordello* so feverish. While the plays do not suggest a conflict of *genres* identical with the confusion of the novel, the allegory, and the narrative poem, and the direct, narrative, and dramatic modes of discourse typical of *Sordello,* the plays are nevertheless the battleground of a contest between the *original* and *imitative* energies of the poet.

These observations lead naturally to the opinion that Browning's imitative plays, along with *Pauline, Paracelsus,* and *Sordello* constitute the laboratory of his poetic imagination, an opinion which, if accepted, makes the loss of his juvenile *Incondita* a less and less tearful consideration. He probably had every

[13] *Ibid.,* p. 88. "One great characteristic of this time is, of course, the interest in Elizabethan literature. . . . This was the period when the long buried works of the minor Elizabethans were unearthed; this, too, was the period when the criticism of Coleridge, Schlegel, Hazlitt and a host of others revealed a profundity in Shakespeare which had hardly been felt before."

[14] *Ibid.,* p. 71. "One might, therefore, have expected that, with their interest in the fortunes and dignity of the theater, some of the many novelists or poets of the period might have given something of dramatic worth to the early nineteenth century stage. Here again, however, we come back to the prevailing weaknesses of the romantic temperament. Among those who were most enthusiastic, Scott, Dickens, and Byron stand out chief; but all of these failed to study dramatic conditions in such a manner as to improve their own work."

reason for destroying *Incondita*. That *Pauline, Paracelsus,* and *Sordello* were the more important divisions of the laboratory is proved by Browning's continued regard for their welfare, although he sometimes pretended his disgust for them, and also by his willingness to give up dramaturgy without another attempt at (significant phrase) "dramatic writing." The genesis of *The Ring and the Book* is to be found in his early *original* poetry, rather than in his imitative works, although its architecture may owe something to the discipline of "dramatic writing."[15]

Furthermore, we must not forget that while Browning was at work in the laboratory, he was also busy in the studio, developing his knowledge of music and painting and, most important of all, modeling the sculptural[16] compactness of his unique dramatic monologue. *Porphyria's Lover* was published, under the title *Porphyria,* in the *Monthly Repository* for January, 1836. It is a poem that marks the discovery of a wholly individual art-form whose possibilities of *compression* deny none of the implications of consummate *expansion*. The brevity of the typical monologue is not the brevity of mere shortness; it is the brevity of a remarkable concentration, comparable to the muscular tension of sculpture which reveals the moment, and the space and time surrounding, preceding, and following the moment. It is a form perfectly suited to the intense personality of Robert Browning, for it resolves the conflict of forms of expression into unity, and permits the fusion of the poet's essential dramatic energy with his interests in other modes of artistic creation.

A search for causes that might explain the diminished force of the star-image in Browning's imitative plays has thus led to an examination of characteristics of the early nineteenth century theatre, and to an attempt to see more plainly the dramatic pattern that Browning followed. The conflict between originality and imitation, which becomes visible through this examination, is the same, I think, that Browning wished to specify in his preface to *Strafford*. The conclusion that we may draw from the recognition of this conflict, and from our observation of the poet's attempt to distinguish the forces opposed, may be thought of as an extension of the opinions already presented in the comparison of *Strafford* and *Paracelsus* in another division of this study.

Browning adopted the "Elizabethan" pattern in much the same spirit, it seems to me, as that in which he clamped the rigid strength of the rhymed couplet upon *Sordello*. In neither instance was he guided by a critical decision. Consequently he failed to discover the artistic possibilities and limitations of both the dramatic pattern and the couplet. He attempted to force them to do

[15] Letter to E. B., February 13, 1846, "I have lost, of late, interest in dramatic writing, as you know, and, perhaps, occasion."

[16] Browning's interest in sculpture is manifest not only in the subject-matter of his poetry, but also in his desire to become a sculptor as the result of his friendship for the American sculptor, W. W. Story.

things that they were never intended to do, and yet he succeeded partially in realizing their outward semblances. He is conscious, for example, of the details of dramatic organization: characters, setting, plot, acts, scenes, and the dramatic unities, but he is constantly forcing them to do the work of his *original* as distinct from his *imitative* dramaturgy. His interest remains, after all, in the drama of action *within* character, for it is the conflict *within* character, rather than the conflict *among* characters, with which he is concerned. He does not take the course of the great dramatist who, thoroughly conscious of the conflicts *within* character, seeks to represent them on the stage by actions that mirror the natural phenomena of conflicts *among* characters, thus to gain the approval of the knowing, who can see through the externalities of dramatic imagery, and the delight of the multitude, who are fascinated by the verisimilitude of the physical action.

Browning's imagistic technique, the development of which we have observed by examining the star-images in *Pauline, Paracelsus,* and *Sordello,* had gained too strong a hold upon his general artistic method to permit his getting rid of it entirely for the purpose of writing for the stage; yet he seems to have tried to do this very thing. It is as if his eagerness to succeed with the new pattern had brought with it the decision to eliminate everything that did not seem to belong. Thus he would quickly observe that the problems of design and organization, to the solution of which he had brought the full effects of his poetic imagery in other works, were to be solved by the dramatist by means of plot, incident, and the actions of characters. He would therefore restrict his imagery arbitrarily. We have noted that he did so.

But, without becoming frankly allegorical, Browning tries to make images and even symbols of his characters. Thus Strafford represents loyalty to the governmental idea of monarchy and comes into conflict with Pym, who stands for the ideal of democracy; Tresham represents social convention coming into conflict with the natural law of youthful love; Luria represents the warm truth of the heart as opposed to the cold knowledge of the brain. Furthermore, it is these abstractions, rather than vivid personalities, that clash in his imitative plays. In attempting to make his characters *act like symbols,* he lost the opportunity of making them act like people. It is all very well, poetically, to let Tresham and Luria drink their symbolical poisons, but it isn't the thing we should expect either of them to do in real life. There are so many other ways out of the situations in which they find themselves.[17]

The diminished *number* of poetical images in these plays may be explained as a result of Browning's serious attempt to cut to pattern; the diminished *force* of the images, as the result of the conflict between imitative and original energy, for through this struggle, in combination with the literary rather than dramaturgical ambitions of the poet, some of the life of the drama has been driven out. Under such conditions one should not expect to find either

---

[17] See T. R. Lounsbury, Chapter III, and pp. 147-155 of Chapter IV.

imagery or characterization accomplishing the effects of projection of which we know Robert Browning to have been otherwise capable. It is therefore natural to expect these imitative plays to be less efficient conductors of both dramatic and imagistic force than the dramatic monologues whose unique form perfectly suited Browning's unconventional spirit.

In spite of the less effective quality of the imitative plays, there were certain advantages for the poet to be gained from his act in composing them. I have maintained elsewhere that an examination of the imagery in these plays reveals a young artist in the process of submitting for the first time to the dictates of prescribed form. It is significant, I think, that he never again becomes involved in obscurities as puzzling as those of *Pauline* and *Sordello*, save incidentally in a poem like *Fifine at the Fair.* That the plays disclose a somewhat sudden emergence from the obscurity of the early original poems is a fact which is attributable in no uncertain degree to the disciplinary labors of composition to pattern. Even *Paracelsus,* regardless of the reputation it has acquired because of its many similarities to *Pauline,* qualifies, as we have seen, as work that is both logically and structurally superior. Suddenly the poet had achieved order, at a time in his life when he was also creating the apparent disorders of *Sordello.*

Throughout the tumultuous conflict of *Sordello* we have observed the poet's effort to realize the artistic control of the forces of compression and expansion, and we have, consequently sympathized with his passionate desire for discipline. The confessional manner of the latter books of *Sordello* has suggested the personal sincerity of his declarations. We have also witnessed his decision regarding the social responsibility of the poet, in which the conviction is implicit that with the realization of social responsibility the poet shall achieve discipline. In this confession and conviction there is an unmistakable insistence upon the discipline of the soul as distinct from the discipline of the body, a fact which implies the belief that once the heart is sure of its direction, the hand must follow.

In the midst of his work on *Sordello* Browning turned to writing plays, and thereby, since it was in response to another's suggestion, and since it involved his following a pattern that was not his own invention, to the discipline of the hand. In *Sordello* he was trying his heart; in the plays he was trying his hand. In two, and possibly three of his plays, *Paracelsus, Pippa Passes,* and *In a Balcony,* he was trying both heart and hand. The difference between these original plays and the imitative plays is noteworthy. This generality is not an attempt to state an indisputable truth; it is another means of coming to a clearer understanding of the artistic fact represented in the composition of the plays; it is another attempt to explain the quality of the star-images which occur in these plays.

That Browning's hand never became the "forthright craftsman's hand," which he deplored in *Andrea del Sarto,* is well proved by the simple fact that he never became as successful in writing plays as Andrea became in painting madonnas. Had he been a more skillful imitator and less an original artist, he might have fitted perfectly into the mould of the nineteenth century dramatist, with money and questionable fame in his pocket.

The discipline of the hand was nevertheless advantageous. Among other things, which his pattern forced upon him, was an important departure in the consideration of character. In his earlier poems it was his habit to concentrate upon one character. The Elizabethan pattern demanded many characters. Therefore, even though the characters of his plays continue to "talk like Robert Browning" (as Shakespeare's seem to talk like Shakespeare) and try to act symbolically, their increased numbers nevertheless demand the poet's thinking of them as distinct entities. The consequence is that Browning escapes noticeably from his tendency to absorb and to be absorbed by the characters he creates. He is forced into the attitude of artistic detachment, so important to the creation of poetry "dramatic in principle," an attitude that serves to restrain the confessional mannerism of the earlier poems, and that gives the poet freedom within artistic limits. Henceforth he must become in turn, and imaginatively, *all* of the characters he creates, without permitting all of them to become, unimaginatively, as many different aspects of himself.

Another aspect of the disciplinary consequence of following the Elizabethan pattern is evident in Browning's regard for the dramatic unities. It is possible that, with Browning's general artistic development in mind, we may be able to answer one of the questions that was raised by Professor Lounsbury, who, in speaking of Browning's "distinct hankering" for the unities, wrote as follows:[18]

> Before taking leave of the plays, it may be well to note that Browning, in no respect a follower of any school, in many respects a law unto himself, in his method of expression almost defiantly free from the trammels of the conventional—that Browning of all men should have been the only great writer of our day, at all events of our race, to deliver himself of his own accord into the bondage of the unities, and if not to accept fully that antiquated superstition, to be profoundly affected by it. . . . It was sometimes impossible to carry through the action of his drama within the limits required by his doctrine. Accordingly, he divided into two parts—as in "King Victor and King Charles" and in "A Soul's Tragedy"—what is really one play. So an artificial unity is gained at the expense of a natural one; for in each of these parts the action is limited to a single day. . . . In "A Blot in the 'Scutcheon" the stress of circumstances compels the extension of the time somewhat beyond the prescribed twenty-four hours. In general, the difficulties in which he involves himself by encumbering his motions with these fetters have been successfully surmounted; though in certain of them, and especially in "Luria," there is always present to the mind the perpetually recurring flaw in the observance of the unities, the moral impossibility of the events taking place in the limited time in which

[18] T. R. Lounsbury, pp. 153-155.

they are described as happening, and too often the physical impossibility. Why Browning should have voluntarily entered into a bondage which France had then flung off, it is not easy to say.

In answer may we not say that in cutting to pattern it was only natural that Browning should have been eager to comply with any details of the Elizabethan form that seemed at all definite? Furthermore, this, as well as other disciplinary exercises, may have been a good thing for an undisciplined poet.

In *Sordello* we have seen the insistent motion of the poet's mind towards compression and his use there of a literary pattern, the rhymed couplet, with which he evidently hoped to attain compression. The process had resulted, however, in squeezing his material into a congested and rather inarticulate mass, which to the casual reader looks like anything but compression. But the formula of the dramatic unities holds as one of its virtues a means of systematic compression in which structural joinery is a most important quantity. In the hands of a skillful dramatist it may therefore become the instrument of artistic restraint and emphatic condensation, which is of course a different thing from mere compression. At any rate, whether the conjecture be a good one or not, the dramatic monologues show that in some effective way Browning had learned the secret of condensation, and the comparison of *The Ring and the Book* with *Sordello* shows that he had also discovered a superior, if not perfect method of narrative articulation. That is to say, the poet was in the process of discovering artistic freedom, a liberty of expression aided rather than repressed by external injunction, the freedom which distinguishes excellent sonnets from those written by poets who cannot command the sonnet law. The difference between Browning and the accomplished sonneteer is that Browning invented his forms as well as his content, a fact which means that his experiments in the laboratory of poetry were ever the process of his becoming an original as distinct from a traditional poet. If this be barbarism, Mr. Santayana was and is pontifically right.

Perhaps the clearest evidence disclosing the poet's original presence in all of his plays is to be found in the similarity of their several themes with the interest in social theses which Browning "confessed" in *Sordello*. It would not be an exaggeration to say that all the social and political problems, which in turn the plays present separately in a manner characteristic of the orderly pattern that the poet follows, may be picked out of the intense though original confusions of *Sordello*. The mind of the poet continues its preoccupation with the general theme of social responsibility as he turns to the composition of plays coincident with and following his work on *Sordello*. Thus *Paracelsus* sets forth the opposition of Demogorgon to Promethean vision; *Strafford,* the conflict of monarchy and democracy; *Pippa,* the effects of uncalculating goodness upon the affairs of the scheming world; *King Victor,* social justice eclipsed by selfishness and weakness in the characters of rulers; *The Return of the Druses,* the strange companionship of gross deception and lofty political ambition; *A Blot,* social convention in conflict with natural law; *Colombe's Birthday,* the union of love and social justice; *Luria,* a conflict of civilizations; *A Soul's Tragedy,* moral disintegration before the social fact; *In a Balcony,* love and political policy. In addition to these the familiar themes of aspiration, love, and spiritual conflict are everywhere present in the plays. In *Sordello* Browning has attempted to see society as a whole; in the plays he is satisfied to regard its separate elements.

Our somewhat discursive approach to the specific analysis of the functions of star-image in these plays has been the result of attempting to examine the causes that account for the less effective force of the image, particularly as it appears in the imitative plays. The process of analysis again and again became involved in considerations of the nineteenth century stage, the Elizabethan dramaturgy, the matter of artistic discipline, and the conflict between imitative and original art. I have felt, therefore, the necessity of presenting a continuous discussion of these problems, for by that means I have been able to avoid a discussion that would have been both fragmentary and excessively repetitive. As I proceed with the details of specific analysis, I shall assume that the general statements that have been made need be referred to only in the instance of discussing exceptions to the rule.

PIPPA PASSES, 1841

Our analysis begins with one of the original plays. It is significant that in *Pippa Passes* seven of the nine images of the star attach to the story of Luigi. He has been inspired to give his life to a cause, and has evidently been led to his decision through contemplation of the "symbols of immensity":

> *Luigi.* Escape? To even wish that, would spoil all.   (III, 64)
> The dying is best part of it. Too much
> Have I enjoyed these fifteen years of mine,
> To leave myself excuse for longer life:
>
> . . . .
> I can give news of earth to all the dead
> Who ask me:—last year's sunsets, and great stars
> Which had a right to come first and see ebb
> The crimson wave that drifts the sun away—
> Those crescent moons with notched and burning rims
> That strengthened into sharp fire, and there stood
> Impatient of the azure—and that day
> In March, a double rainbow stopped the storm—
> May's warm slow yellow moonlit summer nights—
> Gone are they, but I have them in my soul!

In this passage the star is but one of a number of images of light that represent forces acting upon the soul of the young idealist. The eternity in which they originate makes the span of a man's life seem insignificant. They have fused into one truth, one "orb," in Luigi's soul. The passage recalls the opening lines of Book VI in *Sordello* where the decision was not to be made with such unquestioning dispatch.

The relationship of these lines to thematic as well as artistic elements in *Sordello* is corroborated by external evidence that has been set down as follows:

> It is easy to see that *Pippa Passes* is a happy by-product of the Poet's labors on *Sordello*. In his travels in northern Italy in June, 1838, in search of local color for *Sordello*, Browning came upon "delicious Asolo," a town he was to celebrate in his very last volume of poems. It was his imaginative observation of the life in that small city which gave him his materials for *Pippa Passes*. But the poem was certainly written on the spot in 1838, for we know from the letter which Browning wrote to Miss Haworth upon his return to England late in July of 1838 that he "did not write six lines while absent (except a scene in a play, jotted down as we sailed through the straits of Gibraltar)." It is possible that this "scene in a play" may be the present Part III of *Pippa Passes*, the scene between Luigi and his mother: the matter dealt with there, the questions of tyranny and revolt, of high and noble action, is the matter of *Strafford, Sordello, King Victor and King Charles,* and *The Return of the Druses,* poems which were much in Browning's mind at that time.[19]

As the scene reaches its climax, it is studded with star-images that show the originality of the poet's composition as clearly as they add emphasis to the contrast of character between Luigi and his mother. Theirs is a debate grounded upon the different faiths that they represent. The mother knows her son as a human being, but she cannot understand his superhuman aspiration; it is she who invokes the aid of age-old human arguments compact of basic paganism and a knowledge of human susceptibility to the charms of earthly love; it is she who calls upon *Jupiter, Juno,* and *Chiara* in an effort to substitute her "orb" for the one she cannot see, but which she knows intuitively to possess her son's imagination. She is a mother, perfectly human and womanly wise, jealous for her son's happiness, reluctant to see him throw himself away upon a cause she cannot understand. Luigi invokes the "bright and morning star" of God, the light of his superhuman resolve. But Luigi is almost persuaded to accept his mother's more "tangible" faith, when Pippa's song recalls his resolution:

> *Mother.*   Why go to-night?   (III, 145)
> Morn's for adventure. Jupiter is now
> A morning-star. I cannot hear you, Luigi!
>   *Luigi.* "I am the bright and morning star," saith God—
> And, "to such an one I give the morning-star."
> The gift of the morning-star! Have I God's gift
> Of the morning-star?
>   *Mother.*   Chiara will love to see
> That Jupiter an evening-star next June.

[19] W. C. DeVane, *Handbook*, p. 86.

Luigi. True, mother, Well for those who live through June!
Great noontides, thunder-storms, all glaring pomps
That triumph at the heels of June the god
Leading his revel through our leafy world.
Yes, Chiara will be there.
  Mother.   In June: remember,
Yourself appointed that month for her coming.
  Luigi. Was that low noise the echo?
  Mother.   The night-wind.
She must be grown—with her blue eyes upturned
As if life were one long and sweet surprise:
In June she comes.
  Luigi.   We were to see together
The Titian at Treviso. There, again!
   From without is heard the voice of
     Pippa singing—
   A king lived long ago,
   In the morning of the world,

. . . .

The mother has lost her son, for though his arguments were less persuasive
than her old wives' wisdom, he has seen the light of a new faith that trusts
only in God, that transcends argument, and that abjures the superstitions of
the old world which his political convictions have forced him to renounce.
Pippa sings, and Luigi knows,

  'Tis God's voice calls: how could I stay? Farewell!

There are two star-images in *Pippa Passes,* Part IV, Night. The second,
since it occurs in one of Pippa's songs, where we have good reason to expect it,
does not present much difficulty of interpretation. The first, however, is
momentarily a puzzle. It occurs in one of Monsignor's speeches. He is a
character from whom, we might argue, on basis of evidence drawn from
previous analysis, the association of the star should be withheld, just as it is
withheld from the characters of Ottima and Sebald. But closer examination
of this image reveals two interesting facts of both symbolic and structural
significance. Symbolically, this image is marked as "a falling star," an idea
appropriate to Monsignor; structurally, it occurs at the beginning of his
dark converse with Ugo, just as the second star-image, in Pippa's song, marks
the dissolution of Monsignor's dismal schemes, for it is Pippa's song which
recalls his lost vision of light.

 Scene.—*Inside the Palace by the Duomo.* Monsignor *dismissing his* At-
  tendants.
 Monsignor. Thanks, friends, many thanks! I chiefly desire life now, that
 I may recompense every one of you. Most I know something of already.
 What, a repast prepared? *Benedicto benedicatur* . . . ugh, ugh! Where was
 I? Oh, as you were remarking, Ugo, the weather is mild, very unlike
 winter-weather: but I am a Sicilian, you know, and shiver in your Julys here.
 To be sure, when 't was full summer at Messina, as we priests used to cross

in procession the great square on Assumption Day, you might see our thickest yellow tapers twist suddenly in two, each like a falling star, or sink down on themselves in a gore of wax. But go, my friends, but go! [*To the* Intendant.] Not you, Ugo! [*The others leave the apartment.*] I have long wanted to converse with you, Ugo.

Little more than a descriptive beauty attaches to the comparison of the "falling star" until one makes the structural and symbolical connection that the "stars" of Pippa's song require, for it is her innocent music which compels Monsignor to rise from the "gore of wax" into which he has so miserably sunk.

> *From without is heard the voice of* Pippa *singing—*
>
> Overhead the tree-tops meet,   (IV, 223)
> Flowers and grass spring 'neath one's feet;
> There was nought above me, nought below,
> My childhood had not learned to know:
> For, what are the voices of birds
> Ay, and of beasts,—but words, our words,
> Only so much more sweet?
> The knowledge of that with my life begun.
> But I had so near made out the sun,
> And counted your stars, the seven and one,
> Like the fingers of my hand:
> Nay, I could all but understand
> Wherefore through heaven the white moon ranges;
> And just when out of her soft fifty changes
> No unfamiliar face might overlook me—
> Suddenly God took me.
>   Pippa *Passes.*

The star-image in this song is the last in the "drama." One is tempted to wonder why the star was not more frequent in its occurrence in a poem whose principal character is herself an image of light. Furthermore, one may ask why the star is not directly associated with Pippa. I think there is an explanation. In the first place, Pippa's image of light is the sun, for hers is a general radiance shining upon all things, the just and the unjust. In the second place, Pippa's day, and the momentous events to which she innocently gives occasion during her day, have not been the result of strenuous resolution on her part. She does not know or need to know the experience of deliberate and intense devotion to an *orb,* for, without willing it, and without being able to escape God's influence, she has become, or is, a part of universal light. The star, in the many examples we have previously examined, is likely to imply effort of the soul and the will on the part of the individual who seeks his *orb*. It is interesting to note, furthermore, that in both the story of Luigi and of Monsignor Pippa's music impels these characters to resolve upon orbs of activity that will have both religious and social consequences, while the final action in the stories of Ottima and Sebald, and Jules and Phene, from which the star-image has been withheld, point to personal rather than social consequences. Thus the song that Monsignor hears is intended to have the same effect upon him as the "symbols of immensity" have had upon Luigi.

A brief analysis of Pippa's song to Monsignor shows, in fact, the similarity of its pattern to that of the dramatic lyric spoken by Luigi in Part III, lines 64-83, most of which has been quoted above. The imagery in both of these lyric passages is in many instances the same. Both sing of the beauty of the world in its manifold variety, although Luigi's "song" perhaps concentrates more upon the beauty of light. The concluding phrases are similar in their implications. Luigi says:

> Gone are they [the beauties of the earth], but
> I have them in my soul!

Pippa sings:

> Suddenly God took me.

Both indicate the possession of God's truth, although Luigi's achievement has been the result of active aspiration, and Pippa's the result of passive receptivity. That there is consequently less concentration in Pippa's song upon images of light is a fact which not only suits her character, but also the purpose of her song, the recall of Monsignor from the path of many vices to the path of many virtues. Such, in spite of the straining of plot in this part of the "drama," a fact which has made the transformation of Monsignor seem doubtful to many readers, was evidently the intention of the poet.

It is also interesting to observe that the lyrics of Luigi and Pippa recall associations that have been noted in earlier poems. Luigi's "Gone are they, but I have them in my soul" suggests the "consummate orb" and the compression of "the starriest into one star" of *Sordello;* his "gift of the morning-star," the "lode-star" of *Pauline* and *Paracelsus.* Not as clearly, perhaps, the line, "And counted your stars, the seven and one," in Pippa's song, suggests the lode-star of God's beauty to which Monsignor is reminded to return.

More interesting as an indication of Browning's artistic development, than as a further interpretation of the structural and symbolic nature of the images in the two lyric passages mentioned above, is the imagistic design common to both of them. We have noted that in neither of these passages does the star become a dominant image, but that it is one of a number of harmoniously blended images. This is a peculiarity in design that we have observed in *Pauline* and *Paracelsus,* and also in the sixth book of *Sordello.* In these poems this phenomenon of style was often associated with "confessional" poetry or with groups of lines that implied the "confessional" attitude of the poet. In *Pippa* it is associated with lyric poetry; in the instance of Pippa's song, with pure lyric; in the instance of Luigi's, with dramatic lyric. The change, I think, is significant. It shows a greater artistic detachment; for, while it does not deprive the author of personal expression, the lyric form being most capable of expressing personal vision, it nevertheless withholds him from a too obvious appearance in the faces of his characters.

The strong probability that the scene between Luigi and his mother was composed in 1838 means, of course, that even at the time in which Browning was engaged in the composition of *Sordello,* he had developed an artistic control which a reading of that poem does not lead one to suspect. His development as an artist is, therefore, not to be explained as a regular chronological progress, but as a development which was regular or interrupted in accord with his attitude towards the subjects upon which he chose to write, and his knowledge of the *genres* in which he worked. The confessional mannerisms of *Sordello* may well have arisen from the nearness of the subject to the poet's own experience; the artistic control of the Luigi scenes, from an aesthetic power that was developing at the same time. The same difference may be observed in his identification of himself with the drama of Paracelsus, in contrast to his truly dramatic detachment in *Porphyria's Lover,* a poem which belongs to the same period of production.

KING VICTOR AND KING CHARLES, 1842

The single star-image of *King Victor and King Charles* is in a sense misleading; for, while it is the only literal star-image in this play, it is connected with several verbal suggestions or associations with stars that give it a degree of symbolic and structural importance. It is the image of the star in eclipse. The play tells the story of the eclipse of political justice through the selfishness of King Victor on the one hand, and the weakness of King Charles on the other. The selfishness of King Victor is obvious, but the weakness of King Charles takes its origin in a form of human behavior that is usually considered virtuous: the act of filial obedience. The story of King Charles represents, therefore, the sort of paradoxical truth that Browning delighted to investigate: evil as the product of nominal good, or, *vice versa,* good as the outcome of evil. The "Note" prefixed to the first edition of *King Victor and King Charles,* and since retained in most modern editions of Browning's works, contains certain phrases that seem to warrant eliminating from this play an image whose characteristic associations with human virtue we have come to know through our examination of other poems and plays:

> So far as I know this Tragedy is the first artistic consequence of what Voltaire termed "a terrible event without consequences;" . . . I cannot expect them [his readers] to be versed, nor desirous of becoming so, in all the detail of the memoirs, correspondence, and relations of the time. From these only may be obtained a knowledge of the fiery and audacious temper, unscrupulous selfishness, profound dissimulation, and singular fertility in resources, of Victor—the extreme and painful sensibility, prolonged immaturity of powers, earnest good purpose and vacillating will of Charles— the noble and right woman's manliness of his wife—and the ill-considered rascality and subsequent better-advised rectitude of D'Ormea.

While we have no foundation for a strict rule that would eliminate the use of the star-image from any poem or play Browning might choose to write, we have acquired, nevertheless, a sense of its inappropriateness to the kind of subject and the kind of characters which this "Note" announces. The peculiar nature of the star-image in the play confirms such an opinion, I think, and at the same time represents one of the most interesting applications of the image to unfamiliar content.

King Victor and King Charles was written for the stage. It is to be expected, therefore, that what poetical imagery it may contain will be of a variety less effective, artistically, than the imagery of the original plays. Nevertheless, when the star-image in this play is considered alone, and when the sum of its one literal and several suggested occurrences, with their comparatively regular distribution, has been noted, one may see a slight, if not wholly important, variation from the imitative norm to which the stage-plays, in general, conform. Dramatically speaking, however, the count of these occurrences of the image is not sufficient to produce a noticeable heightening of effect, even though they assume, poetically, somewhat more than a casual importance.

A comparison of *King Victor and King Charles* with other plays written for the stage shows that in not only these, but in other respects, it varies from the imitative norm. We may recall that in the letter urging the production of *A Blot in the 'Scutcheon* Browning said, "I have written a spick and span new Tragedy [*A Blot*] (a sort of compromise between my own notion and yours—as I understand it at least) . . . ." *King Victor and King Charles* and *The Return of the Druses* were his "own notion." It is only reasonable, therefore, to anticipate a noticeable variation in comparing the design of *King Victor and King Charles* with the designs of the more strictly imitative plays.

Unlike the plays that conform to the Elizabethan pattern, *King Victor* does not follow the five-act plan of organization, nor does it attempt to realize fully the scheme of the dramatic unities. Its division is indicated by an organization into the following parts: "First Year, 1730.—King Victor, Part I and Part II"; "Second Year, 1731.—King Charles, Part I and Part II." In the amount of its imagery *King Victor and King Charles* shows a decline that accords with the general falling off in the amount of imagery in the more strictly imitative plays. The effects of its imagery are noticeable, however, through a number of verbal suggestions of the literal star-image, in the last speech in the play, and, as a general rule, in the longer speeches of the four principal characters of the play: Victor, Charles, Polyxena, and D'Ormea. Among these are the speech of Polyxena to Charles in "Second Year" II, lines 648-688, and the soliloquy of D'Ormea in "Second Year" II, lines 409-432. In addition to their imagistic effects, these speeches also possess a lyric quality similar to that which has been noted in some of the speeches in *Pippa Passes*.

There is in this play a sufficient distribution of verbal suggestions or associations with the star-image to suggest its structural significance. But the symbolic function of both literal and suggested instances of the eclipsed star is clear only when they are imaginatively related to each other by the reader. This relationship, I think, can be made more easily by a reader than by a member of an audience in a theatre. Consequently, the poetic virtues of the image do not carry over into dramatic effects as well as one might hope. The nature of these images may be seen in the following quotations from the play wherein, in quoting them, I have italicized words and phrases that I have considered suggestive of the eclipsed star. The literal image appears in the last quotation of the series.

First Year, 1730—King Victor.

> *Charles.*   Because I felt as sure, as I feel sure   (I, 17)
> We clasp hands now, of being happy once.
> Young was I, nor quite neglected, nor concerned
> By the world's business that engrossed so much
> My father and my brother: *If I peered*
> *From out my privacy,—amid the crash*
> *And blaze of nations, domineered those two.*
> *'T was war, peace*—France our foe, now—England, friend—
> In love with Spain—*at feud with Austria!*

> *Victor.*   D'Ormea!—for patience fails me, tread-   (II, 314)
>   ing thus
> Among *the obscure trains* I have laid, my knights
> Safe in the hall here—in the anteroom,
> My son,—D'Ormea, where? Of this, one touch—
>   [*Laying down the crown.*]
> *This fireball to these mute black cold trains—*
> then
> Outbreak enough!
> [*Contemplating it.*]   To lose all, after all!
> *This, glancing o'er my house for ages—shaped,-*
> *Brave meteor, like the crown of Cyprus now,*
> Jerusalem, Spain, England, *every change*
> The braver,—and when I have clutched a prize
> *My ancestry died wan with watching for,*
> To lose it! by a slip, a fault, a trick
> Learnt to advantage once and not unlearned
> When past the use,—"just this once more"
>   (I thought)
> "Use it with Spain and Austria happily,
> "And then away with trick!"

> *Charles.*   Hush—*a new world*   (II, 667)
> *Brightens* before me; *he is moved away*
> *—The dark form that eclipsed it, he subsides*
> *Into a shape supporting me like* you,
> And *I, alone, tend upward,* more and more
> *Tend upward: I am grown* Sardinia's King.

Second Year, 1731—King Charles.

> *Polyxena [seizing his hand].*   King Charles!   (II, 661)
> > *Pause here upon this strip of time*
> *Allotted you out of eternity!*
> *Crowns are from God*: you in his name hold yours.
> Your life's no least thing, were it fit your life
> Should be abjured along with rule; but now,
> Keep both! Your duty is to live and rule—
> You, who would *vulgarly look fine enough*
> *In the world's eye, deserting your soul's charge,*—
> Ay, you would have *men's praise,* this Rivoli
> Would be *illumined!* While, as 't is, no doubt,
> *Something of stain will ever rest on you*;
> No one will rightly know why you refused
> To abdicate; they'll talk of deeds you could
> Have done, no doubt,—nor do I much expect
> *Future achievement will blot out the past,*
> *Envelope it in haze*—nor shall we two
> Live happy any more. 'T will be, I feel,
> *Only in moments that the duty's seen*
> *As palpably as now*: the months, the years
> Of *painful indistinctness* are to come,
> While daily must we tread these palace rooms,
> Pregnant with memories of the past: your eye
> May turn to mine and find no comfort there,
> Through fancies that beset me, as yourself,
> Of *other courses, with far other issues,*
> We might have taken *this great night*: such bear
> As I will bear! What matters happiness?
> Duty! There's man's *one moment*: this is yours!
> *Putting the crown on his head, and the sceptre in*
> > *his hand, she places him on his seat: a*
> > *long pause and silence.*

> *Charles [to Polyxena].* I love you now.   (II, 752)
> > indeed.
> [*To Victor*] You never knew me.
> *Victor.*   Hardly till this moment,
> When I seem learning many other things
> Because the time for using them is past.
> If 't were to do again! That's idly wished.
> Truthfulness might prove policy as good
> As guile. Is this my daughter's forehead? Yes:
> I've made it fitter now to be a queen's
> Than formerly: I've ploughed the deep lines there
> Which keep too well a crown from slipping off.
> No matter. Guile has made me King again.
> *Louis*—'twas in King *Victor's time:—long since,*
> *When Louis reigned and, also Victor reigned.*[20]

---

[20] These two lines are italicized in the text of the play.

How the world talks already of us two!
God of eclipse and each discoloured star,
Why do I linger then?
                    Ha! Where lurks he?
D'Ormea! Nearer to your King! Now stand!
[*Collecting his strength as D'Ormea approaches.*]
You lied, D'Ormea! I do not repent.   [*Dies*]

In addition to those marked in the passages quoted above there are other examples of this kind to be found in other parts of the play. Their delicacy of suggestion, however, precludes their quotation as evidence of an artistic method that these clearer but not quite obvious examples are intended to illustrate. With the larger purposes of the present study in mind, perhaps the most interesting fact to be observed in the examination of the star-image in *King Victor and King Charles* is its peculiar form, the eclipsed star, and its association with human frailty rather than with human strength, an association which recalls the mythological stars, the stars of fancy, and the false stars of *Paracelsus* and *Sordello*.

A BLOT IN THE 'SCUTCHEON, 1843

A Blot in the 'Scutcheon was first published on the day of its presentation in Drury Lane Theatre, February 11, 1843. It was Number V in the series "Bells and Pomegranates." It was a play "written expressly for the stage. On September 5, 1839, Macready, the tragedian and manager of Drury Lane, had refused *King Victor and King Charles,* and on September 17, 1840, he had given back to Browning *The Return of the Druses.* With these rejections in mind, therefore, Browning seems to have written, sometime during the fall of 1840, *A Blot in the 'Scutcheon.* Before the end of the year the new tragedy was ready to send to Macready. . . ." I quote these details from Professor DeVane's *Handbook*[21] to show that in writing this play Browning was evidently striving to adapt his work to the demands of the great actor-manager. That these demands cannot be construed as a statement of the essential requirements for excellence in dramatic composition may be surmised from what has been stated previously. We have noted elsewhere that Browning thought of *A Blot in the 'Scutcheon* as a compromise of dramatic *notions*.[22] Browning's notion is exemplified, as we have seen, in *King Victor and King Charles;* Macready's, with even greater vagueness, in the attitude of an actor-manager, a strange combination of artistic, commercial, personal, and competitive animus.

The "compromise" did not please Macready, for, among other things, he was beginning to grow just a little weary of the insistent young poet who was so eager for success. Furthermore, he knew that the rôle of Lord Tresham would be a difficult one to act before an audience that was in the habit of

---

[21] W. C. DeVane, *Handbook*, p. 124.   [22] See above, p. 105.

taking its drama straight, for Tresham's conflict is against an intangible villain. The poison that kills him is in itself a symbol of defeat, rather than the inevitable consequence of a great action. Macready thought it would be better to end the play with Tresham's voluntary retirement to a monastery.

If compromise there be in this play, and certainly there are qualities in it that distinguish it from the other plays, it is possible that it exists only within the mind of Robert Browning, and without reference to any of the things that Macready really wanted. There is evidence in this play of Browning's having gone directly to Shakespeare for instruction. Macready himself, who was working on *Much Ado* at the time he was engaged in his controversy with Browning over *A Blot in the 'Scutcheon,* evidently made some of the suggestions which produced the similarity between the pairs of lovers in both plays. The connection with *Romeo and Juliet* may be seen at once.[23]

It so happens that the imagery of this play, to the extent in which it is concerned with light—particularly the light of the moon—suggests another "compromise" that Browning surely did not realize, for it turns out to be a compromise between the pseudo-Elizabethan form of drama and a method of production common to the theatre of our own day. For example, we have only to compare the recent acclaim by fourteen dramatic critics of Maxwell Anderson's *Winterset*[24] with the failure of *A Blot in the 'Scutcheon* on the stage of 1843 to come to a clearer realization of this opinion. *Winterset,* like *A Blot,* is poetical drama, but it has been produced with the assistance of a technique in stage-scenery and stage-lighting that was unknown to the theatre of the early nineteenth century and that certainly was essential to *Winterset's* excellent presentation. It is technical assistance of this kind that Browning unconsciously demands for his *A Blot in the 'Scutcheon.* Had his pattern been truly Elizabethan, he might have followed the method of Shakespeare who created his effects in lighting imaginatively, as he moved from one scene to another. But the stage directions in *A Blot,* as well as its imagery, reveal the poet to have been attempting to create an atmospheric stage-setting which, if perfectly realized, might have cast over his audience a spell powerful enough to convince them of the verisimilitude of his characters and their actions. Furthermore, for the creation of such an atmosphere he depends very largely upon the effects of light. In none of his plays does Browning "see" the action of his characters in a setting more vivid, with the contrasts of light and shade, and color, than he does in *A Blot in the 'Scutcheon.*

> Act I, Scene iii.—Mildred's *Chamber. A painted window overlooks the park.* Mildred *and* Guendolen.
>
> . . . .
>
> *She lifts the small lamp which is suspended be-*

[23] W. C. DeVane, *Handbook,* p. 129; G. R. Elliot, "Shakespeare's Significance for Browning," *Anglia,* XXXII, 90-162; T. R. Lounsbury, pp. 50-72, and 147-155.

[24] Drama Section, *New York Times,* Sunday, April 5, 1936.

*fore the virgin's image in the window
and places it by the purple pane.*

. . . .

*The window opens softly, A low voice sings.
A figure wrapped in a mantle appears at the
window.*

. . . .

Act III, Scene i.—*The end of the Yew-tree Avenue
under Mildred's window. A light seen through a
central red pane.*
     Enter Tresham *through the trees*

. . . .

*He retires behind one of the trees. After a
pause, enter* Mertoun *cloaked as before.*

Mertoun. Not time! Beat out thy last voluptuous beat   (III, 31)
Of hope and fear, my heart! I thought the clock
I' the chapel struck as I was pushing through
The ferns. And so I shall no more see rise
My love-star! Oh, no matter for the past!
So much the more delicious task to watch
Mildred revive: to pluck out, thorn by thorn,
All traces of the rough forbidden path
My rash love lured her to! Each day must see
Some fear of hers effaced, some hope renewed:
Then there will be surprises, unforeseen
Delights in store. I'll not regret the past.
     The light is placed above in the purple pane.
And see, my signal rises, Mildred's star!
I never saw it lovelier than now
It rises for the last time. If it sets,
'Tis that the re-assuring sun may dawn.
          *As he prepares to ascend the last tree of the
          avenue,* Tresham *arrests his arm.*
Unhand me—peasant, by your grasp! Here's gold
'Twas a mad freak of mine. I said I'd pluck
A branch from the white-blossomed shrub beneath
The casement there. Take this and hold your peace.
   Tresham. Into the moonlight yonder, come with me!
Out of the shadow!
   Mertoun.   I am armed, fool!
   Tresham.   Yes,
Or no? You'll come into the light, or no?
My hand is on your throat—refuse!—

[Tresham and Mertoun fight. Mertoun is slain. As he
is dying he sees the light of the "love-star" in Mildred's
window.]
          *As he endeavors to raise himself, his eye
          catches the lamp.*

. . . .

Mertoun.   And she sits there   (III, 158)
Waiting for me now! Now, say you this to her—
You, not another—say, I saw him die
As he breathed this, "I love her"—you don't know
What those three small words mean! Say, loving her
Lowers me down the bloody slope to death
With memories. . . .

. . . .

Tresham. Ho, Gerard!   (III, 177)
          Enter Gerard, Austin *and* Guendolen, *with*
          lights.
                    No one speak! You see what's done.
I cannot bear another voice.
          Mertoun.   There's light—
Light all about me and I move in it.
Tresham, did I not tell you—did you not
Just promise to deliver words of mine to her
To Mildred?
          Tresham. I will bear those words to her.
          Mertoun. Now?
          Tresham. Now. Lift you the body, and leave me
The head.
          As they have half raised Mertoun, *he turns*
          suddenly.
          Mertoun. I knew they turned me: turn me not
                    from her!
There! stay you! there!   *Dies.*

The picture in Browning's mind of Mertoun's death is well stated in one
of the speeches of Tresham to Mildred in Act III, Scene II:

                    Why, as he lay there,
          The moon on his flushed cheek, I gathered all
          The story ere he told it.

While they do not specify effects in lighting, nevertheless, such stage-directions as two of those quoted above, *The window opens softly, A low voice*
sings, and *A figure wrapped in a mantle appears at the window* are full of the
suggestion of melodramatic moonlight. Their suggestions are made particular
in the other stage-directions, and even in the descriptive lines of the dialogue.
The business of lights in the window shows clearly the poet's desire to combine his symbolic "love-star" with the mechanics of theatrical effects, a practice
which is always dubious even with the best stage equipment, for it is one
of the most obvious methods of calling attention to the mechanism of stage
production, and of thereby endangering the effect of poetical imagery that
otherwise might have carried a dramatic force. The symbolistic drama of the
Continent, of the later nineteenth and early twentieth century, has often been
the subject of ridicule because of its attempt to translate poetic imagery into
the terms of scenery, costume, properties, make-up, and lighting, as well as

character. Thus the poetical stars of *Paracelsus* attempt to become stage effects in *A Blot in the 'Scutcheon*. An actor such as Macready, could not be blamed if he felt a play of this sort denied him theatrical bread and butter, the lung-filling passions that swept audiences to glorious applause.

COLOMBE'S BIRTHDAY, 1844

Colombe's Birthday, "Bells and Pomegranates," Number VI, was published on April 20, 1844. It was prepared expressly for Charles Kean and his wife, Ellen Tree, but hustled into print with the characteristic impatience of its author, and thereby denied immediate production on the stage.[25] Later, 1853, it was produced with the success which its unexpected happy ending permitted. The rôle of Colombe was played by Helen Faucit.

If any image characterizes the action of this play, it is the image of the unfolding flower that represents the character and the experience of Colombe. Like the other plays *Colombe's Birthday* cannot be said to depend upon imagery for much of its dramatic projection, unless we are to imagine the audience before whom it was played to have been made up of individuals peculiarly sensitive to the charms of poetry as distinct from the persuasive motions of first-rate drama.

The star-images in *Colombe* have only that structural and symbolic importance that arises from their appearance at the right places in the course of the action, and from their association with ideas and emotions that we have begun to regard as characteristic of Browning's use of the image. Significantly the star-images appear in the scene in which Valence pleads the cause of Berthold and, in spite of himself, succeeds in confessing his own love to the highly amused Colombe. Quotations from this scene will at once disclose the familiar conceptions of the "guiding star" (the "lode-star"), the "orb" (or cause), together with a blending and clustering of images, which, as in *Pippa Passes,* is another indication of the poet's development of the *confessional* into the *lyric* manner of expression. In the quotation that follows I have italicized the literal images and also those phrases which connotatively suggest the association of the star with other images.

Act IV, Evening, Scene—An Antechamber.

. . . .

Valence. I am to say, you love her? (IV, 176)
Berthold. Say that too!
Love has no great concernment, thinks the world,
With a Duke's marriage. How go precedents
In Juliers' story—how use Juliers' Dukes?
I see you must have them here in goodly row;
Yon must be Luitpold—ay, a stalwart sire!
Say, I have been arrested suddenly

---

[25] See above, p. 105, Letter to Dowson.

In my ambitious course, its rocky course,
By this *sweet flower*: I fain would gather it
And then proceed: so say and speedily
—(Nor stand there like Duke Luitpold's brazen self!)
Enough, sir: you possess my mind, I think.
This is my claim, the others being withdrawn,
And to this be it that, i' the Hall to-night,
Your lady's answer comes: till when, farewell!
                                        He retires.
    Valence [*after a pause*]. The *heavens* and
                    earth stay as they were; my heart
Beats as it beat: the truth remains the truth.
What falls away, then, if not *faith* in her?
Was it my faith, that she could estimate
Love's value, and, *such faith still guiding me,*
Dare I now test her? Or grew *faith* so strong
Solely because no power of test was mine?
                        Enter the Duchess
    The Duchess. My fate, sir! Ah, you turn
                    away. All's over.
But you are sorry for me? Be not so!
What I might have become, and never was,
Regret with me! What I have merely been,
Rejoice I am no longer! What I seem
Beginning now, in my new state, to be,
Hope that I am!—for, once my rights proved void,
This heavy roof seems easy to exchange
For *the blue sky* outside—my lot henceforth.
    Valence. And what a lot is Berthold's!
    The Duchess.   How of him?
    Valence. He gathers earth's whole good into his
                    arms;
Standing, as man now, *stately, strong* and wise,
Marching to fortune, not surprised by her.
One great aim, like a guiding-star, above—
Which tasks *strength, wisdom, stateliness, to lift
His manhood to the height that takes the prize;*
A prize *not near*—lest *overlooking earth*
He rashly *spring to sieze it*—nor remote,
So that he rest upon *his path* content:
But day by day, *while shimmering grows shine,
And the faint circlet prophesies the orb,*
He sees so much as just *evolving* these,
The *stateliness,* the *wisdom* and the *strength,
To due completion,* will suffice this life,
And lead him *at his grandest* to the grave.
After this star, out of a night he springs;
A beggar's cradle for the *throne of thrones*
He quits; so, *mounting,* feels each step he *mounts,*
Nor, as from each to each exultingly

He *passes, overleaps* one grade of joy.
This, for his own good;—with the world each gift
Of God and man,—reality, tradition,
Fancy and fact—so well environ him,
That *as a mystic panoply they serve*—
Of force, untenanted, *to awe mankind*
And works *his purpose* out with half the world,
While he, their master, dexterously slipt
From such encumbrance, is meantime employed
With his own *prowess* on the other half.
Thus shall he prosper, every day's success
Adding, to what is he, *a solid strength*—
An aery might to what encircles him,
Till at the last, so *life's routine* lends help
That as the Emperor only breathes and moves,
His *shadow* shall be *watched,* his step or stalk
Become *a comfort or a portent*, how
He trails his ermine take significance,—
Till even his *power* shall cease to be *most power*
And men shall *dread his weakness* more, nor dare
Peril their earth its *bravest*, first and best,
Its *typified invincibility*.
Thus *shall he go on, greatening*, till he ends—
The man of men, the spirit of all flesh,
The fiery centre of an earthly world!
    The Duchess. Some such a fortune I had dreamed
                 should rise
Out of my own—that is, *above my power*
Seemed other, *greater potencies* to *stretch*—
    Valence. For you?
    The Duchess. It was not I moved there, I think:
But one I could,—though *constantly* beside,
And aye *approaching*,—still keep *distant* from,
And *so adore*. 'Twas *a man* moved there.
    Valence.   Who?
    The Duchess. I *felt the spirit, never saw the face.*
    Valence. See it! 'T is Berthold's! He enables you
To realize *your vision.*

    The Duchess, of course, is unmoved to acquiescence in the requests of
Berthold, but she is secretly delighted with the fervor of Valence's invitation,
and her own words declare that Valence is her star. It is fitting that the star-
image should illuminate Valence's speech, and it is interesting that he should
translate the "rocky course" of Berthold's path to fortune into the luminous
course of his own ambition, thus blending the images of Berthold's earth
with his own heaven. It is therefore entirely in keeping with the character
of Valence that, in Act V, Guibert, speaking of him to Berthold, should
describe Valence as follows:

> *Guibert.*   Sir, there's one Valence, the pale fiery man
> You saw and heard this morning—thought, no doubt,
> Was of considerable standing here:
> I put it to your penetration, Prince,
> If aught save love, the truest love for her
> Could make him serve the lady as he did!

Again, in the same act, another of the speeches of Valence reveals his ideal of the Duchess:

> *Melchoir.* . . . . (V, 995)
>   What we want is, your own witness,
> For, or against—her good, or yours: decide!
>   *Valence [aside].* Be it her good if she accounts it so!
> [*After a contest.*] For what am I but hers, to choose
>   as she?
> *Who knows how far, beside, the light from her*
> *May reach and dwell with, what she looks upon?*

Beauty and nobility are transformed by the resolute soul of Valence into images of his inevitably luminous vision. Just as his loyalty in personal trust persuaded him to translate the course of Berthold's earthly ambition into a pathway of light, so his love for flowerlike Colombe inspires his conception of her adorable radiance; the flower and the star become one through love. The lyric fervor of Valence's character and action is thus enhanced by the poet's blending of images.

LURIA, 1846

Luria was published April 13, 1846. With it appeared *A Soul's Tragedy,* whose publication had been urged by Elizabeth Barrett, to make "Number VIII and Last" in the series, "Bells and Pomegranates." *Luria* is Browning's *Othello.* Luria, the hero, is the embodiment of honor and good faith, with a determination to stand for his idealized conception of the civilization of Florence, even when Florentine hypocrisies have been unmasked. In a larger sense, Luria is the protagonist of the heart against the brain, in the eternal debate as to which of these human powers is the proper instrument for discovering truth. It is this debate that is the central theme of the play. Luria himself is the battleground of the struggle between *heart* and *brain*. His several soliloquies center upon this fundamental conflict. In Act V (lines 228-262), he states the problem in terms of the differences between Orient (heart) and Occident (brain), so that the play becomes involved in actions of a somewhat metaphysical nature, at the expense of losing the dramatic movement usually associated with human nature.

It is not surprising to find images of light, the star among them, in a play which is thus concerned with the problem of truth. As we shall note later, it is the sun, rather than the star, that is the image more characteristic of Browning's conception of Luria. The star-image is restricted, indeed, to two literal appearances. The first of these occurs in Luria's soliloquy in Act II. Tiburzio, his friend, has urged Luria to desert Florence and to join his forces to the cause of Pisa. He goes, leaving Luria to ponder the claims of cool intellectualism against his native *belief*:

> *Luria.* . . . .   (II, 269)
> Oh world, where all things pass and nought abides,
> Oh life, the long mutation—is it so?
> Is it with life as with the body's change?
> —Where, e'en tho' better follow, good must pass.
> Nor manhood's strength can mate with boyhood's
>   grace,
> Nor age's wisdom, in its turn, find strength,
> But silently the first gift dies away,
> And though the new stays, never both at once.
> Life's time of savage instinct o'er with me,
> It fades and dies away, past trusting more,
> As if to punish the ingratitude
> With which *I turned to grow in these new lights*,
> And *learned to look with European eyes.*
> Yet *it is better, this cold certain way,*
> Where Braccio's brow tells nothing, Puccio's mouth,
> Domizia's eyes reject the searcher: yes!
> For on *their calm sagacity* I lean,
> Their sense of right, deliberate choice of good,
> Sure, as they know my deeds, they deal with me.
> Yes that is better—that is best of all!
> Such faith stays when mere wild belief would go.
> Yes—when the desert creature's heart, at fault
> Amid the scattering tempest's pillared sands,
> Betrays its step into the pathless drift—
> The *calm instructed eye* of man holds fast
> By *the sole bearing of the visible star,*
> Sure that when slow the whirling wreck subside,
> The boundaries, lost now, shall be found again,—
> The palm-trees and the pyramid over all.
> Yes: I trust Florence: Pisa is deceived.

Thus Luria, against his nature, resolves to know the ways of a foreign civilization, for it is the resolute energy of the Florentine which is symbolized by the star, in contrast to the sunlit radiance of the Orient which is the soul of Luria.

The second literal occurrence of the star-image is in one of the speeches of the lady Domizia in Act IV. Luria has been informed of the plot of the Florentines to bring him to trial and disgrace, lest in their opinion he exert his power over the city, now that his army has won their victory. Husain, the Moor, Luria's friend and comrade, strongly urges revenge:

> Take revenge!   (IV, 165)
> Wide, deep—to live upon, in fleeing now,—

And, after live, in memory, year by year
And, with the dear conviction, die at last!
She lies now at thy pleasure: pleasure have!
Their *vaunted intellect that gilds our sense,*
And *blends* with life, to show it better by,
—How think'st thou?—I have turned that light on
                    them!

Domizia, realizing the power at Luria's command and the loyalty of his soldiers, seeks, nevertheless, to persuade him to save Florence from destruction. She reminds him that Florence was founded by one who followed his star as faithfully as Luria has followed his sun, and she points out the waste and uselessness of destroying a noble civilization, even though its faults may be many. Luria is moved by her plea.

Act IV, Evening.

Husian *goes.*

Luria. Have I heard all?   (IV, 188)
Domizia [*advancing from the background*]. No,
            Luria, I remain!
Not from the motives these have urged on thee,
Ignoble, insufficient, incomplete,
And pregnant each with sure seeds of decay,
As failing of sustainment from thyself,
—Neither from low revenge, nor selfishness,
Nor savage lust of power, nor one, nor all,
Shalt thou abolish Florence! I proclaim
The angel in thee, and reject the sprites
Which ineffectual crowd about his strength,
And mingle with his work and claim a share!
Inconsciously to the augustest end
Thou hast arisen: second not in rank
So much as time, to him who first ordained
That Florence, thou art to destroy, should be.
Yet him a star, too guided, who broke first
The pride of lonely power, the life apart,
And *made the eminences, each to each,*
Lean o'er the level world and let it lie
Safe from the thunder henceforth 'neath their tops;
So the few famous men of old *combined,*
And let the multitude rise underneath
And reach them and unite—so Florence grew:
Bracchio speaks true, it was well worth the price.

While verbal suggestions of both the star and the sun-images are to be found frequently in *Luria,* it is only natural that those of the star should be the less emphatic, for it is images of such aspects of light as the sun and fire which hold the greater symbolic importance for Luria. The "orb," for example, which has often suggested the star in other poems, is here specifically identified with the sun. In one of Luria's speeches in Act IV he declares:

> Ah, we Moors get blind   (IV, 299)
> Out of our proper world, where we can see!
> The sun that guides is closer to us! There—
> There, *my own orb! He sinks from out the sky.*
> . . . .
> . . . . . Night wipes blame away
> Another morning from my East shall spring
> And find all eyes at leisure, all disposed
> To watch and understanu its work, no doubt.
> *So praise the new sun,* the successor praise,
> Praise the new Luria and forget the old!

Near the beginning of the play an interesting astrological image appears
which also shows the importance of the sun-image and which at the same
time reveals a star that is meteoric and erratic, rather than calm and steady.

> Act I, Morning.
>
> *Secretary.*   Do but you think too,   (I, 110)
> And all is saved! I only have to write,
> "The man seemed false awhile, proves true at last,
> "Bury it"—so I write the Signory—
> "Bury this trial in your breast forever,
> "Blot it from things or done or dreamed about!
> "So Luria shall receive his meed today
> "With no suspicion what reverse was near,—
> "As if no meteoric finger hushed
> "The doom-word just on the destroyer's lip,
> "Motioned him off, and let life's sun fall straight."

In so far as these images of light enter the plot of the play, it is not an
exaggeration to say that the conflict of heart and brain has been transformed
into a battle between sun and star. Perhaps the most interesting of the verbal
suggestions or associations of these images is the one occurring near the beginning of Act II:

> *Luria.* Oh, their reward and triumph and the rest   (II, 72)
> They round me in the ears with, all day long?
> All that, I never take for earnest, friend!
> Well would it suit us,—their triumphal arch
> Or storied pillar,—thee and me, the moors!
> But gratitude in those Italian eyes—
> That, we shall get?
> *Husain.*   It is *too cold an air.*
> *Our sun rose out of yonder mound of mist:*
> Where is he now? So, I trust none of them.
> *Luria.* Truly?
> *Husain. I doubt and fear. There stands a wall*
> *'Twixt our expansive and explosive race*
> *And those absorbing, concentrating men.*
> *They use thee.*

Luria.   And I feel it, Husain! yes,
And care not—yes, an alien force like mine
Is only called to play its part outside
Their different nature; where its sole use seems
To fight with and keep off an *adverse force,*
As alien,—which repelled, mine too withdraws:
Inside, they know not what to do with me
Thus I have told them laughingly and oft,
But long since am prepared to learn the worst.

The phrases "expansive and explosive race" and "those absorbing, concentrating men" not only stand, respectively, as interesting connotations of the sun and star in this play, but also recall scores of similar meanings with which the poet has been preoccupied in his earlier works, especially in *Pauline, Paracelsus,* and *Sordello.* Once more the star has been identified with positive resolution as opposed to expansive radiance. Among the plays this distinction between sun and star as revelations of the poet's thought has been most clear in *Pippa Passes* where the sun of Pippa's innocent generosity has been compared to the star of Luigi's concentrated ambition.

Before turning our attention to *In a Balcony,* it may be well to comment, though hardly with the hope of offering an adequate explanation, upon the two plays which exclude the star-image. These are *The Return of the Druses,* published in 1843, as "Bells and Pomegranates," Number IV, and *A Soul's Tragedy,* which appeared with *Luria* in Number VIII. I feel that a detailed explanation of this exclusion might run into a lengthy discussion with the consequent danger of seeming to imply a greater dramatic significance for the poetical star-image than it actually possesses. Ultimately such an explanation would arrive at a conclusion which, it seems to me, may be stated quite · simply.

We have noted, certainly, in all of the plays, both "imitative" and "original," that the star-image is associated with an important character, either through his own words, or the words of other characters who so describe him. He is a character distinguished for singleness of purpose, an idea which can be tastefully symbolized with the singular clarity and unique brilliance of the star. A Paracelsus may indeed waver from the line of single purpose to behold a star of fancy, but his waverings are not sufficiently frequent to suggest a fundamental duplicity such as is represented in the characters of Djabal in the *Druses* and Chiappino in the *Tragedy.* Compact in the single personality of Djabal is at once an immense religious deception and a noble political ambition. The devotion of Anael to Djabal is blind. The conflict of good and evil is a subject in which Browning delighted, but his interest does not commit him to the necessity of marking the character who embodies that conflict with the sign of his approval, the star-image, even though his sympathies for such a one as Djabal may be great. Chiappino's story is one of moral disintegration. His one act of courage was an accident, "He was," as Mrs. Orr says, "shamed into nobleness."[26]

IN A BALCONY, 1855

For reasons previously stated, I have included *In a Balcony* among the plays. According to the distinctions I have made between the "imitative" and the "original" varieties of Browning's "dramas," *In a Balcony* is, at once, both and neither. Although it has been called fragmentary, it is so only in the sense that it does not fill the conventional form of the stage-play, and only as all of Browning's most interesting dramatic monologues are fragmentary through artistic necessity. Yet *In a Balcony* is not a dramatic monologue. Unique as it is among all of Browning's works, it seems to me to combine the technique of the forms which have been mentioned: the original drama, the imitative drama, and the dramatic monologue. Its resemblance to original drama is manifest in the vitality of its imagery as compared to the rather casual effects of the imagery in the imitative plays. Its approximation to the imitative plays is borne out by the fact of its actual production on the stage, by its clarity of design, its unity of time, its organized, as well as its organic one-ness. Its relationship to the dramatic monologue is evident in its superior analysis of character, the versimilitude of its characters, and its suggestive conclusion. It was written (1853) and published (1855) at a time when Browning was well on the way toward, if he had not indeed arrived at, the artistic position of disciplined control, and to the perfection of a new literary form which remains even today distinctly his own. From his effort to write for the stage, he had realized the effects of the dramatic unity of time; from his original development of the dramatic lyric and the dramatic monologue, he had discovered the method of compressing "the starriest into one star" and of realizing at the same time the expansion of his soul.

It is hardly possible that these achievements in the development of the artist can be seen in those passages of *In a Balcony* which contain the star-image, for they are but pieces of a whole from which Browning's artistic growth has made the extraction of illustrative quotations much less satisfactory than the removal of such passages from his earlier works has been. It is almost necessary to take *Pauline* apart in order to see it whole, for *Sordello* the same process holds. *Paracelsus* marks a tightening of the joints and a distinct approach to, if not the attainment of logical and imagistic unity. The dramatic lyrics and monologues, because of their compactness (but not merely for that reason), collapse when one begins to tinker with their machinery. The lines of *In a Balcony* that attach to the star-image are nevertheless clear in their illustration of Browning's continued use of the star-image for purposes that have evidently become fixed associations in his mind: Norbert speaking to Constance of his love for her says,

26 Mrs. Sutherland Orr, *Handbook*, p. 69.

                              How was it to be?   (161)
I found you were the cousin of the Queen:
I must then serve the Queen to get to you.
No other way. Suppose there had been one,
And I, by saying prayers to some white star
With promise of my body and my soul,
Might gain you,—*should I pray the star or no?*
Instead, there was the Queen to serve! I served,
Helped, did what other servants failed to do.
Neither she sought nor I declared my end.

. . . .

                              Love has been so long   (232)
Subdued in me, eating me through and through,
That now 't is all of me and must have way.
Think of my work, that chaos of intrigues,
These hopes and fears, surprises and delays,
That long endeavour, earnest, patient, slow,
Trembling at last to its assured result:
Then think of this revulsion! I resume
Life after death, (it is no less than life,
After such long unlovely labouring days)
And *liberate to beauty life's great need*
O' the beautiful, which, while *it prompted work,*
Suppressed itself erewhile. *This eve's the time,*
This eve intense with yon first trembling star
We seem to pant and reach: scarce aught between
The earth that rises and the heaven that bends;
All nature self-abandoned, every tree
Flung as it will, pursuing its own thoughts
And fixed so, every flower and every weed,
No pride, no shame, no victory, no defeat;
All under God, each measured by itself.

. . . .

                              I understand your soul.   (678)
You live, and rightly sympathize with life,
With action, power, success. This way is straight;
And time were short beside, to let me change
The craft my childhood learnt: my craft shall serve.
Men set me here to subjugate, enclose,
Manure their barren lives, and force thence fruit
First for themselves, and afterward for me
In the due tithe; the task of some one soul,
Through ways of work appointed by the world.
I am not bid create—men see no star
Transfiguring my brow to warrant that—
But find and bind and bring to bear their wills.
So I began: tonight sees how I end.

    Besides the lyric quality of the blended images, the most interesting detail
that these quotations show is the strict association of the star-image with the
character of Norbert; for it is he, rather than Constance or the Queen, who

approaches truth. It is therefore reasonable to declare that in all of Browning's plays the star-image is constant in its symbolical implications, and to maintain also that, in spite of numerous modifications, the prototypes of all these symbolical meanings may be found in *Pauline* and *Sordello*. The poetic force of the image, however, is generally speaking not as strong in the plays, with the exception of *Paracelsus*, as it is in the earlier poems. Browning's imitative labors tend to weaken its effects, and, simultaneously, his development of greater artistic control and his discovery of original forms of expression have a tendency to subject the use of poetical imagery in general to a functional position which equals, but no longer transcends, the importance of other ele-ments of expression and poetic form. Chronologically speaking, of course, *In a Balcony* does not belong to the period of the stage plays, but to the period of the famous volume, "Men and Women."

A study of the imagery in the earlier poems amounts in a large measure to a study of the very substance of the poetry and the chief artistic method of the poet. In the poems of the middle and latter periods of Browning's career the consideration of meter, rhythm, stanza form, and the other notable elements of poetic design is quite as essential to an understanding of the poet's art and thought as the examination of his imagery. As one of his favorite images, the star consequently loses, or, to state it otherwise, is relieved of the many burdens placed upon it during the years when it stood for the ideal of an artistic compression and expansion not yet achieved. Then, since the poet was incapable of actual control, he could aspire to artistic supremacy only by keeping his star ever before him; now, when artistic control is a fact in his poetical experience, he can detach the star-image from himself, or at least reserve it for characters whose actions remind him of his early struggles, or for others whose achievements, either in life or in art, ever inspire his approach to an ultimate consummation.

CHAPTER V

DRAMATIC AND LYRIC POETRY, 1840-1864

URING the years between the appearance of *Sordello*, in 1840, and the publication of *Dramatis Personae*, in 1864, Robert Browning wrote a great number of poems that, with increasing success, marked the ascendance of his poetical power and attracted a growing number of readers. Furthermore, these were times filled with experiences of a more personal nature, which, without much doubt, had their effect upon Browning's development as a poet. They included such events as the Letters between Robert Browning and Elizabeth Barrett, the marriage of the two poets, their life in Italy, and the death of Elizabeth Barrett Browning. With the possible exception of the imitative plays, the forms of which suggest a digression from the main line of his progress, the poetry of this period established Browning's literary reputation and laid the foundations upon which the lasting value of his art may be said to rest.

In a literary sense these years began with a series of pamphlet volumes, eight in number, called "Bells and Pomegranates." This series included all of Browning's plays (except *Paracelsus*, 1835, *Strafford*, 1837, and *In a Balcony*, 1855), his *Dramatic Lyrics*, and *Dramatic Romances and Lyrics*. The "Bells" were followed by *Christmas-Eve and Easter-day*, *Men and Women*, in two volumes, and *Dramatis Personae*. That many of the works in these collections were considered by their author to be poems "dramatic in principle" is a fact clearly indicated by their style and by their collective titles.

The star-image is sporadic rather than constant in its occurrence among these poems. This phenomenon, however, does not indicate a weakening in the artistic effect of the image, nor a lessening of the poet's regard for the symbolic appropriateness of the star as an image of resolution, aspiration, and supreme attainment. Real weakness in the effects of imagery, as the preceding examination of Browning's imitative plays is intended to show, is the result of a general weakness in the whole of a given composition. That the star-image does not lose its symbolic importance in the mind of the poet, but that Browning continues to reserve it for the expression of experiences with which it has become profoundly associated in his earlier works, is a fact which its functions in many poems of the middle period continually suggest. The sporadic occurrence of the star-image points, rather, to a threefold change in Browning's development. *First*, Browning's interests multiplied and the variety of his imaginative experiences increased, so that the variety of his images likewise increased to give vivid expression to as many new conceptions of life and of human nature; *second*, Browning's conception of poetic form matured to a degree that made possible his recognition of other means of communicative expression as the forceful equivalents of the imagistic technique; *third,* in consequence of a clearer conception of form, Browning realized that imagery is integral to, but not necessarily dominant in the composition of a poetic design.

A maturing interest in the varieties of imaginative experience is what we may regard as the result natural to the development of native genius. But the general improvement in the poet's conception of form is the result of his earlier experiments in the studio and in the laboratory of poetry. For a time the effort to overcome a tendency to reproduce "obscurities," similar to those of *Pauline,* had been relieved only by occasional flashes of artistic clarity, like the more luminous passages of *Paracelsus,* or the dramatic excellence of *Porphyria's Lover.* In the middle period of his life, however, clarity of form, rather than obscurity, was to predominate. The dramatic monologue, the dramatic lyric, and the argumentative poem were to attain, with remarkable consistency, their most perfect forms. Furthermore, these forms were to depend for their clarity not upon excellent imitations of preëstablished patterns, but, in each instance, upon Browning's having invented designs of expression peculiarly suited to his genius and his purpose.

It was inevitable that in the process of inventing new forms the poet should make changes in his technique. These changes are noticeable especially in his versification and stanza-form. Professor Harlan H. Hatcher, in his *The Versification of Robert Browning,* has observed that from *"Transcendentalism* to *Imperante Augusto* Browning's blank verse bears the stamp imprinted by the dramatic monologue. With few exceptions the meter is rough and often rebellious in the restraint of the pattern. In many instances this seems to be by design."[1] The *design* of the poet is certainly clear in the illustrations that Professor Hatcher mentions, among them the blank verse of *Cleon* as compared to the blank verse of *Caliban;* the blank verse of *Pompilia* as compared to the blank verse of *Sludge.* Furthermore, in the matter of dramatic rhythm, there is a noticeable contrast between the undistinguished uniformity of both the first and last periods of authorship and the significant variations among the monologues of the middle period. The speeches of various characters in the imitative plays and in *The Inn Album* are rhythmically undifferentiated, while the lines of various dramatic monologues are interesting for their rhythmical variety.

It seems reasonable to assume, therefore, that the characteristic "ruggedness" of Browning's most effective blank verse is often the result of an intentionally imposed conflict between a conventional literary pattern and the intellectual or emotional *rhythm* of the character who is speaking the lines. In rhythm and poetic tone, and their infinite possibilities of expression, the poet has discovered something quite different from the "tones" of painting

[1] Harland H. Hatcher, p. 40.

and music, which, tentatively, he tried to introduce into the composition of *Pauline* and *Sordello*.

> What does it all mean, poet? Well
> Your brains beat into a rhythm, you tell
> What we felt only; you expressed
> You hold things beautiful the best,
>   And place them in rhyme so, side by side.
> 'T is something, nay 't is much:
>   (from Stanza VII, *The Last Ride Together*)

If the couplets of *Sordello* may be said to reveal the poet's failure to adapt his versification to his subject, the couplets of *My Last Duchess* may be regarded as a perfect example of Browning's technical advancement. Fanatically strict as they are, even to the syllable count, perfectly rhymed, these couplets are so manipulated rhythmically as to give the impression of dramatic conversation. They have no small part in making the poem at once memorable but in no sense does the traditional rigidity of their form constrict the flow of action. For the reader they produce a stimulating conflict between prescribed form and the rhythm of dramatic speech. In *Sordello* Browning seems to have assumed that of itself the couplet pattern would transform chaotic thinking into clarity; in *My Last Duchess* he no longer regards this literary device as in itself a security against formlessness. He now understands thoroughly that any life which the couplet may possess is essentially his own energy transformed; renewed, in fact, by his having mastered both the pattern and the substance of his poem.

If the blank verse of *Pauline* and the imitative plays shows Browning's limited appreciation of the possibilities of rhythmic variation *within* a prescribed pattern, one has only to turn to *Giuseppi Caponsacchi* and then to *Pompilia* for a contrast of rhetorical brilliance with lyric charm, to hear in these blank verses the distinct variations in tone that, in no small measure, account for the reader's clear conception of the differences between Caponsacchi and Pompilia. The apparent subtlety of the rhythmic variations in *Pauline* that, in the instance of a group of about eight lines, beginning,

> Thou wilt remember one warm morn when winter,

make it possible to read the verses either as pentameters or tetrameters, suggests to me the poet's probable imitation of the poetical music of Shelley, rather than his mastery of a specific technique. In a certain sense Browning seems to have produced these charming lines accidentally, in a moment similar to that which prompted Sordello to improvise his brilliant prize song. In creating such poetic music as the lyric solemnity of *A Grammarian's Funeral*, however, Browning was thoroughly conscious of his versification. Professor Hatcher's comment, even briefly stated, makes the point clear: "The meter of *A Grammarian's Funeral* is often considered difficult, but beautiful and strange. . . . The long lines are couplets. . . . The short lines are adonics so familiar in the Odes of Horace."[2] But the poetical music of this poem is dependent less upon the poet's mere knowledge of couplets and adonics than upon his mastery of total form. He can do what he will, a point that is illustrated by Professor Hatcher's having noted that the serene tones of *A Grammarian's Funeral* and the choppy rhetoric of the Prologue to *Ferishtah's Fancies* have both been cast in the same metrical pattern.[3]

Experimentation in verse-form led to, or followed naturally, the invention of stanza-forms whose constructions were conspicuously omitted from the compositions of earlier years. Browning, having realized that the rhythm of poetry is essentially different from the rhythm of music or the rhythm of painting, has felt the necessity of devising a variety of structural forms that will assure his reader a more effective communication of the rhythms of his mind. The painter's rhythm is expressed in the visible patterns of lines and in rapid or delayed "echoes" of color. The musician's rhythm is transfixed with the mathematical exactness of notes, rests, and bars that guarantee its repetition through the skill of a competent performer. The poet's rhythm depends for its projection upon the patterns of verse and stanza-forms that must be capable not only of suggesting the characteristic movement of the poem, but also of allowing for variations in tone, speed, syncopation, and the many indescribable subtleties of human speech. When the poet entrusts his observations or his visions to the printed page, he must take infinite pains to perfect the technique of his art against the probable distortion of his meaning.

Consequently, as Robert Browning sees more clearly the possibilities and limitations peculiar to the art of poetry, he shows less and less inclination to compose as if he were a painter or a musician writing poetry, and more and more of the desire to master such elements of literary technique as verse-form and stanza-form. Without becoming the avowed imitator of his predecessors, he has become the originator of a poetic technique whose fundamental principles nevertheless accord with the basic laws of the poetic tradition.

Observations such as these are but a means of calling attention to specific aspects of the poet's general development of a clearer conception of total form. That this conception approaches almost complete realization in practice is evident in the perfection of such a form as the dramatic monologue, and also in the ability of the poet to adapt his knowledge of other arts to the uses of poetry. The musical pattern which we call the *fugue,* for example, is transformed into a poetic design in *Waring* and in *A Grammarian's Funeral*. But the unmistakable sign of the poet's conception of total form is the symmetrical ordering of poetical forces, the harmonious fusion of the characteristic elements of poetic expression, diction, meter, stanza-form, imagery, and rhythm, into a unity from which each element becomes inseparable. Thus, rhythm itself now acquires a symbolical importance that was

[2] Harland H. Hatcher, p. 28.   [3] *Ibid.*, p. 139.

attained in Browning's earlier poems chiefly by his imagery. That is to say, the *tone* of the poem is now as much of a concern for the poet as the *color* of the poem.

We are thus confronted with an artistic phenomenon that cannot be explained without our becoming involved in an analysis of Browning's art taken at the full tide of its creative power. The dissection of earlier imperfections was much less trying than the present vivisection of his approach to perfection. The anatomy of these greater accomplishments in poetic design reveals the poet's changed conception of the functions of poetic imagery; specifically, his having conceived of a clear relationship between imagery and total or enveloping design.

In considering Browning's imitative plays we assumed that the diminished force of his star-images was to be explained largely by the general weakness of the plays themselves, a condition that was attributable to his attempt to conform to the vaguely conceived design of an "Elizabethan" pattern. While the poems of the middle period of Browning's development represent a reduction in the number of star-images, similar in amount, indeed, to the reduced number of star-images in the imitative plays, the reasons for this reduction are now quite different. Furthermore, the change in the degree of the artistic effects of these star-images must be recognized as a change obedient to the laws of new and originally conceived notions of poetic design, rather than as a change emanating from the relaxed or retarded energies of an imitative playwright. If the star-images in the original poetry of Browning's middle period have been reduced in numbers, it is because they have been used only when artistically necessary; if they have now less structural significance than they had in the early poems, it is because Browning has invented other means of reënforcing the organization of his poems; if they seem to possess now and again less symbolic vigor, it is because the poet intends they shall. In other words, the sporadic occurrence and the diminished force of the star-image are now intentional; not the lacklustre result of painstaking imitation.

The star-image has thus become integral to a total or enveloping design. Its structural force, so important in *Pauline, Paracelsus,* and *Sordello,* is distinctly limited, and, while its symbolic meaning clings to associations established in the earlier poems, its symbolic influence is less constantly felt, because the ideas for which it stands are now but a part of the poet's enlarged conception of life, rather than his chief intellectual concern. The poet has become very much alive to the significance of total design. He realizes that the structure of his verses, his stanzas, the larger divisions of his longer poems, his diction, and his imagery have everything to do with the creation of unified impressions. It is the harmonious integration of these elements that determines the characteristic rhythm or tone of the poem, or of a particular division of a poem, and that assures the reader's closer approach to a correct appreciation of the poet's meaning.

It is noteworthy that in the argumentative poems of this period the star-image is likely to become a "point" in the outline of a casuistical discourse, to hold a position still related to structural organization, therefore, but no longer, as in *Pauline,* to stand as the principal indication of structural design. In lyric poems the star-image is likely to occur in clusters, or in passages in which it blends with other images, as it did in the lyric speeches of Luigi in *Pippa Passes.* In the poetry of the earliest period of composition the employment of this method was often the sign of the poet's "confessional" manner. The change therefore suggests that Browning has developed a lyric style that both absorbs and conceals his inclination towards confession, even though he may continue to present many of his individual beliefs, and sign them with the star-image, the mark of his personal approval. His art has become a more effective instrument of detachment, so that the characters who speak his lyric lines may remain artistically intact, free from confusion with the author's personality.

By the very nature of its form, as distinct from poetry that is chiefly dramatic, narrative, didactic, or argumentative, the lyric depends for its effect much less upon technical elements that point out divisions in its structure than upon those elements that secure and maintain a continuous tone. Furthermore, the lyric is characteristically short; so that, while the action of memory is to a degree essential to the reader's appreciation of the lyric, the poet is released to a great extent from the necessity of inventing methods of logical or narrative recall to assure a unity of impression. If a story should run through a lyric poem, as one does in *In A Gondola,* the poet is bound to emphasize separate details in the story much less than he is committed to emphasize the essence or characteristic tone of the entire sequence of episodes. The lyric poet does not intend to lead his reader to a dramatic, narrative, or argumentative conclusion; he tries to surround his reader immediately and continuously with a single impression compact of tone and rhythm.

Structurally considered, therefore, the effects of the star-image in Browning's lyric poetry have been subordinated in general to a clarified conception of total form. Just as his stars and other images often become "points" in the outline of an argumentative design, so they may become supporting "tones" in a lyric composition. In the dramatic monologue, since the flow of action is almost never independent of an argumentative or lyric accompaniment, the star-image may be either a "point" or a "tone," or a mixture of both, depending upon which of the two complementary motifs predominates.

The consistency with which the star-image maintains its characteristic symbolic meaning, in spite of the limitation of its symbolic influence, may be understood not only by observing the presence of the star-image in many poems, but also by noting its significant omission from such works as *The Lost Leader, Soliloquy of the Spanish Cloister, The Laboratory, My Last Duchess, The Statue and the Bust,* and *The Bishop Orders His Tomb.* In poems like these one would anticipate the elimination of an image that stands characteristically for truth, aspiration, hope, and resolution, but the omission of the star-image from such poems as *Cleon, Rudel to the Lady of Tripoli,* and *One Word More* is more difficult to explain. However, our previous examination of the functions of the star-image in *Pippa Passes* and in *Luria,* supplies evidence for a probable explanation. In both *Pippa Passes* and *Luria* images of light were important elements in the poet's design. But for the leading characters, Pippa and Luria, the sun-image, rather than the star, represented the outstanding attributes of personality. Both Pippa and Luria represent a general radiance of human personality; they are persons whose conception of truth and goodness comes naturally and directly from heaven. The experience of intellectual aspiration or of intellectual resolve is foreign to characters whose intuitive awareness of the goodness of God is sufficient to create their positive charm. For similar reasons, it seems to me, the sun has become the principal image of light in *Cleon,* the sun and the flower in *Rudel to the Lady of Tripoli,* and the moon, because of its suggestion of romantic love, in *One Word More.* In a few poems, the best example being *A Face,* the presence of the star-image may be felt only through the force of verbal association. In all of these instances, of inclusion or elimination of the star-image, the poet's decisions seem to have been made by design. Browning's developing conception of the proper function of poetic imagery has caused him to discriminate ever more sharply among the symbolical differences that have become fixed associations with various images of light.

As a means of presenting the more detailed observations that follow, I have employed a somewhat arbitrary plan of procedure. Many of the points of evidence to be drawn from an examination of the poems of the middle period are of themselves too slight to require separate and lengthy discussion. Only when several of them have been gathered together in support of a single opinion do they become wholly significant as illustrations of a particular use of the star-image. Among the many poems included in this part of our study, only a few, *Saul, A Death in the Desert,* and *Abt Vogler,* require detailed analysis. I have therefore made a division of these poems into groups that were suggested in each instance by peculiarities in the use of the star-image. For the reader's convenience the headings of these groups may be listed here as follows:

    I. The Star-image and Browning's Argumentative Style.
    II. The Star-image and Browning's Lyric Style.
    III. The Star-image and Total Poetic Form.

IV. The Incidental Star-image.
    A. "Painter Poems."
    B. Theological Poems.
V. *Saul, A Death in the Desert,* and *Epilogue* to *Dramatic Personae.*
VI. *Abt Vogler.*

It will be observed at once that these headings are not intended to suggest groupings according to *genre,*[4] but merely a method of expository arrangement that has been dictated, generally, by the varieties of evidence drawn from investigation. However, it has been impossible to detach the analysis of functions of the star-image entirely from a consideration of *genre,* since observations regarding the structural relation of the star-image to total form, or the symbolic association of the star with poet's attitude towards his subject, often suggest the distinctions among poetic *genres,* or the fusion of poetic *genres.* Accordingly, those considerations of *genre* that seemed to be significant as explanations of the functions of the star-image have been set down when and where they have been considered appropriate.

While no great significance may attach to the fact, it may be well to remark that the poems to which our analysis leads at present are to be found chiefly among those originally published in the two volumes of *Men and Women* and in *Dramatis Personae.* In the editorial arrangements followed from the time of publishing the collected editions, 1863, 1868, and 1888, there have been many changes in the printed order of the poems, especially among these of the middle period. Consequently, even the fair suggestion of the chronology of composition, which the first editions naturally represented, has been rather completely obscured by the plans followed thereafter. With these brief statements of the general problems of *genre* and of chronology in mind, we may

---

[4] Real difficulties attend one's attempt to classify the poems of Browning's middle period according to *genre,* or even to discover the principles upon which Browning based the groupings of these poems when he made arrangements for the publication of the revised and final edition of his works. Such headings as "Dramatic Lyrics," "Dramatic Romances," and "Dramatis Personae" are titles rather than strict classifications; nor are the headings under which many of these poems were published originally any more clear. Professor Thomas M. Parrott has stated this problem very clearly in a dissertation entitled *An Examination of the Non-Dramatic Poems in Robert Browning's First and Second Periods,* Leipzig, 1893, pp. 29 ff.: "Browning was not very accurate in the nomenclature of his poems, nor does he seem to have been very well satisfied with it, as the frequent changes of arrangement show. Of the 14 poems entitled *Dramatic Lyrics* which constitute the 3rd number of *B.* and *P.* we find but four included under the *Lyrics* of the edition of 1863, the others being assigned to the *Dramatic Romances* and the group entitled *Men and Women.* . . . Of the 47 poems included in the last edition under the heading, 'Dramatic Lyrics,' 15 cannot by any stretch of the definition of a lyric be considered as such. . . . Since, then, this confusion of nomenclature exists, let us try as simply as possible to rectify it. We may include under the head of *Dramatic Lyrics* such poems as are the song-like expression of a single mood, the mood, however, being not the poet's own but that of an imaginary or historical character in whom the poet has sunk his own personality. . . ." "Under the head of *Dramatic Romances* we may include such poems as are essentially narrative in form, containing an incident, or incidents, about which the thoughts and reflections gather."

turn to the more particular discussion of the following divisions of this chapter.

The Star-Image and Browning's Argumentative Style

JOHANNES AGRICOLA IN MEDITATION, 1836

Like *Porphyria's Lover,* with which it was first published[5] in *The Monthly Repository* for January, 1836, *Johannes Agricola in Meditation* is a poem whose form anticipates the poetry of Browning's middle and later years. It is less satisfactory than *Porphyria* as an example of the dramatic monologue, but as such it often has been classified without much difficulty. In another sense, it is anticipatory of the argumentative monologues which, like *Mihrab Shah, Plot Culture,* and *A Bean Stripe,* are characteristic of the last period of the poet's career. Nevertheless it would be wrong, I think, to insist that with *Johannes Agricola* Browning invented the form of his last poems. It is simply interesting to note that the argumentative style of many of the later monologues, "dramatic in principle," shows itself at this early date in the poet's life.

Since this argumentative manner of expression may be found in a great number of Browning's works, from *Pauline* to *Asolando,* it is difficult to make a real classification of his poems into those that are argumentative and those that are not. But I think it is true, generally, that as the confessional manner shows most clearly in the early poems, so the argumentative manner shows most clearly in the poetry of the last years. Professor DeVane in his *Browning's Parleyings,* p. xiii, says quite positively, "Inspiration had departed after *Balaustion's Adventure,* in 1871, and only argument was left to fill its place. The judgment which he [Browning] had made in 1855 against the author of 'Transcendentalism: A Poem in Twelve Books' is the most apt and just criticism of Robert Browning himself in the last two decades of his life.

> Stop playing, poet! May a brother speak?
> 'T is you speak, that's your error. Song's our art. . . .

For Browning, a philosophical poet in the best of his time, finally took philosophy as his main business in life. . . . Consequently his poetry had in it more and more of the ingenuity of the metaphysician, and less and less of the spontaneous wedding of idea and music."

An examination of *Johannes Agricola in Meditation* reveals less of the ingenuity of disputation and more of the harmony of thought and music

[5] In 1842 both of these poems appeared in *Dramatic Lyrics* ("Bells and Pomegranates," Number III) under the heading *Madhouse Cells:* I [*Johannes Agricola*] and II [*Porphyria*]. They appeared in print first in *The Monthly Repository* (edited by Rev. W. J. Fox), X, N.S. (January, 1836), as *Porphyria,* pp. 43-44, and *Johannes Agricola,* pp. 45-46. Later (1849) their titles were changed to *Porphyria's Lover* and *Johannes Agricola in Meditation.* (See *The Complete Poetical Works of Robert Browning,* Macmillan Edition, 1917, p. 1319; Griffin-Minchin, p. 73; W. C. DeVane, *Handbook,* pp. 111-114, where the later adventures of these poems are recorded.)

than the *Parleyings with Certain People of Importance in Their Day,* and yet its star-images, in their relation to total form, are responsive to the demands of a "dramatic" argument which requires a subordination of imagistic effects similar to that which may be observed in the Parleying *With Francis Furini.* In a certain sense the stars in these poems become "points" in an argument, a fact that deprives them of values such as we have observed in *Pauline, Paracelsus,* and *Sordello.*

> There's heaven above, and night by night
>   I look right through its gorgeous roof;
> No suns and moons though e'er so bright
>   Avail to stop me; splendour-proof
>   I keep the broods of stars aloof:
> For I intend to get to God,
>   For 't is to God I speed so fast,
> For in God's breast, my own abode,
>   Those shoals of dazzling glory passed
>   I lay my spirit down at last.
> I lie where I have always lain,
>   God smiles as he has always smiled;
> Ere suns and moons could wax and wane,
>   Ere stars were thunder girt, or piled
>   The heavens, God thought on me his child;
> Ordained a life for me, arrayed
>   Its circumstances every one
> To the minutest; ay, God said
>   This head this hand should rest upon
>   Thus, ere he fashioned star or sun.

These are the first twenty lines of *Johannes Agricola.* Obviously the star-images in Johannes' argument are not intended to suggest his character; they are the "shoals of dazzling glory" that he wishes to pass; they are *examples* of the kind of thing from which he desires to remain aloof. Thus, while the symbolic meaning of these star-images, in this instance the *laws* of God,[6] is not unlike that in other poems, which discuss religious and theological questions, the principal function of these images is to color Johannes' argument, rather than to signify his character. It is this fact that seems to me to subordinate the function of the star-image to the design of argument, rather than to allow it to stand a primary element in an imagistic pattern, similar to those which constitute the enveloping designs of *Pauline* and *Sordello.* Here logic rather than imagery is the basis of structure.

---

[6] This poem as a whole is a statement, in brief, of the arguments of the Antinomians who rejected the necessity of living under the Mosaic Law. DeVane, *Handbook,* p. 112, quotes the note which, in *The Monthly Repository,* prefaced the poem, and which begins as follows: "Antinomians, so denominated for rejecting the Law as a thing of no use under Gospel dispensation: they say that good works do not further, nor evil works hinder salvation; that the child of God cannot sin. . . ."

In the last part of the poem the occurrence of another star-image calls attention to the rhetorical design of Johannes' argument, for in this instance it is not only the image itself that recalls the first part of the poem, but also the sentence pattern of line 55, "Before God fashioned star or sun!" which is almost identical with the pattern of line 20.

> Priest, doctor, hermit, monk grown white   (51)
>   With prayer, the broken hearted nun
> The martyr, the wan acolyte,
>   The incense-swinging child,—undone
> Before God fashioned star or sun!
> God whom I praise; how could I praise
>   If such as I might understand,
> Make out and reckon on his ways
>   And bargain for his love, and stand,
> Paying a price, at his right hand.

The period of production to which *Johannes Agricola* belongs is the period of *Sordello* and *Paracelsus*. Its form, however, in so far as its star-images are concerned, points to the poet's having composed it in response to an idea that, in its totality, differs from the ideas that inspired *Sordello* and *Paracelsus*. It was an idea that prompted the statement of opinion, rather than the expression of poetic visions, so that the poet had no choice but to become argumentative, rather than largely imagistic, in the conception of his design.

THE STAR-IMAGE AND BROWNING'S LYRIC STYLE

According to the evidence that investigation supplies, it now becomes possible to discuss several poems in one group. The common denominator of the seven works here selected is that their star-images point chiefly to one of the poet's characteristic manners of expression, his lyric style. With the exception of *In a Gondola*, all these poems were first published in *Men and Women*, 1855, a fact that provides a chronological, as well as a stylistic reason, for the proposed grouping. In no sense, however, should this grouping be regarded as a strict classification according to the lyric *genre*, for neither Robert Browning nor the definitive canons of criticism permit it. The seven poems to be considered are: *In a Gondola, The Last Ride Together, My Star, By the Fireside, Two in the Campagna, A Serenade at the Villa*, and *Popularity*.

As a group these poems exemplify the technique of imagistic blending or of otherwise joining a great variety of images into a harmonious unity of impression. We have noted previously[7] that, in his early poems, this practice was associated with the confessional manner of the poet. In *Pippa Passes*, however, where the same technique was employed in one of the speeches of Luigi, we were able to observe in the poet's attitude towards his subject a

---

[7] See above, pp. 143-144.

quality that approached artistic and lyric detachment.[8] It is quite possible that in at least two of the poems in the present group the confessional, rather than the more detached lyric manner, predominates; at least there is abundant commentary to declare that *By the Fireside* and *My Star* are wholly personal, and therefore confessional poems.

There is that abundance of imagery in *In a Gondola*[9] that one might expect to find in a poem that was composed as a lyric description of a famous picture, Maclise's *The Serenade*. Speaking of the picture and the poem in a letter to Miss Fanny Haworth,[10] Browning wrote:

> Oh, let me tell you—I chanced to call on Forster the other day—and he pressed me into committing verse on the instant, not the minute, in Maclise's behalf—who has wrought a divine Venetian work, it seems for the British Institution—Forster described it well—but I could do nothing better than this wooden ware (All the "properties," as we say, were given —and the problem was how to cataloguise them in rhyme and unreason)—
>
> > I send my heart up to thee—all my heart
> >   In this my singing!
> > For the stars help me, and the sea bears part,
> >   —The very night is clinging
> > Closer to Venice—streets to leave one space
> >   Above me whence thy face
> > May light my joyous heart to thee—its dwelling place.
>
> Singing and stars and night and Venice streets in depths of shade and space are "properties," do you please to see. And now tell me, is this below the average of Catalogue original poetry? Tell me—for to that end, of being told, I write it.

Except for minor changes in punctuation, the stanza quoted in the letter to Miss Haworth is the first stanza, as we now have it, of *In a Gondola,* where it is introduced with the notation, *He Sings*. Here the "properties" of the poem are projected with no greater emphasis upon the star than upon "singing," "night," and "Venice streets." With the poet's own explanation of his method before us, we can be certain that he intends the effects of his poem to be realized in part, at least, through the harmonious blending of his "properties." Not the least among them is the form of the stanza itself.

As this original stanza grew into the present poem, it began to tell a story for whose fitting accompaniment the lyric mood was maintained. With the next appearance of the star-image in the poem, it is possible to note its having acquired a characteristic symbolical meaning, and even a slight suggestion of structural importance. At any rate, it is interesting to observe, structurally and symbolically, that as he has composed it in the stories of Valence and Colombe, and Norbert and Constance, Browning has again attached the star

---

[8] See above, pp. 143-144.

[9] First published in "Bells and Pomegranates," No. III, 1842, under *Dramatic Lyrics*; assigned in the collected edition of 1863 (and thereafter) to *Dramatic Romances*.

[10] T. L. Hood, p. 7, where the letter is dated, "(*ca.* December 30, 1841)."

to the lover rather than the mistress. Furthermore, he has assigned it in each of its appearances in this poem to one of the lover's songs.

> Say again, what we are?
> The sprite of a star,
> I lure thee above where the destinies bar
> My plumes their full play
> Till a ruddier ray
> Than my pale one announce there is withering away
> Some . . . Scatter the vision for ever! And now,
> As of old, I am I, thou art thou!

This is the second stanza of the lover's third song. A comparison of the star-image in this stanza with the "property"—star above will show the difference in the force of the two images. It is not possible to regard "The sprite of a star" as a mere "property," for the lover's third song is a lyric in its own right, independent of suggestions from *The Serenade* to give it form. The stanza before us is peculiarly reminiscent, in fact, of themes in *Pauline* that we have every reason to regard as a poem originating in Browning's own experience. Just as the "hero" of *Pauline* is a poet, the lover of *In a Gondola* here becomes a poet. Through such phrases as: "sprite of a star," "above where destinies bar," "my plumes," "ray," "my pale one," "Scatter the vision forever!", this song may be readily interpreted as an expression of the original devotion of Robert Browning to the spirit of poetry, Pauline:

> As of old, I am I, thou art thou!

But whether or not such an interpretation be correct, the attention of the reader never shifts its focus from the characters of *In a Gondola* to the personal preoccupations of the poet who gave them lyric importance. Such meaning as this stanza may possess independently has been artfully absorbed and concealed by the total design of a "dramatic romance." The chief characteristic of the imagery of this poem is the intentional confusion of images, the blending of poetical "properties," into the suggestion of a single impression, compact of the hopes, fears, loyalties, doubts, loves, deaths, and conceptions of man and society that are profoundly intermingled in the characters of the two in a gondola.

The lyric qualities of *The Last Ride Together*[11] are in many respects similar to those of *In a Gondola,* although the presence of the poet himself may be more easily discerned in his verses, through the first-personal style that he has employed, and through the commentary of Stanzas VII and VIII on poetry, sculpture, and music, three of Browning's special interests. The star-images of this poem occur in Stanza III where they are made to harmonize with other images of light.

---

11 First published in *Men and Women,* Vol. I, 1855, but, since 1863, assigned to *Dramatic Romances.*

III

Hush! if you saw some western cloud
All billowy-bosomed, over-bowed
By many benedictions—sun's
And moon's and evening-star's at once—
  And so, you, looking and loving best,
Conscious grew, your passion drew
Cloud, sunset, moonrise, star-shine too,
Down on you, near and yet more near,
Till flesh must fade for heaven was here!—
Thus leant she and lingered—joy and fear!
Thus lay she a moment on my breast.

The Last Ride Together represents as a whole the emotion of hopeless resignation. It is symbolically interesting, therefore, that the star-image should appear in the one stanza of the poem that gives expression to the dream of what might have been. With its associated images of light, this contrasting vision of hope momentarily possesses the poem. The star-image points, therefore, to a particular division in the poem's total structure, a fact which suggests that, in spite of their lyric quality, the stanzas of this poem have been conceived as "paragraphs" in a fundamentally logical plan of presentation.

A Grammarian's Funeral,[12] to which we shall return for further consideration shortly, *My Star*,[13] and *By the Fireside*[13] contain imagistic designs, characterized by the harmonious blending of images, suitable at once to the themes of these poems, and suggestive of the lyric quality of their verses. *My Star* has been regarded, usually, as not only lyric but confessional. It presents the opportunity, indeed, for several biographical interpretations, all of which are plausible in the light of the poem's imagistic harmonies and their several symbolic implications.

All that I know
  Of a certain star
Is, it can throw
  (Like the angled spar)
Now a dart of red,
  Now a dart of blue;
Till my friends have said
  They would fain see, too,
My star that dartles the red and the blue!
Then it stops like a bird; like a flower, hangs furled:
  They must solace themselves with the Saturn above it.
What matter to me if their star is a world?
  Mine has opened its soul to me; therefore I love it.

[12] First published in *Men and Women*, Vol. II, 1855, later (1863) permanently assigned to *Dramatic Romances*.
[13] First published in *Men and Women*, Vol. I, 1855, later (1863) permanently assigned to *Dramatic Lyrics*.

Beyond the possibility that this lyric may refer pointedly to Elizabeth Barrett Browning, there is a larger, and, it seems to me, a more satisfactory interpretation possible. The interesting variety of imagistic detail, which is discernible within the compact limits of this poem, is reminiscent of certain qualities that have been observed in *Sordello,* particularly Browning's habitual association of the image of the star with his conception of poetry itself. Certain details connected with the publication of *Selections from the Poetical Works of Robert Browning* in 1872 have further led me to assume that *My Star* is, indeed, closely related to Browning's conception of his own poetry.

The 1872 volume of *Selections* was dedicated to Alfred Tennyson. The language that Browning has used to express his admiration for Tennyson suggests the star through a familiar verbal connotation, particularly in the words "illustrious" and "consummate": "In Poetry—Illustrious and consummate: In Friendship—Noble and sincere." The preface to the *Selections* concludes with another suggestion of Browning's inclination to associate his poetry with the imagery of light.

> Having hitherto done my utmost in the art to which my life is a devotion, I cannot engage to increase the effort; but I conceive that there may be helpful light, as well as reassuring warmth in the attention and sympathy I gratefully acknowledge.
> London, May 14, 1872.   R.B.

Furthermore, as if by design, *My Star* has been chosen to stand as the first poem in the volume, to signify, it seems reasonable to say, the quality of poetry to be found therein, and to awaken in the reader a sympathetic regard for the poet's art. Thus, not only the internal evidence of a similar use of the star-image in *Sordello* and in *My Star* to signify poetry, but also the external evidence of the circumstances of publication, imply that Robert Browning had both a symbolical and structural reason for heading a collection of his chosen poems with the image of the star.[14]

While the single star-image in *By the Fireside,* Stanza XXXVII, is in no sense extraordinary in its intrinsic force, an attentive reader may readily observe that this star attaches to one of the most significant moments in the poem:

XXXVII
Oh moment, one and infinite!
The water slips o'er stock and stone;
The West is tender, hardly bright:

---

[14] Against this interpretation, however, is the opinion of Professor DeVane, who says in his *Handbook,* p. 202, "It has been suggested, however,—I believe mistakenly—that Browning is referring in *My Star* to his own peculiar poetic genius, and his gift for seeing in events and things a significance hidden from other men."

> How grey at once is the evening grown—
> One star, its chrysolite!

It is the instant that unites two souls who have "caught for a moment the powers at play":

XLVIII

> The forests had done it; there they stood;
>   We caught for a moment the powers at play:
> They had mingled us so, for once and good
>   Their work was done—we might go or stay;
> They relapsed to their ancient mood.

Furthermore, it is quite significant that in *Two in the Campagna*,[15] a poem which by contrast laments the loss of the enchanted moment, the star should again appear to mark the crucial stanzas of this dramatic lyric:

X

> No, I yearn upward, touch you close,
>   Then stand away. I kiss your cheek,
> Catch your soul's warmth,—I pluck the rose
>   And love it more than tongue can speak—
> Then the good minute goes.

XI

> Already how am I so far
>   Out of that minute? Must I go
> Still like the thistle-ball, no bar,
>   Onward, whenever light winds blow,
> Fixed by no friendly star?

The lyric mood of *By the Fireside* is positive, hopeful; the mood of *Two in the Campagna* is wistfully negative, although its hopelessness is relieved by a tentatively fragile vision of what might have been true, "Fixed by no friendly star." The juxtaposition of the stanzas here quoted from these two poems presents the evidence that demonstrates the symbolic importance of their star-images: the positive and negative forms of the "lode-star," or the star of emotional resolution. One may see in this comparison, furthermore, how deftly the image has been worked into the texture of both poems, with the author's undoubted intention of signifying in each instance a moment of lyric intensity.

A Serenade at the Villa[16] exemplifies, in addition to a pattern of imagistic blending, a most unusual function of the star-image, for in this instance the star emphasizes the absence of light. It is the loss of light, rather than the presence of darkness, that is important to the symbolism of this poem; such is the suggestion of the first stanza:

---

[15] First published in *Men and Women*, Vol. II, 1855, later (1863) permanently assigned to *Dramatic Lyrics*.

[16] First published in *Men and Women*, Vol. I, 1855, later (1863) permanently assigned to *Dramatic Lyrics*.

I

That was I, you heard last night,
  When there rose no moon at all,
Nor to pierce the strained and tight
  Tent of heaven, a planet small:
Life was dead and so was light.

Hope has died in the lover's heart, and the verses that compose his song of lament repeat the imagery of the first stanza:

IX

"When no moon succeeds the sun,
  "Nor can pierce the midnight's tent
"Any star, the smallest one
  "While some drops, where lightning rent,
"Show the final storm begun—"

Finally, the lover admits the darkness:

XII

Oh how dark your villa was,
  Windows fast and obdurate!
How the garden grudged me grass
  Where I stood—the iron gate
Ground its teeth to let me pass!

Consequently, while the "planet" and the "star" may not possess unique importance in the imagistic design of *A Serenade at the Villa,* their association with such images as the "sun," "moon," "glow-worm," and "firefly" is peculiarly satisfactory as a means of emphasizing the death of light, the absence of hope.

Popularity,[17] a poem addressed to the memory of John Keats, is unquestionably lyric in its stanza-form. According to opinions previously stated, in connection with the discussion of other poems, the lyric quality of *Popularity* is suggested also by the fusion of most of its images into a poetical harmony. But it is important to observe the exception that the star-images of *Popularity* are withheld from participating fully in the imagistic fusion thus created. This fact therefore suggests peculiarities in both imagistic and total designs that distinguish *Popularity* from the other poems in the group to which it has been assigned for discussion.

The star-image is here but one of a number of images such as: the feast, the fisher, Tyrian blue, scepter, crown and ball, the sea, Solomon's cedarhouse, blue bell and drunken bee, extract of Tyrian blue, and porridge, to mention them in order but not to give a complete list, all of which contribute equally to the total effect of the poem. But the structural and symbolic effects of the star-image stop short, it seems to me, with the conclusion of the

[17] First published in *Men and Women,* Vol. II, 1855, later (1863), and thereafter, assigned to *Dramatic Lyrics.*

first two, or possibly three stanzas. The influence of the star is not felt, through verbal connotation or the technique of blending, throughout the remaining stanzas. In direct contrast to this functional peculiarity of the star-image, it is interesting to note that the images of Stanzas IV to XIII, beginning with the image of the regal feast and ending with the image of humble porridge, are inextricably fused with one another and, at the same time, dominated by the symbolical Tyrian blue.

These phenomena suggest confusing though interesting conclusions to the present analysis. At least two explanations are possible. The first is that *Popularity* is, actually, a structural *arrangement* in which two poems, one of three stanzas and the other of ten, have been artfully combined into one. The second explanation is that *Popularity* is a lyric poem in which the first three stanzas have been composed as a prelude whose lyric tone and imagistic pattern differ, and are intended to differ, from the tonal and imagistic designs of the latter ten stanzas.

In support of the first of these explanations, that *Popularity* is, indeed, two poems artfully combined into one, is the evidence to be drawn from examining the symbolical nature of the star-images of the first two stanzas. These star-images are peculiarly reminiscent of those stars in *Pauline* that signified the poetical genius of Percy Bysshe Shelley. The first three stanzas of *Popularity* may be read, in fact, as though they were an apostrophe to Shelley, and Browning himself the "one man" of the fourth line in Stanza I:

I

Stand still, true poet that you are!
  I know you; let me try and draw you.
Some night you'll fail us: when afar
  You rise, remember one man saw you,
Knew you and named a star!

II

My star, God's glow-worm! Why extend
  That loving hand of his which leads you
Yet locks you safe from end to end
  Of this dark world, unless he needs you,
Just saves your light to spend?

III

His clenched hand shall unclose at last,
  I know, and let out all the beauty:
My poet holds the future fast,
  Accepts the coming ages' duty,
Their present for this past.

The star is obviously the dominant image of these stanzas; to interpret it as signifying the genius of Shelley requires no violent distortion of the meaning of the verses. Consequently, this section of *Popularity* may be regarded as a satellite of *Pauline,* and as in itself complete.

In support of the second explanation, that *Popularity* is a lyric poem in which the first three stanzas have been composed as a prelude to the imagistic and tonal differences of the last ten stanzas, is the evidence to be drawn from the final stanza of *Adonais* where Shelley clearly refers to Keats as a star:

> The soul of Adonais, like a star,
> Beacons from the abode where the eternal are.

With this interpretation in mind the reader of the poem may suppose the "one man" of Stanza I to be not Browning, but the author *Adonais.* The imagery of the last ten stanzas of the poem is unified by its dominant color, *blue.* The star-image does not appear in this section of the poem; so that it cannot here confuse the reader's appreciation of direct references to John Keats with the suggestion of Browning's reminiscences of his early devotion of Shelley.

Further evidence in support of this second explanation is to be found in the details of the poem's expository structure. In Stanza I Browning says:

> Stand still, true poet that you are!
> I know you; let me try and draw you.

Repeating himself in the first two lines of the fifth stanza, and thereby welding together the two divisions of the poem, he says:

> Meantime I'll draw you as you stand,
> With few or none to watch and wonder:

For a moment let us recall what has been said about the functions and the effects of the star-image in such poems as, *By the Fireside, Two in the Campagna,* and *A Serenade at the Villa.* In each of these poems only one image of the star appears. At first thought it would seem, therefore, that these single star-images must be less effective elements of expression than the two prominently displayed stars of *Popularity.* But in discussing the functions of the star-image in *Popularity,* it was necessary to resort to alternative explanations, because a question arose as to the exact relationship of the image to the total form of the poem. In discussing *By the Fireside, Two in the Campagna,* and *A Serenade at the Villa,* no such question arose, because the relationship of the star-image to the total form of each of these poems was seen to be thoroughly organic, structurally secure, and symbolically effective. In *By the Fireside* and *Two in the Campagna* the star marked the crucial "moments" of lyric themes. Although the evidence immediately before us is slight, it points to the important, though perhaps obvious fact, that the best effects of imagery are to be attained not so much by increasing the number of images to be used, but by assuring each image its proper place and function in a completed design. Only when Browning fully controls a total design, can he most effectively release the structural and symbolic forces of his imagery.

The Star-Image and Total Poetic Form

Inevitably the attempt to consider a group of poems whose star-images suggested the lyric manner of expression has led to considerations of poetic structure as well as poetic charm. There are several poems in the middle period of Browning's career that may be regarded as clear illustrations of the poet's adaptation of his earlier conceptions of the functions of imagery to his maturer conceptions of total design. Among these poems there are at least four containing the star-image that exemplify the poet's methods, *Evelyn Hope, Master Hugues, Waring,* and *A Grammarian's Funeral.*

Evelyn Hope,[18] both by its religious theme and a slight suggestion of the argumentative manner, recalls some of the structural characteristics of *Johannes Agricola.* The "good stars" in the third stanza of *Evelyn Hope* rather lose the general symbolic force that we have learned to regard as characteristic of Browning's stars, for they have been absorbed into the more ordinary conception of astrological superstition,

> The good stars met in your horoscope, . . ?

As its characteristic symbolism has been sacrificed to the demands of the theme, so the structural potentialities of this star-image have been reduced to conform to the total design, rather than released to control the form of the poem. This image, as the stanza shows, is a detail in the rhetorical question that demands the negative reply (but the implied positive assertion) of the succeeding divisions of the poem.

III

> Is it too late then, Evelyn Hope?
>   What, your soul was pure and true,
> The good stars met in your horoscope,
>   Made you of spirit, fire and dew—
> And just because I was thrice as old
>   And our paths in the world diverged so wide,
> Each was nought to each, must I be told?
>   We were fellow mortals, nought beside?

Light, in fact, has been deliberately shut out from the lives of Evelyn Hope and her lover by the surrounding darkness of a superstitious civilization, which does not permit the unconventional union of "fellow mortals" whose ages and whose "paths in the world diverged so wide." Light has been shut out, except for the "two long rays" of the sun, which represent the lovers, and which promise the consummation lyrically projected in the final stanzas of the poem. In Stanza I we may read:

> The shutters are shut, no light may pass
>   Save two long rays thro' the hinge's chink.

---

[18] First published in *Men and Women,* Vol. I, 1855; later (1863), and thereafter, assigned to *Dramatic Lyrics.*

But the "two long rays," when traced to their origin, the sun, unite in the single orb of God's Light that dispels the darkness of conventional belief, and promises the hope of the lovers' final union:

VI

. . . .
And I want and find you, Evelyn Hope!
What is the issue? let us see!

VII

. . . .
You will wake, and remember, and understand.

The star-image has thus been subjected symbolically and structurally to the necessities of a total design that is both lyric and rhetorical in nature.

In *Master Hugues of Saxe-Gotha*[19] I have found the clearest example, as illustrated by the use of the star-image at least, of the adaptation of imagistic detail to the pattern of stanza-form. Since the lyric stanza of this poem is itself a structural element existing within a total or enveloping design, the star may be regarded here as of third rank in structural importance. The dominant imagery of this poem is, in a sense, the musical pattern of the fugue, although the fugue-pattern is perhaps more completely realized in terms of poetic design in such compositions as *A Grammarian's Funeral* and *Waring*. Browning's colloquy with Master Hugues, on the subject of the fugue, nevertheless supplies the musical terms that constitute much of the imagery of the poem, even to the description of Master Hugues himself:

IX

Sure you were wishful to speak?
    You, with brow ruled like a score,
Yes, and eyes buried in pits on each cheek
    Like two great breves, as they wrote them
        of yore,
Each side that bar, your straight beak!

In a manner somewhat similar to the appearance of the star at moments of consummation in *A Grammarian's Funeral* and *Waring*, as we shall see, the star-image of *Master Hugues* occurs at that point where Browning asks the most profound questions regarding the meaning of the fugue-design. Addressing Master Hugues he says:

XXII

Is it your moral of Life?
    Such a web, simple and subtle,

---

[19] First published in *Men and Women*, Vol. I, 1855; later (1863), and thereafter, assigned to *Dramatic Lyrics*.

Weave we on earth here in impotent strife,
  Backward and forward each throwing his
      shuttle,
Death ending all with a knife?

XXIII

Over our heads truth and nature—
  Still our life's zigzags and dodges,
Ins and outs, weaving a new legislature—
  God's gold just shining its last where that
      lodges,
Palled beneath man's usurpature.

XXIV

So we o'ershroud stars and roses,
  Cherub and trophy and garland;
Nothings grow something which quietly closes
  Heaven's earnest eye: not a glimpse of the
      far land
Gets through our comments and glozes.

The detail to which I would call attention is the instance of mathematical precision with which, to the very syllable, the images "stars" and "roses" in Stanza XXIV have been matched with their symbolic interpretations "truth" and "nature" in the first line of Stanza XXIII. This, with other artistic phenomena here observable, the blending of images, the melody of the verses, the coherence of the stanzas, produces a poetic structure that is at once imagistically, lyrically, and logically compact.

But the poetic embodiment of the fugue-pattern is more perfectly realized in two of Browning's finest poems, *Waring*,[20] published as early as 1842, and *A Grammarian's Funeral*.[21] In both of these poems a single literal image of the star marks the moment of lyric consummation.

Grove's *Dictionary of Music and Musicians* defines the fugue as "a musical movement in which a definite number of parts or voices combine in stating and developing a single theme, the interest being cumulative."[22] Browning's explanation of the fugue may be said to have been stated in *Master Hugues of Saxe-Gotha*. But the poetical adaptation of this musical pattern required the translation of such quantities as the "definite number of parts or voices" into the terms of poetry: words, ideas, images, rhythms, meters, and stanza-forms. In one aspect of design both the poetical and musical forms of the fugue agreed; that is, in "the interest being cumulative." For Browning this interest became intensified by the effort to achieve consummation. It is this artistic

---

[20] First published in 1842 in "Bells and Pomegranates," Number III, under the title heading, *Dramatic Lyrics*. In the volume of poems published in 1849 it was assigned to *Dramatic Lyrics and Romances;* in 1863, and thereafter, to *Dramatic Romances*.

[21] First published in *Men and Women*, Vol. II, 1855, later (1863), and thereafter, assigned to *Dramatic Romances*.

[22] H. C. Colles (editor), *Grove's Dict. of Mus. and Musi.*, II, 320.

reality which he sought to create in *Waring* and *A Grammarian's Funeral,* and upon which he set the mark of his most appropriate image.

In *Waring* the "number of parts and voices" that combine to present the "single theme" of friendship are Browning's biographical and fanciful recollections of his friendship with Alfred Domett. From its apparently casual beginning, the simple statement of the fugue theme, the poem rises to its quasi-mystical conclusion. Accordingly, the poet has written a sort of evolution of friendship, which begins with mere acquaintance and runs through the natural course of first impressions, and proceeds thence to meetings and visits, to the discovery of mutual interests, to the birth of affection and admiration. Follows the companionship in art, music, nature, poetry, drama, politics, and *belles lettres* with its culmination in friendship. To give this exhilarating theme its poignancy, to enhance its emotional grandeur, an undertone of loss and separation combines with it, to the running accompaniment of imagery that symbolizes the vastness of the world, its great distances and remote regions. Finally, all is resolved into the image of consummation which concludes the poem:

> Oh, never star
> Was lost here but it rose afar!
> Look East, where whole new thousands are!
> In Vishnu-land what Avatar?

The design of *A Grammarian's Funeral,* though not identical with it, is essentially similar to that of *Waring.* The poem proceeds with rhythmical solemnity from the descriptive simplicity of its opening stanzas to the question, Who was this man? and thence to the lyric expression of the Grammarian's character, culminating in the realization of his lofty serenity. It is the ascent from the "unlettered plain" to the "tall mountain, citied to the top":

> Well, here's the platform, here's the proper place:
>   Hail to your purlieus,
> All ye highfliers of the feathered race,
>   Swallows and curlews!
> Here's the top-peak; the multitude below
>   Live, for they can, there:
> This man decided not to Live but Know—
>   Bury this man there?
> Here—here's his place, where meteors shoot, clouds form,
>   Lightnings are loosened,
> Stars come and go! Let joy break with the storm,
>   Peace let the dew send!
> Lofty designs must close in like effects:
>   Loftily lying,
> Leave him—still loftier than the world suspects
>   Living and dying.

The line, "Lofty designs must close in like effects:" is a virtual commentary of the poet upon his art. It will be noted, however, that while the star-image here participates in producing effects appropriate to "close" the "lofty design" of *A Grammarian's Funeral,* it does not, like the star of *Waring,* become the unique symbol of consummation. Both structurally and symbolically the forces of the star of *Waring* are superior to the inherent values of the lyrically harmonious "stars" that "come and go" about the Grammarian's mountain peak.

> Here—here's his place, where meteors shoot, clouds form,
> Lightnings are loosened,
> Stars come and go! Let joy break with the storm,
> Peace let the dew send!

The Incidental Star-Image

"painter poems" and theological poems

In a number of the most famous poems of Browning's middle career the star-image, though consistently retaining its familiar symbolic meanings, is structurally almost negligible; it is incidental, rather than structurally assertive within the form of these poems. This peculiarity of function is common to a number of poems that, when arranged in two distinct groups, have a most reasonable and natural association with each other. These are (1) three of Browning's poems on the subject of painters and painting, *Old Pictures in Florence, Fra Lippo Lippi,* and *Andrea del Sarto,* and (2) seven of his theological, didactic, or religious poems, *Christmas-Eve and Easter-Day, An Epistle . . . of Karshish, Bishop Blougram's Apology, Holy-Cross Day, Rabbi Ben Ezra, Mr. Sludge, "The Medium,"* and *Caliban upon Setebos.*

For purposes of contrast I shall add *Pictor Ignotus* to the discussion of the "painter poems," and *Saul, A Death in the Desert,* and the *Epilogue* to *Dramatis Personae* to the discussion of the theological poems. While the star-images in these poems, especially in *Pictor Ignotus* and in *Saul,* are anything but incidental, there is a certain expository advantage to be gained in keeping the natural grouping that our analysis has otherwise suggested. Furthermore, it may thus be observed that other considerations aside from subjects, in this case, painting and, in the broadest sense of the term, theology, have determined Browning's uses of the star-image, a fact, indeed, that prevents our considering *How They Brought the Good News* an intruder into the group of poems marked by the "incidental star."

When, in the mad gallop of *How They Brought the Good News from Ghent to Aix,*[23] "At Boom, a great yellow star came out to see," there was little more than a frankly narrative and descriptive beauty to be felt in the

---

[23] First published in 1845, in "Bells and Pomegranates," Number VII, under the title heading, *Dramatic Romances and Lyrics,* in 1849 it retained this assignment, but in 1863, and thereafter, it became one of the *Dramatic Lyrics.*

image, even though it is one of the best elements in a thoroughly enjoyable poem. Structurally it may be said to assist in marking the time and the progress of the horsemen; symbolically it is again associated with the idea of attaining the objective of a spirited resolution. It is possible that this association, as well as the purely descriptive phenomenon of the stars in the sky, has suggested its use in this poem.

"PAINTER POEMS"

First in the group of poems on the subject of painters and painting is *Old Pictures in Florence*.[24] In this poem the star-image appears as the adjective "starry" with which Browning has qualified the artistry of one of the early Italian painters. Its symbolic meaning is characteristic, but its structural value is negligible. Its function is to suggest that Stefano painted, as did *Pictor Ignotus,* with the vision of pure art in his mind's eye.

IX

. . . .
What, not a word for Stefano there,
   Of brow once prominent and starry.
Called Nature's Ape and the world's despair
   For his peerless painting?   (See Vasari)

The interpretation of these lines is best supplied, perhaps by the nineteenth stanza of the poem where the objectives of an art such as Stefano's are stated:

XIX

On which I conclude, that the early painters,
   To cries of "Greek Art and what more wish you?"—
Replied, "To become now self-acquainters,
   And paint man, man, whatever the issue!
Make new hopes shine through the flesh they fray,
   New fears aggrandize the rage and tatters:
To bring the invisible full into play!
   Let the visible go to the dogs—what matters?"

If it were necessary to prove, therefore, that the "incidental" star-image is in no sense a mark of the poet's carelessness in composition, one might point simply to the characteristic symbolism of the "great yellow star" of *How They Brought the Good News,* or to Stefano's "brow once prominent and starry." More convincing proof lies in the comparison of the star-images in *Fra Lippo Lippi*[25] and *Andrea del Sarto*.[25] While these images have been frankly subordinated to other elements of expression and design, their elimination would prove only the necessity of their presence. They are the deft brush-strokes of an artist whose portraiture here approaches perfection. The reader

---

[24] First published in *Men and Women,* 1855; in 1863 it became one of the *Lyrics,* and in 1868 was assigned to its permanent position in the *Dramatic Lyrics.*

[25] First published in *Men and Women,* 1855, and since retained in this classification.

has only to remind himself of the essential qualities of these poems to realize that over these apparently insignificant details of composition Browning has worked as though they were of utmost importance, as, in an artistic sense, they really are. In *Andrea del Sarto* he has set the evening-star, in *Fra Lippo,* the morning-star.

Fra Lippo, the champion of healthy realism in art says:

> You understand me: I'm a beast, I know,   (270)
> But see, now—why, I see as certainly
> As that the morning-star's about to shine,
> What will hap some day. We've a youngster here
> Comes to our convent, studies what I do,
> Slouches and stares and lets no atom drop:
> His name is Guidi—he'll not mind the monks—
> They call him Hulking Tom, he lets them talk—
> He picks my practice up—he'll paint apace,
> I hope so—though I never live so long,
> I know what's sure to follow.

Fra Lippo has hope and confidence in the future of his art.

Andrea del Sarto, on the other hand, hopelessly resigns himself to his lamentable fate—for him, as for Strafford, shines night's "first, supreme, forsaken star." To Lucrezia, Andrea confides his lingering but spiritless desire:

> If you would sit thus by me every night   (205)
> I should work better, do you comprehend?
> I mean that I should earn more, give you more.
> See, it is settled dusk now; there's a star;
> Morello's gone, the watch-lights show the wall,
> The cue-owls speak the name we call them by.
> Come from the window, love, come in, at last,
> Inside the melancholy little house
> We built to be so gay with. God is just.

The stage-setting for both of these poems is at once sympathetic, symbolic, and, in a measure, responsible for the occurrence of the star-images we have noted: in *Fra Lippo Lippi,* the realistic city streets whose carnival lights pale before the morning; in *Andrea del Sarto,* "the melancholy little house," silvered with "a common greyness," which deepens into dusk and night. Although setting may have been partially responsible for their appearance, it may be observed also, that the star of morning illuminates a moment of hope, and that the star of evening transfixes a memorable despair.

From a purely expository point of view, it is unfortunate that *Pictor Ignotus*[26] does not fit neatly into the group of "painter poems" that the incidental use of the star-image has suggested. In point of time it is the

---

[26] First published in 1845, in "Bells and Pomegranates," Number VII, under the title heading, *Dramatic Romances and Lyrics;* in 1849 this assignment was retained, but in 1863, and thereafter, the poem was assigned to *Men and Women.*

first of Browning's compositions to express his specific interest in the Italian painters, for, like *How They Brought the Good News,* it belongs to the seventh number of the series, "Bells and Pomegranates." Its publication in 1845 therefore classifies it as a comparatively early poem; it is even more interesting to see in the design revealed by its star-images an imagistic pattern that suggests *Pauline,* rather than the companion pieces, *Old Pictures in Florence* and *Fra Lippo Lippi.* In *Pictor Ignotus* the star-image is both symbolically and structurally important. It occurs, either specifically or through verbal association, at the beginning, the middle, and the end of the poem. The symbolic suggestions of these images, though not in any sense obscure, are peculiar; so that the analysis of their functions runs into difficulties similar to those encountered in the study of *Pauline.*

The first lines of this unknown artist's apology for his apparent failure disclose the image of the star in one of its most peculiar uses:

> I could have painted pictures like that youth's
> Ye praise so. How my soul springs up! No bar
> Stayed me—ah, thought which saddens while it soothes!
> —Never did fate forbid me, star by star,
> To *outburst on your night* with all my gift
> Of *fires from God*: nor would my flesh have shrunk
> From seconding my soul, with *eyes uplift*
> *And wide to heaven,* or, straight like thunder, sunk
> To the centre, of an instant; *or around*
> *Turned calmly and inquisitive,* to scan
> The licence and the limit, *space and bound,*
> Allowed to *truth made visible in man.*[27]

In the worldly "night" that surrounds him, never did fate forbid his genius from flashing "star by star"; his pictures might have become glorious in men's sensuous eyes; Popes and Emperors, cities and towns might have become jealously competitive to possess them; his fame might have increased

> Till it reached home, where learned age should greet   (33)
> My face, and youth, the star not yet distinct
> Above his hair, lie learning at my feet!—
> Oh, thus to live, I and my picture, linked
> With love about, and praise, till life should end,
> And then not go to heaven, but linger here,
> Here on my earth, earth's every man my friend,—
> The thought grew frightful, 't was so wildly dear!
> But a voice changed it.

Our first inclination is to regard these star-images as explicit in their suggestion of the familiar conception: the "lode-star," the "star to men," the star of genuine achievement, aspiration, artistic resolution, and truth. These interpretations are all the more insistent because of the meanings implicit

---

[27] I have italicized, in this quotation, those words that seem to me to be clear verbal associations with the star-image.

in the connotations of the lines that immediately follow the first appearance of the image, "—Never did fate forbid me, star by star, To outburst on your night. . . ." Such phrases as, "fires from God," "eyes uplift And wide to heaven," "Turned calmly and inquisitive," "space and bound," and "truth made visible in man," inform the star-image with the serenity of the unknown painter's character.

But Pictor Ignotus has refused the star, whereupon such an interpretation as this breaks down. His words imply that it is the young, popular artist's pictures that have become stars, that he himself "could have painted pictures like that youth's" that would have forced the youth, "the star not yet distinct Above his hair," to sit at his feet. Pictor's character, as it is thus revealed, persuades us to consider another interpretation of the image, to give it a meaning not unfamiliar to the reader of *Sordello,* to see it as the star of fame or of earthly glory. It was earthly fame that tempted Pictor Ignotus until *a voice* changed his attitude towards life and art. Henceforth, no stars of popular fame would light his path, no scrabbling merchant would knock down his very life to the fattest purse.

We are faced, then, with two interpretations of the symbolical implications of the star-image in this poem. We accept the first largely through habit, but not entirely so, for the verbal associations that we have noted reënforce our first notion. We incline towards the second interpretation because of the conception of Pictor's character that engages our minds as the poem continues. Consequently, our poet seems to have failed to give his work its anticipated imagistic unity.

Whether or not the solution to this question is the one I shall propose, I would suggest it may be found very interestingly stated in the last part of the poem where Pictor Ignotus says:

> Wherefore I chose my portion. If at whiles   (57)
>   My heart sinks, as monotonous I paint
> These endless cloisters and eternal aisles
>   With the same series, Virgin, Babe and Saint,
> With the same cold calm beautiful regard—
>   At least no merchant traffics in my heart.

The connotation of "the same cold calm beautiful regard" seems to me most emphatic: Pictor has not forsaken the star of truth and art; he is *painting* his stars. Just as his poet, Robert Browning, reveals himself in his art, so Pictor is painting the image of his soul in his pictures. We may see him at his work, illuminating his saints and madonnas with the "cold calm beautiful regard" of his own face. He himself has become a star. So Browning would have us think; for he sympathized with the devotion of the early Italian painters, whose tradition Pictor followed, as much as he enjoyed the realistic exuberance of Fra Lippo. Without attempting to be artificially emphatic, one may conclude that these star-images clarify the meaning of the poem. For Pictor Ignotus Browning's star-image would have a most natural attraction; Pictor, even in his attempt to visualize worldly fame, could not conceive a star bereft of "fires from God."

THEOLOGICAL POEMS

Christmas-Éve and Easter-Day, published as a separate volume of poetry, April 1, 1850, has retained its single identity in the collected editions of Browning's works. It is the first in the present group of theological poems in which the star-image assumes its comparatively incidental rôle. Such artistic force as the image may possess in *Christmas-Eve and Easter-Day* depends upon its association with numerous images of light and contrasting images of darkness. As a whole the poem is rich in imagery. In *Christmas-Eve,* it is the sun, the rainbow, the moon, and the clouds that become dominant images. It is also this part of the poem that contains the excellent description of the Independent Chapel, and the pictorial as well as symbolical vividness of such lines and phrases as: "Like yonder spots of our roadside lamps, Haloed about with the common's damps," "the full fruition Of the moon's consummate apparition," "The black cloud-barricade was riven,"

> For see, for see, the rapturous moment   (569)
> Approaches, and earth's best endowment
> Blends with heaven's; the taper-fires
> Pant up the winding brazen spires
> Heave loftier yet the baldachin;
> The incense-gaspings, long kept in,
> Suspire in clouds . . . . . .

As *Christmas-Eve* sweeps through its more than thirteen hundred and fifty lines, which so curiously blend controversial, lyric, and descriptive modes of expression, the quest for light is ever the important theme. It is the general radiance of God's truth that the poet strives to see, as his triangular debate sharpens the distinctions among the powers of revelation ascribed to Protestantism, Catholicism, and Higher Criticism. It is not inconsistent, then, with the poet's characteristic use of the star-image that its luminous companions, sun, moon, and rainbow, should have here become the symbols of God's enveloping radiance, and that the star itself should have been restricted to two specific occurrences.

The first appears in the section of the poem that attacks the higher criticism of the lecture halls of Göttingen:

> Truth's atmosphere may grow mephitic   (900)
> When Papist struggles with Dissenter,
> Impregnating its pristine clarity,
> —One, by his daily fare's vulgarity,
> —Its gust of broken meat and garlic;
> —One, by his soul's too-much presuming
> To turn the frankincense's fuming

> And vapours of the candle starlike
> Into the cloud her wings she buoys on.
>   Each, that thus sets the pure air seething
>   May poison it for healthy breathing—
> But the Critic leaves no air to poison;
> Pumps out with ruthless ingenuity
> Atom by atom, and leaves you—vacuity.

The second occurs in the twentieth division of *Christmas-Eve,* where the poet seeks to resolve his opinions into unity:

> The world rolls witnessing around me   (1188)
> Only to leave me as it found me;
> Men cry there, but my ear is slow:
> Their races flourish or decay
> —What boots it, while yon lucid way
> Loaded with stars divides the vault?
> But soon my soul repairs its fault
> When sharpening sense's hebetude,
> She turns on my own life!

Although the appearance of the star-image is restricted, similarly, to three instances in *Easter-Day,* its force has been increased to emphasize changes in content and in the author's attitude towards his subject. While it would not be appropriate to present here a lengthy interpretation[28] of the two parts of the poem, it is perhaps necessary to mention the principal result of a comparison of *Christmas-Eve* and *Easter-Day* that partially explains the greater force of the star-image in *Easter-Day: Christmas-Eve* resolves itself into the declaration of an opinion: that among three kinds of revelation, the ways of Protestantism, Catholicism, and Higher Criticism, the Protestant way is best. Having made this intellectual decision, the poet then proceeds, in *Easter-Day,* to the much greater task of spiritual resolve. The problem before him is now,

> How very hard it is to be   (1)
> A Christian! . . . .
> . . . . . . hard, I mean for me and you
> To realize it, more or less,
> With even the moderate success
> Which commonly repays our strife
> To carry out the aims of life.

The plan of *Easter-Day* falls into two divisions approximately equal in length. The first division is a colloquy between *you* and *me;* that is to say, a friend and the poet himself. The second division relates the poet's vision of the Day of Judgment. At midnight before the dawn of Easter-Day, the heavens are filled with fire, the "Voice" speaks to the poet; it is God speaking

---

[28] See E. M. Naish, *Browning and Dogma,* Lectures IV, V, and VI; also F. R. G. Duckworth, *Browning: Background and Conflict,* "The White Light," Chap. IX, and M. G. Machen, *The Bible in Browning,* pp. 55-72.

to Man. The pleasures of Earth are compared to the joys of Heaven; the labors of the body and the mind, with the duties of the spirit, until the poet has finally resolved upon a way of life that promises immediate and eternal salvation.

It is in this colloquy of God and Man that images of the star appear, significantly interwoven with the words of the "Voice," and attached to lines that smooth out the tangle of argument in which the poet has become involved in his effort to realize what it is to be a Christian. One may see in the opening lines of the following quotation certain verbal associations with the star that may be said to prepare the way for the specific appearance of the star-images themselves. The "Voice" speaks to the poet:

> ". . . . . This world,   (667)
> "This finite life, thou hast preferred,
> "In disbelief of God's plain word,
> "To heaven and to infinity.
> "Here the probation was for thee,
> "To show thy soul the earthly mixed
> "With heavenly, it must choose betwixt.
> "The earthly joys lay palpable,—
> "A taint, in each, distinct as well;
> "The heavenly flitted, faint and rare,
> "Above them, but as truly were
> "Taintless, so, in their nature, best.
> "Thy choice was earth: thou didst attest
> " 'T was fitter spirit should subserve
> "The flesh, than flesh refine to nerve
> "Beneath the spirit's play. Advance
> "No claim to their inheritance
> "Who chose the spirit's fugitive
> "Brief gleams, and yearned, 'This were to live
> " 'Indeed, if rays, completely pure
> " 'From flesh that dulls them, could endure,—
> " 'Not shoot in meteor-light athwart
> " 'Our earth, to show how cold and swart
> " 'It lies beneath their fire, but stand
> " 'As stars do, destined to expand
> " 'Prove veritable worlds, our home!'
> "Thou saidst,—'Let spirit star the dome
> " 'Of sky, that flesh may miss no peak,
> " 'No nook of earth,—I shall not seek
> " 'Its service further!' Thou art shut
> "Out of the heaven of spirit; glut
> "Thy sense upon the world: 't is thine
> "For ever—take it!"

The association of the star with the "Voice," in the lines here quoted, leaves one in little doubt as to the momentary importance of the substantive "stars" and the verb "star." The only other reference to the star-image in

Easter-Day is the adjectival "starry," which is again spoken by the "Voice" in the course of instructing the poet as to the differences between nature and art, power and beauty:

> "What was the world, the starry state   (815)
> "Of the broad skies,—what, all displays
> "Of power and beauty intermixed,
> "Which now thy soul is chained betwixt,—
> "What else than needful furniture
> "For life's first stage? God's work, be sure,
> "No more spreads wasted, than falls scant!
> "He filled, did not exceed, man's want
> "Of beauty in this life. But through
> "Life pierce,—and what has earth to do,
> "Its utmost beauty's appanage,
> "With the requirement of next stage?"

Interesting and excellent though the poems themselves are as examples of Robert Browning's achievement, it would be ridiculous to insist that in *An Epistle . . . . of Karshish,*[29] *Bishop Blougram's Apology,*[29] and *Holy Cross Day*[30] the star-image is of great artistic consequence. In the *Epistle,* the single appearance of the image is, both structurally and symbolically, of little importance:

> . . . . when, being young,   (169)
> We both would unadvisedly recite
> Some charm's beginning, from that book of his,
> Able to bid the sun throb wide and burst
> All into stars, as suns grown old are wont.

While the lines themselves are reminiscent of others in which the force of the star-image is of great moment, Karshish's particular association of stars with a book of charms here denies the image its characteristic meaning. Furthermore, the very interesting personality of Karshish would have been weakened had Browning attempted to confuse it with a symbolical light, which, though perfect as a qualification of the attitude of St. John (in *A Death in the Desert*) towards Christ, would not have been appropriate to the irrepressible curiosity and learned skepticism of the Arab physician.

Similarly, the usual significance of the star is not exactly compatible with the character of Bishop Blougram, nor with the temper of his argument. The Bishop is as picturesque in his rhetoric as any of Browning's casuistical disputants, but he prefers the practical symbolism of the ship-image, from tops to steerage, to the idealistic image of the star. When he does use it, once in his argument, it is with a symbolic sense familiar to the reader of Browning's poetry, but also, in its application, rather characteristic of the Bishop.

---

[29] First published in *Men and Women,* Vol. I, 1855, and since retained in this classification.

[30] First published in *Men and Women,* Vol. II, 1855; in 1863, and thereafter, assigned to *Dramatic Romances.*

. . . . But whom, at least do you admire?   (433)
Present your own perfection, your ideal,
Your pattern man for a minute—oh, make haste,
Is it Napoleon you would have us grow?
Concede the means; allow his head and hand,
(A large concession, clever as you are)
Good! In our common primal element
Of unbelief (we can't believe, you know—
We're still at that admission recollect!)
Where do you find—apart from, towering o'er
The secondary temporary aims
Which satisfy the gross taste you despise—
Where do you find his star?—his crazy trust
God knows through what or in what? it's alive
And shines and leads him, and that's all we want.
Have we aught in our sober night shall point
Such ends as his were, and direct the means
Of working out our purpose straight as his,
Nor bring a moment's trouble on success
With after-care to justify the same?
—Be a Napoleon, and yet disbelieve—
Why, the man's mad, friend, take his light away!

Holy-Cross Day, one of the most entertaining of Browning's poems, combines the grotesque humor of its descriptive first division with the composed serenity of the "sermon," which is founded upon "Ben Ezra's Song of Death."

XII

For Rabbi Ben Ezra, the night he died,
Called sons and sons' sons to his side,
And spoke, ...

It is "Ben Ezra's Song of Death" that contains a reference to starlight, so slight in its imagistic effect as to be no more than descriptively significant.

XV

"God spoke, and gave us the word to keep,
"Bade never fold the hands nor sleep
"Mid a faithless world,—at watch and ward,
"Till Christ at the end relieve our guard.
"By His servant Moses the watch was set:
"Though near upon cock-crow, we kept it yet.

XVI

"Thou! if thou wast He, who at mid-watch came,
"By the starlight, naming a dubious name!
"And if, too heavy was sleep—too rash
"With fear—O Thou, if that martyr-gash
"Fell on Thee coming to take thine own,
"And we gave the Cross, when we owed the Throne—"

The gravely didactic *Rabbi Ben Ezra*[31] is almost disguised, as a serious statement of moral and philosophical meditation, by the lyric profusion of its images. Though comparatively insignificant when judged by the effects produced by the famous metaphor of the "Potter's wheel," the "stars" of Stanza II possess their brief moment of characteristic meaning; the aspiration of youth in contrast to the deliberation of age:

II

Not that, amassing flowers,
Youth sighed "Which rose make ours,
"Which lily leave and then as best recall?"
Not that, admiring stars,
It yearned "Nor Jove, nor Mars;
"Mine be some figured flame which
        blends, transcends them all!"

Caliban upon Setebos; or, Natural Theology in the Island[31] is perhaps the most curious among all of Browning's theological poems, and one of the most original of his psychological studies. Star-images occur in only two lines of this poem; they are associated with Caliban's groping but cunning speculations upon "the Quiet." He has stolen time from his work for Prospero to engage in such meditation as his luxurious posture will permit. He sprawls,

(. . . . . . now that the heat of day is best,   (1)
Flat on his belly in the pit's much mire,
With elbows wide, fists clenched to prop his chin.

He feels secure, kicking "both feet in the cool slush," talking to himself as he pleases:

Letting the rank tongue blossom into speech.)   (23)
Setebos, Setebos, and Setebos!
'Thinketh, He dwelleth i' the cold o' the moon.
'Thinketh He made it, with the sun to match,
But not the stars; the stars came otherwise;
Only made clouds, winds, meteors, such as that:
Also this isle, what lives and grows thereon,
And snaky sea which rounds and ends the same.

For Caliban, stars signify the being of remote mystery; they are the outposts of another realm of power, superior and disinterested,

—the something over Setebos   (129)
That made Him, or He, may be, found and fought,
Worsted, drove off and did to nothing, perchance.
There may be something quiet o'er His head,
Out of His reach, that feels nor joy nor grief,
Since both derive from weakness in some way.
I joy because the quails come; would not joy
Could I bring quails here when I have a mind:

[31] First published in *Dramatis Personae*, 1864, a classification since retained.

This Quiet, all it hath a mind to, doth.
'Esteemeth stars the outposts of its couch,
But never spends much thought nor care that way.
It may look up, work up,—the worse for those
It works on! 'Careth but for Setebos
The many-handed as a cuttle-fish,
Who making Himself feared through what He does,
Looks up, first, and perceives he cannot soar
To what is quiet and hath happy life; . .. . .

But among all the curiosities in Browning's poetry, there is none more grotesquely amusing than the character of Mr. Sludge, "the Medium."[32] If we may omit from consideration Sludge's allusion to "'. . . . the "Stars and Stripes" set to consecutive fourths,'" and his colloquialism, "thanks his stars," there remain at least two passages in his slap-dash dialectics to present the star-image in a manner that cleverly holds the "tune" of Sludge's voice, and at the same time marks him for what, in Browning's opinion, he is. Sludge has a certain careless regard for the laws of logical sequence that is equaled only by the vehemence of his rhetoric and the insouciance of his attitude towards the "symbols of immensity":

"How last night, I no sooner snug in bed,   (274)
"Tucked up, just as they left me,—than came raps!
"While a light whisked" . . . "Shaped somewhat
        like a star?"
"Well, like some sort of stars, ma'am."—"So we thought!"

'T is easy saying they serve vast purposes,   (912)
Advantage their grand selves: be it true or false,
Each thing may have two uses. What's a star?
A world, or a world's sun: doesn't it serve
As taper also, time-piece, weather-glass,
And almanac? Are stars not set for signs
When we should shear our sheep, sow corn, prune trees?
The Bible says so.
                        Well, I add one use
To all the acknowledged uses, and declare
If I spy Charles's Wain at twelve to-night,
It warns me, "Go, nor lose another day,
"And have your hair cut, Sludge!" You laugh: and why?
Were such a sign too hard for God to give?
No: but Sludge seems too little for such grace:
Thank you, sir! So you think, so does not Sludge!

SAUL, A DEATH IN THE DESERT,

AND EPILOGUE TO DRAMATIS PERSONAE

As the functions of the star-image in *Pictor Ignotus* suggest the evidence of a contrast to the way in which the star-image has been used in other

[32] *Mr. Sludge, "the Medium,"* first published in *Dramatis Personae*, 1864, and since retained in this classification.

"painter poems," so the particular functions of the star-images in one of Browning's most powerful religious or theological poems, *Saul*, supply the evidence of a departure from the imagistic practice that has been common to the theological poems we have just examined. *Saul* has had a peculiar history, for it may be said to belong to both the early and middle career of the poet. Furthermore, as the influence of Shelley's poetry may have been responsible in a large measure for the imagistic peculiarities of *Pauline*, so the poetry of Christopher Smart[33] may have been the source of much that is interesting in the imagery of *Saul*. There are, nevertheless, sufficient indications in both *Pauline* and *Saul* to suggest that even in the technique of borrowing Robert Browning could remain essentially himself:

> As on the works of mighty bards I gazed,
> . . . . I rather sought
> To rival what I wondered at than form
> Creations of my own; if much was light
> Lent by the others, much was yet my own.
> *(Pauline*, line 885 ff.)

When *Saul* was first published as a dramatic romance in *Dramatic Romances and Lyrics*, "Bells and Pomegranates," Number VII (1845), it consisted of nine divisions that, in spite of several changes, are approximately identical with the first nine sections of the *Saul* of later editions. In 1849 it was published again, in the collected edition of that year. In its present form of nineteen sections it first appeared in *Men and Women* (1855); but in 1863 its assignment was changed to *Dramatic Lyrics*, where it has remained.

Whatever the source of the poem was, the "much" that was yet his own has produced in Browning's *Saul* an imagistic pattern that is similar in many respects to the imagistic design of *Pauline*. Here are the same, or nearly the same, symbolic values of the star-image, the verbal associations, the blendings, the clusters, the profuse variety of images. The essential difference between the total designs of the two poems is that beneath the dramatic and lyrical form of *Saul* there is a foundation of logical and argumentative structure, while beneath the lyrical and confessional form of *Pauline* there is nothing more than a thinly meandering narrative or autobiographical outline. The basic structure of *Saul* is therefore clear in its literary and logical divisions, but the basic structure of *Pauline* depends for its clarity upon an imagistic pattern that is evidently intended to mark the important moments in a loosely constructed narrative. Consequently, even though they are integral to the basic design of *Saul*, the star-images in *Saul* are not called upon to assume the structural burdens that they were forced to carry in *Pauline*. In *Saul* they have become, rather, the picturesque accompaniment to the progress of David's argument.

[33] See W. C. DeVane, *Parleyings*, Chapter III, "The Parleying with Christopher Smart," an excellent study of Browning's debt to the poetry of Christopher Smart. . .

In one part of *Saul* there is a marked change in the imagistic pattern; for, beginning at Section XVII and continuing to Section XIX, dramatic argument to an appreciable degree replaces the mood of dramatic lyric. In spite of the occurrence of a significant star-image near the beginning of Section XVII, one may observe in this part of the poem a sharply diminished quantity of imagery. In Section XIX, however, the lyric mood returns with a characteristic profusion of images.

The alterations that Browning made in the text of *Saul* before it was republished in 1849 were insignificant in comparison to those that appeared in the edition of 1855. It was in this final revision that the latter ten sections of the poem first appeared along with significant changes in the nine sections of 1845 and '49. While most of these changes were alterations in diction, word order, and punctuation, a fact which left the imagery of the first nine sections practically intact, there was one important transformation in imagistic effect that is interesting, not only because it involves the image of the star, but also because it reveals the poet at work. This change occurred in the last part of Section IX. I shall set down the versions of 1849 and '55 side by side:

1849	1855

Oh all gifts the world offers singly,
  On one head combine,
On one head the joy and the pride,
  Even rage like the throe
That opes the rock, helps its glad labour,
  And lets the gold go—
And ambition that sees a sun lead it—
Oh, all of these—all
Combine to unite in one creature—Saul!
	"And all gifts which the world offers
	  singly, on one head combine!
	"On one head, all the beauty and
	  strength, love and rage (like the throe
	"That a-work in the rock, helps its labour and lets the gold go)
	"High ambition and deeds which surpass it, fame crowning them,—all
	"Brought to blaze on the head of one creature—King Saul!"

Thus "joy" and "pride" have become "beauty" and "strength"; "love" has been added to "rage"; King Saul, *no longer following the sun,* has himself become a blazing orb, crowned with the brilliance of his ambitious deeds. The sun, image of generous love, no longer leads the King's ambition. The effect of this change is two-fold: it emphasizes the ability of Saul to achieve, without the assistance of external power, and to resolve his energy into one consummate blaze of earthly glory; but it also emphasizes his want of human kindness and the ultimate necessity of his dependence upon heavenly love and mercy, the dominating themes of the additional ten sections of the completed poem. It is the light of Christ's merciful coming that has captivated the soul of David, and it is this vision that he pleads Saul may see, as the poem progresses to its lyric conclusion.

The religious doubts expressed in *Pauline,* and there only partially resolved into firm belief, have given way to the certain convictions of the second *Saul,* for between the composition of the earlier and the later *Saul,* Browning had reached the religious and theological conclusions that he expressed in *Christmas-Eve and Easter-Day*. By making the significant change in Section IX, which has been noted above, Browning was able to integrate the imagistic patterns of the earlier and later divisions of *Saul* to this larger conception of religious truth.

Verbal associations or suggestions of images of light, in the nature of preparatory inferences of a final consummation of light, characterize the imagistic pattern of the first nine sections of the poem. When the reader gives particular attention to these suggestions of light, he may discern the specific progress from "blackness" to the image of Saul's blazing personality. A sunbeam first penetrates the darkness:

III

At the first I saw nought but the blackness; but soon I descried
A something more black than blackness—the vast, the upright
Main prop which sustains the pavilion: and slow into sight
Grew a figure against it, gigantic and blackest of all.
Then a sunbeam, that burst thro' the tent-roof, showed Saul.

The sunbeam reveals Saul in his agony. Then, as David takes his harp to play his soothing music, poetic light adds its illumination to the sun-rays piercing the tent, and the song itself produces the familiar association of music, flowing water, and the star:

V

Then I tuned my harp,—took off the lilies we twine round its chords
Lest they snap 'neath the stress of the noontide—those sunbeams like
    swords!
And I first played the tune all our sheep know, as, one after one,
So docile they come to the pen-door till folding be done.
They are white and untorn by the bushes, for lo, they have fed
Where the long grasses stifle the water within the stream's bed;
And now one after one seeks its lodging, as star after star
Into eve and the blue far above us,—so blue and so far!

But David's song of joy of life stops suddenly, when "here in the darkness Saul groaned,"

VIII

And I paused, held my breath in such silence, and listened apart:
And the tent shook, for mighty Saul shuddered: and sparkles 'gan dart
From the jewels that woke in his turban, at once with a start,
All its lordly male-sapphires, and rubies courageous at heart.
So the head: but the body still moved not, still hung there erect.
And I bent once again to my playing,
. . . .

The theme of David's song now changes to " 'How good is man's life the mere living!' " and finally reaches its conclusion in the apostrophe to Saul, the crown of mankind:

IX

. . . .
"High ambition and deeds which surpass it, fame crowning them,—all
"Brought to blaze on the head of one creature—King Saul!"

As the poem continues, the connotations of the poet's language hold the consummate image of Saul, the blazing crown of earthly glory, before the reader's eye, until the last three sections of the poem introduce the theme of Christ's coming. The images of light are then transformed from the blaze of Saul's power to the trembling stars of Heaven:

XVI

Then the truth came upon me. No harp more—no song more!
    outbroke—

XVII

"I have gone the whole round of creation: I saw and I spoke:

. . . .
"Do I task any faculty highest, to image success?
"I but open my eyes,—and perfection, no more and no less,
"In the kind I imagined, full-fronts me, and God is seen God
"In the star, in the stone, in the flesh, in the soul and the clod

. . . .

XVIII

. . . .
" . . . . O Saul, it shall be
"A Face like my face that receives thee; a Man like to me,
"Thou shalt love and be loved by, for ever: a Hand like this hand
"Shall throw open the gates of new life to thee! See the Christ stand!"

XIX

I know not too well how I found my way home in the night
. . . .
. . . The whole earth was awakened, hell loosed with her crews;
And the stars of night beat with emotion, and tingled and shot
Out in fire the strong pain of pent knowledge: but I fainted not,
For the hand still impelled me at once and supported, suppressed
All the tumult, and quenched it with quiet, and holy behest,
Till the rapture was shut in itself and the earth sank to rest.
. . . .

A Death in the Desert[34] is specifically related, through its attack upon Higher Criticism, to *Christmas-Eve and Easter-Day,* and by certain characteristics of its unique form, to *An Epistle of Karshish.* It was written in direct reply to the statements of such higher critics as Renan and Strauss,[35] and it

[34] First published in *Dramatis Personae,* 1864. In the collected edition of 1868, save for the omission of one line (line 23, "closed with and cast and conquered, crucified,") from the first edition, and a few verbal changes, the poem remains intact and preserves its classification under *Dramatis Personae.*

[35] See W. O. Raymond, "Browning and Higher Criticism," *P.M.L.A.,* XLIV (June, 1929), 590-621.

aims to be a closely reasoned defense of the authenticity of the *Gospel of St. John*. The literary mode of *A Death in the Desert* is inevitably argumentative. While the imagery of this poem is consequently integral to an argumentative design, in many respects similar to that of *Johannes Agricola*, the quality or kind of imagery here employed is the result of Browning's having naturally associated light with the Gospel of St. John and, in a larger sense, with his own search for truth. In contrast, however, to the ravishing effulgence of the images of light in *Christmas-Eve and Easter-Day*, a poem that also approached the question of religious truth both lyrically and argumentatively, the images of *A Death in the Desert* are characterized chiefly by a quiet intensity that accords with the personal intimacy of St. John's revelation. Instead of the rainbows, glowing moons, wide sweeps of sky and cloud, or the vast illumination of the northern lights in *Christmas-Eve and Easter-Day*, the poet has pointed the argument of *A Death in the Desert* with the spark of fire, flaming eyes, Prometheus's fire, "the universal prick of light," "yon sole glimmer in light's place," gleams, the lamp, and the star.

Near the beginning of *A Death in the Desert* Browning has resorted to an imagistic device to make his fundamental proposition clear, that the duty of the religious man is ever to seek those ways of living that will permit the light of Heaven to illuminate his inner darkness.

> But in the midmost grotto: since noon's light   (26)
> Reached there a little, and we would not lose
> The last of what might happen on his face.
> I at the head, and Zanthus at the feet,
> With Valens and the Boy, had lifted him,
> And brought him from the chamber in the depths,
> And laid him in the light where we might see:
> . . . .
> Outside all was noon and burning blue.

As he begins to speak, St. John says, "So is myself withdrawn into my depths."

The proposition before us, to be sure, is not altogether consistent with the statement of the youthful egoist who seemed to imply the opposite when he wrote in his *Paracelsus*,

> Truth is within ourselves; it takes no rise
> From outward things, whate'er you may believe.
> . . . .
> . . . . Watch narrowly
> The demonstration of a truth, its birth,
> And you trace back the effulgence to its spring
> And source within us . . . .
>   (*Paracelsus*, I, 726 ff)

But it is a proposition entirely in agreement with the sentiment of the contemporary *Abt Vogler* in which the great musician's humility of spirit acknowledges God as the ultimate source of all musical beauty and truth. For Abt Vogler the "finger of God" transforms musical harmonies into stars:

> And, there! Ye have heard and seen: consider and bow the head!

As St. John begins to emerge slowly from his "depths," he discourses upon the nature of the three souls of man: the soul that *Does*, the soul that *Knows*, and the soul that *Is*. Life runs back into his dying body like a blown spark of fire on the tip of a burnt stick:

> "Yet, blow the spark, it runs back, spreads itself (107)
> "A little where the fire was:"

John's vision becomes clear once more; it is illuminated by the image of the star and other aspects of light:

> "What if truth broke on me from above (119)
> "As once and oft-times? Such might hap again:
> "Doubtlessly He might stand in presence here,
> "With head wool-white, eyes flame, and feet like brass,
> "The sword and the seven stars, as I have seen—
>
> . . . .
>
> "Since much that at the first, in deed and word,
> "Lay simply and sufficiently exposed
> "Had grown (or else my soul had grown to match,
> "Fed through such years, familiar with such light,
> "Guarded and guided still to see and speak)
> "Of new significance and fresh result;
> "What first were guessed as points, I now knew stars,
> "And named them in the Gospel I have writ."

Wholly significant to the meaning of the argument is the emphatic insistence of the poet that the "stars" of the Gospel have been realized through St. John's having lived constantly in the presence of Truth. As the poem continues, Robert Browning is at pains to show the difference between the direct truth of personal experience and the indirect "facts" of historical investigation. Whether or not his interpretations of Renan and Strauss have been entirely just, the poet is determined to force the issue with certainty, to condemn the "facts" of Higher Criticism, as he conceives them, as an intellectual snare. His vehement disagreement with Higher Criticism is therefore stated in an interesting contrast between personal truth and historical fact that has been sharpened by an ingenious use of the star-image. He says, briefly, that historical fact is like a star seen through an inverted telescope, in other words, through the wrong end of an instrument created by man's inventive intelligence. St. John has seen the star steadily, with his own eyes. He says in effect, "I have seen reality with my very eyes, I have known the Christ personally,"

> ". . . . These [the stars of the Gospel], are, I see; (225)
> "But ye, the children, His beloved ones too,

"Ye need,—as I should use an optic glass
"I wondered at erewhile, somewhere i' the world,
"It had been given a crafty smith to make;
"A tube he turned on objects brought too close,
"Lying confusedly insubordinate
"For the unassisted eye to master once:
"Look through his tube, at distance now they lay,
"Become succinct, distinct, so small, so clear!
"Just thus he needs must apprehend what truth
"I see, reduced to plain historic fact,
"Diminished into clearness, proved a point
"And far away: Ye would withdraw your sense
"From out eternity, strain it upon time,
"Then stand before that fact, that Life and Death,
"Stay there at gaze, till it dispart, dispread,
"As though a star should open out, all sides,
"Grow the world on you, as it is my world."

Historical fact, then, is a view of truth through the inverted optic glass, useful as a means of clarifying one's intellectual vision, but in no sense to be accepted as complete in its realization of the ultimate fact of Life and Death. The intellectual approach to the mystery of God produces the unwholesome satisfaction of an illusion whose apparent clarity depends upon man's having ingeniously increased the distance between himself and the personality of God, Who is

"Diminished into clearness, proved a point
"And far away:"

It is not man's intellect that is at fault, but the improper use of his intellect, and the too certain assumption that his intellect is capable of complete realization. Only through Love, such as St. John's personal love for Christ, can man begin to penetrate the everlasting mystery,

"Stay there at gaze, till it dispart, dispread,
"As though a star should open out, all sides,
. . . .

"For life, with all it yields of joy and woe,   (244)
"And hope and fear,—believe the aged friend,—
"Is just our chance o' the prize of learning love,
"How love might be, hath been indeed, and is;
"And that we hold thenceforth to the uttermost
"Such prize despite the envy of the world,
"And, having gained truth, keep truth: that is all."

Preliminary to the discussion of these passages that contain the literal designation of the star-image in *A Death in the Desert,* I have mentioned other images of light, particularly the dim light of the grotto and the blown spark of fire, that are characteristic of the imagistic content of St. John's discourse. My intention was to suggest that the general image of light, which attaches principally to the first half of the poem, is a composite of several kinds and degrees of luminescence. Just as the imagery of the poem as a whole is integral to an argumentative design, so the image of the star may be seen as integral to the imagistic pattern. It is noteworthy also that the occurrence of different images in this poem is not sufficiently rapid, nor are the images themselves sufficiently various in kind (most of them being images of light) to produce the clusters of color or the harmonious confusions of color that we have noted, frequently, to be characteristic of Browning's lyric as distinct from his argumentative style. The reader's acceptance of the images of light here displayed, as appropriate illustrations of the points in discourse, is dependent, in every instance, upon his close attention to the logical plan of argument. For a poem like *Pauline* the reader must attend first of all to the imagistic design in order to discern the poet's logical outline, such as it is; *A Death in the Desert,* on the other hand, requires the reader to follow closely the logical design of the poem in order to become aware of the interesting effects of its imagery.

Further evidence of the integration of the star with the total imagistic pattern of this poem is to be found in certain examples of that artistic device that has been called verbal association. St. John, speaking of the fleshy veil of youth and strength that enshrouds the spirit of man from the light of truth, insists that through living and learning man may

> ". . . wear the thickness thin and let man see— (202)
> "With me who hardly am withheld at all,
> "But shudderingly, scarce a shred between,
> "Lie bare to the universal prick of light."

Other examples of this sort, but less effective as illustrations when removed from their context, appear at a number of points in the poem.

Thus, while *A Death in the Desert* is not remarkable for the abundance of its imagery, it is interesting as an example of the subordination of imagistic pattern to argumentative design, a subordination that does not result, however, in the poet's failure to create lustrous stars in accordance with the demands of his argument.

In his *Epilogue* to *Dramatis Personae* Browning has written a poem that shows a close relationship to *A Death in the Desert* and to *Christmas-Eve.* Very briefly, the thesis of this poem reintroduces the triangular debate of Catholicism, Higher Criticism, and Protestantism. The poet's point of view has changed sufficiently, however, to cause him to represent these three theological conceptions now as sacerdotal ritualism, Higher Criticism, and religious independence. His "first speaker," David, stands for ritualism; his "second speaker," Renan, for Higher Criticism; his "third speaker," the poet himself, for religious independence. To the "third speaker" goes the victory.

The star-images in this poem are all to be found in the words of the "second speaker," Renan. Either by specific designation or verbal suggestion, the star is present in almost every line that Renan speaks. It is important and

interesting to observe, however, that the star of this passage is the same we
have observed through the optic glass of *A Death in the Desert,* the cool, clear,
distant star of "plain historic fact," "diminished into clearness, proved a point
and far away":

Gone, now! *All gone across the dark so far,*   (22)
    Sharpening fast, shuddering ever, shutting still,
Dwindling into distance, dies that star
    Which came, stood, opened once! We gazed our fill
With upturned faces on as real a Face
    That, stooping from grave music and mild fire,
Took in our homage, made a visible place
    Through many a depth of glory; gyre on gyre,
For the dim human tribute. Was this true?
    Could man indeed avail, mere praise of his,
To help by rapture God's own rapture too,
    Thrill with a heart's red tinge that pure pale bliss?
Why did it end? Who failed to beat the breast,
    And shriek, and throw the arms protesting wide,
When a first shadow showed the star addressed
    Itself to motion, and on either side
The rims contracted as the rays retired;
    The music, like a fountain's sickening pulse,
Subsided on itself; awhile transpired
    Some vestige of a Face no pangs convulse,
No prayers retard; *then even this was gone,*
Lost in the night at last. We, lone·and left
Silent through centuries, ever and anon
    Venture to probe again the vault bereft
Of all now save the lesser lights, a mist
    Of multitudinous points, yet suns, men say—
And this leaps ruby, this lurks amethyst,
But where may hide what came and loved our clay?
How shall the sage detect in yon expanse
    The star which chose to stoop and stay for us?
Unroll the records! Hailed ye such advance
    Indeed, and *did your hope evanish thus?*
Watchers of twilight, is the worst averred?
    We shall not look up, know ourselves are seen,
Speak, and be sure that we again are heard,
    Acting or suffering, *have the disk's serene*
Reflect our life, absorb an earthly flame,
    Nor doubt that, were mankind inert and numb,
Its core had never crimsoned all the same,
    Nor, missing ours, its music fallen dumb?
Oh, dread succession to a dizzy post,
    Sad sway of sceptre whose mere touch appals,
Ghastly dethronement, cursed by those the most
    On whose repugnant brow the crown next falls!

ABT VOGLER

Abt Vogler, published in *Dramatis Personae* in 1864, is generally recognized as one of Browning's finest poems. It is unique in that its style is the harmony of several modes and manners of expression. It is argumentative, lyric, dramatic, religious, mystical, and metaphysical, but, withal, predominantly contemplative. It aims to persuade the reader that music is superior to all other forms of artistic expression. Painting and poetry, great as they may be, are "but art in obedience to laws," while music transcends the laws of art to become one with the laws of God:

> But here [in music] is the finger of God, a
>   flash of the will that can,
> Existent behind all laws that made them and, lo,
>   they are!

The lyric tone of *Abt Vogler* is produced by carefully wrought stanzas and verses. The poem is marked dramatically by Browning's having sought to identify his thesis with the character of a great musician, and by his having ostensibly written in accordance with the scheme of the dramatic monologue. F. R. G. Duckworth, speaking, in his *Browning, Background and Conflict,* of Browning's dramatic propensities, makes this appropriate statement: "And the method which Browning chose was the method of revealing so much of this spectacle of power and beauty as could be seen at work in the minds of a character or a set of characters—in their minds or in their imaginary utterances."[36]

The religious temper of *Abt Vogler* is manifest in the virtual identification of religion and music, or, in a larger sense, of religion and art. Abt Vogler, as he is here represented, like St. John in *A Death in the Desert,* attains to truth and beauty only through humbling himself in love before God and thus seeing ever more clearly the light of Heaven:

> And the emulous heaven yearned down,   (27)
>   made effort to reach the earth,
> As the earth had done her best, in my
>   passion, to scale the sky:
> Novel splendours burst forth, grew familiar
>   and dwelt with mine, . . .

There is no difficulty in interpreting lines such as these as an expression of the religious attitude of the mystic; for the mystic, above all else, yearns for the dissolution of his own personality into unity with God. But there is a certain conscious reluctance in the character of Abt Vogler that checks his mystical enthusiasm just short of a complete self-effacement. Even in the lines quoted above the suggestion that heaven yearns downward to meet Abt Vogler's passion "to scale the sky," together with the insistence on the word "mine,"

---

[36] F. R. G. Duckworth, p. 206.

is the sign of a personality that retains its individual integrity in spite of its moments of genuine humility.

Abt Vogler, like Robert Browning, is a philosophical artist. He can withdraw from the excitement of his argumentative, lyrical, and dramatic themes, or from the ardor of his religious and mystical beliefs, to consider and to meditate with metaphysical detachment. He can examine the effects of his musical improvisation upon himself; he can contemplate the probable impact of his art upon society. Finally, he can formulate certain philosophical opinions that give intellectual meaning to his experience:

> There shall never be one lost good! What   (69)
>   was, shall live. as before;
>   The evil is null, is nought, is silence
>   implying sound;
> What was good shall be good, with, for evil,
>   so much good more;
>   On the earth the broken arcs; in the
>   heaven a perfect round.
>
> . . . .
>
> The high that proved too high, the heroic
>   for earth too hard,
>   The passion that left the ground to lose
>   itself in the sky,
> Are music sent up to God by the lover
>   and the bard;
>   Enough that he heard it once: we shall
>   hear it by-and-by.

This philosophical mood is by no means confined to the lines just quoted; it is present throughout the poem. It is the unifying mood of the poem, for it produces a harmony of many moods, an enveloping tone of contemplative serenity.

No less complex than its characteristic tone is the design of *Abt Vogler*. Its several structural phenomena are difficult to specify. Its logical divisions merge with an imagistic pattern equally important to the turn of the argument, and, while the poem rises with the cumulative insistence of the formal fugue, the impression of the freedom of improvisation remains. In the last section of the poem the lyric stanza-form, though strictly maintained, does not limit the broad sweep of philosophical conclusions. Even the lineaments of a chronological outline are faintly visible in the narrative of Abt Vogler's experience. There is every reason to assume, therefore, that the twelve stanzas of *Abt Vogler,* as well as any single poem that he has written, combine and concentrate the many stylistic modes, and the several most characteristic themes of Browning's poetry.

Looking back for the moment to the intense struggles of *Sordello*, and comparing them with the quiet contemplation of *Abt Volger,* it is possible to see at least the philosophical answer to a former problem. The youth who wrote *Sordello* was oppressed with the fundamental conflict between artistic compression and spiritual expansion; the man who wrote *Abt Vogler,* and perhaps no other poem quite its equal in composure, has resolved the conflict and given it a philosophical solution:

> Give me the keys. I feel for the common   (91)
>   chord again,
> Sliding by semitones, till I sink to the
>   minor,—yes,
> And I blunt it into a ninth, and I stand on
>   alien ground,
> Surveying awhile the heights I rolled
>   from into the deep;
> Which, hark, I have dared and done, for
>   my resting-place is found,
> The C Major of this life: so, now I will
>   try to sleep.

The importance of *Abt Vogler* to the general thesis of the present study is implied in the statements of the paragraphs just concluded, and its relationship to the examination of Browning's use of the star-image is even more specific. The poem as a whole is a significant image of Browning's conception of the artist's creative experience. Aesthetically considered, this poem is a statement of many of Browning's most cherished opinions. It states his conception of the superiority of music to all other forms of art, and in a larger sense it implies that music is but the symbol for all great artistic achievement, as distinguished from the nearly great or imitative.

In his analysis of Abt Vogler's methods of improvisation Browning has expressed his idea of the process of creation. The artist begins with a conception of structure (the temple, or the palace of the first part of the poem) and proceeds to marshal the "keys" of his imagination to build ("Bidding my organ obey, calling its keys to their work,"). When the foundations have been laid and the substantial outlines of his structure (or *genre*) have been established, the artist becomes preoccupied with the injection of life and beauty into a form as yet inert.

> Up, the pinnacled glory reached, and the   (24)
>   pride of my soul was in sight.

> IV

> In sight? Not half! for it seemed, it was
>   certain, to match man's birth,
> Nature in turn conceived, obeying an
>   impulse as I;
> And the emulous heaven yearned down,
>   made effort to reach the earth,
> As the earth had done her best, in my
>   passion, to scale the sky:

Novel splendours burst forth, grew familiar
          and dwelt with mine,
     Not a point nor peak but found and
          fixed its wandering star;
Meteor-moons, balls of blaze: and they
          did not pale nor pine,
     For earth had attained to heaven, there
          was no more near nor far.

This is the element of creation that is called "inspiration." It is the result, according to Browning, of the artist's effort to reach heaven, an "emulous heaven" which yearns down to "reach the earth"; so that no peak of the artist's aspiration but finds and transfixes "its wandering star."

Finally comes realization—the achievement of total form at its best, a form that is responsive to the laws of God, rather than to the laws of man; to universal law, rather than to the conventions of art; the achievement of the soul, as distinct from the achievement of the mind.

VI

All through my keys that gave their   (41)
          sounds to a wish of my soul,
     All through my soul that praised as its
          wish flowed visibly forth,
All through music and me! For think,
          had I painted the whole,
     Why, there it had stood, to see, nor the
          process so wonder-worth:
Had I written the same, made verse—
          still, effect proceeds from cause,
     Ye know why the forms are fair, ye hear
          how the tale is told;
It is all triumphant art, but art in obedience
          to laws,
     Painter and poet are proud in the artist-
          list enrolled:—

VII

But here is the finger of God, a flash of the
          will that can,
     Existent behind all laws that made
          them and, lo, they are!
And I know not if, save in this, such gift be
          allowed to man,
     That out of three sounds he frame, not a
          fourth sound, but a star.
Consider it well: each tone of our scale in
          itself is nought;
     It is everywhere in the world—loud,
          soft, and all is said:

> Give it to me to use! I mix it with two in
> my thought:
> And, there! Ye have heard and seen:
> consider and bow the head!

The "painter and the poet are proud" of their achievements, proud of their abilities to master the laws of triumphant art; the musician is humble, "consider and bow the head," for he has been mastered by the law of God, privileged beyond all other artists to discover the origin of beauty and truth.

It is hardly necessary to note that both the musician's resolution to inform his conception of structure with light and life, and the realization of his achievement of perfect, consummate form have been marked by the image of the star. No ideas in Browning's poetry have been more consistently represented by the image of the star than these: spiritual resolution, and the attainment of perfection. Other ideas that have been so marked have been, indeed, aspects of these two, or their opposites, transfixed by the false, the mythological, the fanciful, and the eclipsed stars of unclarified, or unworthy presumption. Consequently, if within the limits of separate poems the poet has not composed according to a design that was sufficiently systematic to produce the clarity of allegorical symbolism, it is possible to see in the consistency of his general use of the star-image a sufficient regularity of application to warrant our thinking of the star as a veritable symbol in the poet's life and imagination.

Browning's selection, here, of the experience of improvisation as the clearest pattern of the process of artistic creation is a stroke of genius. Improvisation is the act of composing, rather than the act of recording the finished composition. Improvisation is expression in its purest form, untrammeled by the laws of popular appeal, unrestricted by the canons of contemporary criticism, unthwarted by notions of sale and exchange, totally free from preconceived ideas of artistic form. It is an affair which concerns only the artist and the source of all truth and beauty; it is Man and God becoming one and the same personality:

> But God has a few of us whom he whispers
> in the ear;
> The rest may reason and welcome: 'tis
> we musicians know.

It is the mystical and the mysterious experience of creation that Browning seeks to emphasize as the distinguishing ability of every great artist—the rest is the intellectual and the technical labor of modulating experiences of this kind into the "C Major of this life."

The evidence before us constitutes an interesting pattern of aesthetic practice, and its statement in the most philosophically and emotionally composed poem that Browning has written warrants our assuming it to be the design for poetry which he considered noblest and best.

The conclusions that we have been able to draw from this examination of *Abt Vogler* may be said to compose a general conclusion to this division of our study. In the process of analyzing the functions of the star-image in many other poems of Browning's middle period, we have been able to observe, severally, many interesting though perhaps seemingly unrelated details. Fortunately each of these details is to be found again in the design and in the content of *Abt Vogler*. Here they have been drawn together for the first time into a compact body of evidence. *Abt Vogler* is at once an argumentative poem, a lyric, and a dramatic monologue; its theme is philosophical, religious, and artistic; its form is a composite of various modes of expression, ranging from the casuistical discourse to the design of the poetical fugue. The star-images of *Abt Vogler* may be regarded, therefore, as "points" in an argumentative scheme, as supporting tones or "crucial moments" in a lyric design, or as the marks of the poet's emphatic approval of the ideas and the personality that he wishes to present.

We may go a step further to conclude that the evidence at hand points to the establishment of fixed principles in Robert Browning's art for the use of the star-image. First, in contrast to the practice of the earliest period of composition, both the structural and symbolic functions of the star have been restricted to conform to the requirements of a total design. Second, the structural use of the star-image, although reduced in the frequency of its occurrence, is manifest in the mechanical distribution of the image *within* the plan of a given poem, in its occurrence at important "turns" in the development of a poem, in the emphasis it may give to the high points of a dramatic action, in its relation to other significant images, and even in its solitary appearance in a poem at the moment of consummate realization. Third, the symbolical force of the star-image is its power of revealing the attitude of the poet towards his subject. Finally, although the remark may partially anticipate the discussion of the following chapters, we may assume, I think, that these observations are true for all the poems that, through their inclusion of the star-image, enter the scope of the present study. Depending mainly upon the nature of their functions, though to some extent upon the frequency of their occurrence, star-images, to a degree consistent with their poetic force, continue throughout the remainder of Browning's career to point to details of structure within a total or enveloping design, and to qualify the manner or attitude of the poet towards his subject.

CHAPTER VI

THE RING AND THE BOOK, 1868-1869

THE *Ring and the Book* is in many respects Browning's greatest poem. Critics disagree, of course, as to the exact position it should occupy in the scale of Browning's accomplishments. Recent commentaries raise the question as to whether or not it should be regarded as his nearest approach to artistic perfection. Unfortunately, one cannot hope to find a clear answer to this question, even by comparing *The Ring and the Book* with other notable poems. It is certain, only, that *Andrea del Sarto,* to mention but one of the ingenious dramatic monologues, gives the reader an immediate, rather than a delayed, or hardly won sense of aesthetic satisfaction; or that *Abt Vogler* attains to a poetic and philosophic composure that makes it unique among Browning's works. There can be no real comparison of *The Ring and the Book* with other works so widely different in purpose, in form, and in length. If the great dramatic monologues are to be regarded as the crown of Browning's art, one must remember, also, that *The Ring and the Book* is composed, for the most part, of an integrated series of excellent dramatic monologues; if attainment to the mood of contemplation is to be admired as the poet's greatest achievement, one must recognize the aesthetic impossibility of suggesting that a spirit of serenity should or could pervade *The Ring and the Book,* a poem that seeks to explore the labyrinth of human society. Abt Vogler's greatest music is the expression of a soul capable of a mystical identification of itself with God; his improvisations are the creations of a mind that is able to isolate itself, temporarily at least, from the affairs of human society. *The Ring and the Book,* on the other hand, takes for its subject the very complexities of the social order from which *Abt Vogler* has been withdrawn. Only once, perhaps, in *The Pope,* does *The Ring and the Book* presume to leave the level of human contradiction for the summits of divine wisdom. But even in this instance Browning's intention is evidently to show the necessity of applying the Pope's wisdom to the solution of the social problem.

It seems to me quite essential to an understanding of Browning's artistic development that the examination of any one of his poems should begin with the assumption that the poem in question is in many respects unique. While there are certain fundamental ideas, habits of expression, and favorite themes that generally distinguish the works of Robert Browning from all other English poets, there are also peculiarities of form, of purpose, and of intellectual interest that singularize each of his poems. On the other hand, it is certainly true that in the middle and later periods of his poetic career there is observable a cumulative development of Browning's powers that is the direct result of former acts of composition and experiment. The singularity of *The Ring and the Book* is in many ways the result of Browning's having reexamined many of his former interests with a totally new purpose in mind, of his having reechoed the old themes with a new music. To borrow a familiar figure from *Sordello,* one may say without exaggeration that *The Ring and the Book* is the "consummate orb" of Browning's poetical experience. In this, if in any poem, Browning has composed the scattered lights of his visions of God and Man into one constellation. It is this artistic fact which gives *The Ring and the Book* its novelty and, at the same time, its "familiar" quality.

To the degree in which such a comparison is permissible, *The Ring and the Book* was to Browning what *Paradise Lost* was to John Milton, the culmination for which the works of youth and early maturity were the vigorous preparation. Beneath the impetuosity of Browning's character one increasing purpose, to reveal Man to men, seems to have maintained its steady existence, a force comparable to the passionate and continuous meditations of John Milton to justify the ways of God to men. There may be great differences between *At a Solemn Musick* and *Pauline,* between *Lycidas* and *Sordello,* between Horton and Camberwell, but there is an interesting similarity in the patterns of development that permit both Browning and Milton to draw the thoughts of youth into the creations of maturity.

For Browning the intense anticipations of *Sordello* have been realized in *The Ring and the Book. Sordello* revealed his search for artistic and spiritual discipline, his determined quest for truth as distinguished from appearances, his interest in the paradox of good and evil. Tortured as he was by the conflicts of hand and brain and heart, the author of *Sordello* nevertheless emerged with a clearer notion of the state of Man in Society, with the discovery of the poet's social function: to reveal Man to men. These interests of youth have been now transformed into artistic realities, and wrought into the fabric of *The Ring and the Book* to produce the long awaited consummation:

> Why take the artistic way to prove so much?   (XII, 841)
> Because, it is the glory and good of Art,
> That Art remains the one way possible
> Of speaking truth, ...
> . . . . wherein man nowise speaks to men
> Only to mankind,—Art may tell a truth
> Obliquely, do the thing shall breed the thought,
> Nor wrong the thought, missing the mediate word.
> So may you paint your pictures, twice show truth,
> Beyond mere imagery on the wall,—
> So note by note, bring music from your mind,
> Deeper than ever e'en Beethoven dived,—
> So write a book shall mean beyond the facts
> Suffice the eye and save the soul beside.

The accomplishments of Browning's middle years have had their large share in producing the book that "shall mean beyond the facts," for the fruitful labors of this period, which produced the dramatic monologue, and the variety of experiments in metrical innovation, have all contributed to vivify the personalities of Pompilia, Caponsacchi, Guido, the inimitable lawyers, the Pope, the frustrated Comparini; to merge many themes into symphonic unity, to record the distinguishing tunes of many voices, to construct the curious ring of circumstance which is *The Ring and the Book*.

A consideration of this poem that attempts to relate it to the general artistic development of the poet requires that we reconsider the importance of "The Old Yellow Book" as a principal source of poetic material. In a recent dissertation entitled, *Sidelights on Robert Browning's "The Ring and the Book*,"[1] Miss Louise Snitslaar makes the following interesting comment: "The Old Yellow Book was a godsend to Browning in every respect. The story itself being one great unsolved problem, he found in it moreover, all his beloved themes—the lover, the great hater, the tender woman, the wise philosophic religious old man, the Italian landscape, a crowded Roman scene, the casuistry of the Law. He can bring into it the clever reasoning of Bishop Blougram or Mr. Sludge, the tenderness of his many love-poems, the grotesqueness and the rude rhymes of his Caliban, and Holy-Cross Day, the Italian atmosphere of the Englishman in Italy, the contemplative and philosophic moods of Rabbi Ben Ezra and A Death in the Desert; in short, his poems of hatred and heroism and sacrifice, his descriptions of mean and noble characters. So no wonder that when he chanced on The Old Yellow Book, it had at once such a mighty attraction for him that he could not stop reading it, that it took possession of his mind and inspired him to his most powerful creation."[2]

According to this interpretation, which seems to me quite reasonable, Browning's discovery of "The Old Yellow Book" is the occasion without which the poem could not have been written; it is the moment that Browning awaited. "The Old Yellow Book" suggested a ground plan, a plot; it supplied a mass of detail, and a complete set of characters that wanted transformation into the design, the episodes, the moods, and the personalities of *The Ring and the Book*; it presented, in other words, the opportunity that made possible the expression of years of observation and the realization of a number of artistic ambitions conceivable. While this point of view does not minimize the importance of "The Old Yellow Book" as the most specific and tangible of the various sources from which Browning drew his material, it implies what seems to me the essential fact: "The Old Yellow Book" is no more and, at the same time, no less important to a consideration of the

[1] Dissertation, University of Groningen, July, 1934; published by "Pronto," Amsterdam, 1934.
[2] L. Snitslaar, p. 17.

form and the content of *The Ring and the Book* than the accumulated reserves, both intellectual and artistic, of the poet's continuous development.

The difficulty of accepting this point of view is that "The Old Yellow Book" itself has been carefully preserved in the Balliol College Library, that its Latin and Italian text has been twice translated into English, by Professor C. W. Hodell and by Mr. Gest, and that Professor Hodell's translation, with his interesting *Essay,* has been made readily accessible in *Everyman's Library*. Consequently, "The Old Yellow Book" is likely to stand in the way of one's attempt to see the other less clearly demonstrable, but equally important sources of Browning's vision, and to demand a degree of attention that may exceed its importance.[3]

This tendency to overemphasize the importance of one source at the expense of others less palpable, though equally significant, undoubtedly accounts for the legalistic reputation that *The Ring and the Book* sometimes holds, and it explains partially the rise of the critical controversy as to whether or not Browning in writing the poem was faithful to his "source." Mr. John Marshall Gest, in his study of *The Old Yellow Book*,[4] has left his readers in no doubt as to his belief that Browning has proved himself thoroughly incompetent as an investigator of legal practice, and also that certain parts of *The Ring and the Book* are nothing but gross misrepresentations of the innate nobility of the legal mind. Professor DeVane, in his *Handbook,* has prepared a most judicious résumé[5] of the critical controversy regarding Browning's use of the materials in *The Old Yellow Book*. The purport of his conclusions may be surmised from the following sentences: "*The Ring and the Book* was called in the nineteenth century 'the greatest spiritual treasure since Shakespeare.' This praise has often seemed to me to be misguided,

[3] L. Snitslaar, p. 85. "The deeper we penetrate into the Poem, the more we come to the conclusion that The Ring and the Book and The Old Yellow Book are two documents widely differing in many respects. We may consider The Old Yellow Book the warp upon which Browning wove his wonderful tapestry, but no more. By absolutely idealizing the figures of Pompilia and Caponsacchi he changed the whole tenor of the story. Most curious is it to see how often Browning's readers and critics confuse the people of The Old Yellow Book with those of The Ring and the Book. This is a tribute to the greatness of Browning's art; he makes his readers forget that these persons are not entirely his own creations, that their originals existed, and that his art recast them and shows them to us in a new light. But on the other hand his critics give a false view of things when they confound Browning's creations with their originals, and especially when they discuss the legal proceedings in this way."

[4] John Marshall Gest, *The Old Yellow Book, Source of Browning's "The Ring and the Book," A New Translation with Explanatory Notes and Critical Chapters upon the Poem and its Source,* Philadelphia: University of Pennsylvania Press, 1927.

[5] W. C. DeVane, *Handbook,* pp. 286-305. Here the various arguments for and against Browning's "faithfulness" to his source have been carefully considered: Professor Hodell's essay, "The Making of a Great Poem, An Essay on the Relationships of the 'Ring and the Book' to The Old Yellow Book," in his *The Old Yellow Book, Source of Browning's "The Ring and the Book."* . . . Washington: The Carnegie Institution, 1908; studies by Professor W. O. Raymond, Mrs. Frances Theresa Russell, Professor J. E. Shaw, Mr. Gest, and A. K. Cook's *A Commentary upon Browning's "The Ring and the Book,"* London & New York: Oxford Press, 1920.

notably in this, that a much truer comparison may be drawn to the *Paradise Lost*. For Browning's poem, like Milton's, is finally an attempt to justify the ways of God to man, to show that everywhere in the world God has set himself to meet evil in mortal combat. Above all, Browning has given us, not history, but an idealized reading of life, and though he cautions us in the last Book against reading into his story too cheerful a confidence in the chances of virtue in this world, to view the chances hopefully was habitual with Browning throughout his life."[6]

> From the book, yes; thence bit by bit I dug   (I, 458)
> The lingot truth, that memorable day,
> Assayed and knew my piecemeal gain was gold,—
> Yes; *but from something else surpassing that,*
> *Something of mine,* which mixed up with the mass,
> Made it bear hammer and be firm to file.
> Fancy with fact is just one fact the more.

"Something of mine." An Italian murder-case and the action of the courts of law are merely part of a larger theme that represents society as a whole: the home, the family, the church, the court, officialdom, the social group, and the social individual. The characters of the poem are not the originals of the "Old Yellow Book"; they are types of Man that the poet has attempted to show to men. He has not drawn the analytical portraits of actual persons, but he has represented in each character the clearer form of his imagination. "Fancy with fact is just one fact the more." In no sense is *The Ring and the Book* a legal case, or a legal judgment; it is a poet's judgment of society, in other words, a poet's criticism of life. To quote Professor DeVane again, ". . . . Browning was gifted with that peculiar strong-mindedness of the great figures of nineteenth-century literary men, which warped all history to their purposes. Macaulay wrung the history of England to prove a political thesis; Carlyle bent French history to satisfy a personal philosophy; Browning made a section of obscure Italian history into a reading of life as he viewed it in his own day."[7]

The course of the present investigation of the use of the star-image in Browning's poetry has pointed again and again to the necessity of seeing as clearly as possible the total design of each poem that enters the scope of this study. Furthermore, it may be stated with reasonable certainty that, in every instance observed, the total design of each poem has been determined, save in the instance of the imitative plays, by the poet's dominant purpose. Even in the instances of *Pauline* and *Sordello,* whose designs, in a literary sense, are none too clear, one may say that imperfections in design are but the manifestations of imperfectly realized intentions. If it is correct to assume, then, that *The Ring and the Book* is intended to be a criticism of life, not of the life of the late seventeenth century to be sure, but of the life of the later

[6] W. C. DeVane, *Handbook*, p. 305.   [7] W. C. DeVane, *Handbook*, p. 299.

nineteenth century in England and on the Continent, it would be natural to suppose that the total design of *The Ring and the Book* should show a direct relationship to the fundamental purpose of the poet. When this design is seen, the functions of the star-images in the poem may be more clearly observed.

A comparison may help to make the following observations regarding total or enveloping design clear, a comparison of the designs of *The Ring and the Book* and *Sordello*. In the design of *Sordello* we have noted not only a confusion of *genres* and modes of discourse,[8] but also an apparent contest among these forms of expression for individual supremacy. In the mind of the author of *Sordello*, the artist contended with the psychologist; the poet with the novelist. In *The Ring and the Book* it is possible that even a greater number of *genres* and modes of discourse have been used, and that to the intentions of the artist, the psychologist, the poet, and the novelist Browning has added the purpose of the critic, or judge. It is the poet's purpose to express a judgment of society that gives form and unity to *The Ring and the Book*. In other words, Browning has clearly conceived his proper function; he can apply it practically to his task. It is this very function that he sought to realize when he composed *Sordello*, but which then he could not practice, which then he could express only in the form of an intellectual concept: that the poet's function was to reveal Man to men. He can now translate theory into practice, for he can realize his concept of the poet's function in terms of his art. In composing *The Ring and the Book* he is free to give full play to his artistic skill. He therefore escapes from repeating the confusions of *Sordello* and produces the well-wrought framework of a critical design beneath and through which runs a profusion of narrative, argumentative, rhetorical, dramatic, and lyric designs. Within this complicated design a great variety of related themes, the "number of parts and voices,"[9] merge into the single grandeur of the poem. Even the mode of direct commentary, here, as in *Sordello*, signifies occasionally the personal presence of the poet, and it is certainly worth noting that, as he had chosen the couplet as the verse-form of *Sordello*, Browning's original plan was to write *The Ring and the Book* in couplets.[10] The division of the poem into twelve books enables the poet-judge to review his evidence several times over, to examine and to reexamine the testimony of his chief witnesses in turn, and to hear the accompanying voices of public opinion.

> And this corroborates the sage,
> That Art,—which I may style the love of loving, rage
> Of knowing, seeing, feeling the absolute truth of things

---

[8] See above, pp. 96-97.   [9] See above, pp. 159-160.

[10] W. C. DeVane, *Handbook*, p. 286, quoting from the Diary of William Allingham, May 26, 1868, "I [Browning] began it in rhymed couplets, . . . but thought by and by I might as well have my fling, and so turned to blank verse."

For truth's sake, whole and sole, not any good, truth brings
The knower, seer, feeler, beside,—instinctive Art
Must fumble for the whole, once fixing on a part
However poor, surpass the fragment, and aspire
To reconstruct thereby the ultimate entire.
Art, working with a will, discards the superflux,
Contributes to defect, toils on till,—*fiat lux,*—
There's the restored, the prime, the individual type!

(from Section XLIV of Fifine at the Fair)

Unlike *Sordello,* in which the divisions of the basic narrative have been marked by images, *The Ring and the Book* does not present a chronological sequence of "episodes in the development of a soul," but, rather, "developed" souls whose contacts produce a circumstantial ring of social "episodes." This ring of circumstance, with its interlocking elements, moves the poet to call Society to the bar of judgment, in a valiant effort to decide which aspects of Man are good, which evil. But within the framework of this general plan lie divisions of the poem, like the Book of Pompilia, that are chiefly narrative or lyric, and others, like the Book of Caponsacchi, that are chiefly rhetorical. While the controlling purpose of the poem requires an enveloping design that must be logical in kind, it nevertheless admits sub-divisions and minor divisions of narrative, rhetorical, lyric, and dramatic quality.

In *Sordello* Browning promised himself the realization of two distinct though related forms of artistic achievement: the compression of the "starriest into one star," and the expansion of his poetic soul into one "consummate orb" of truth. If we are willing to accept the dramatic monologue as the unique realization of the first of these ambitions, we may readily accept *The Ring and the Book* as the achievement of the second. Truth in its many forms and interrelationships among men has come into the poet's grasp. At least he has made every possible effort to convince himself and his British public that he is telling *the whole truth,* and he has therefore brought all the powers of his mind and art to bear upon the story of Pompilia.

The Ring and the Book abounds in images. For every important character or significant action in the poem appropriate images have been conceived that may be said to accompany that character or denote that action throughout the poem. For the poem as a whole a symbol, the-ring-and-the-book, has been specifically created. The logical, rhetorical, or narrative unity of almost every one of the several main divisions, or "books," of the poem has been reenforced by a dominant image or a dominant group of images. Over all, however, stands the controlling philosophical or critical design, demanding conformity to the fundamental purpose in the poet's mind.

Consistent, therefore, with the demands of a design that is basically logical, the images of this poem have been composed into a kind of logical hierarchy. At the top is the image of the-ring-and-the-book. Immediately subordinated to this general image are the dominant images of each of the twelve books.

These dominant images are most clearly conceived in the image of the feast, or the banquet of briefs, of *Dominus Hyacinthus de Archangelis*; in the image of the garden, or the garden of the arts, of *Johannes-Baptista Bottinius*; in the contrasting colors, red and white, darkness and lustre, of *Pompilia;* and in the fusion of images of "white light" of *The Pope*. In the third rank in this hierarchy are scores of images, abundant in their variety, that show, when examined separately, a number of logical transformations or natural metamorphoses. One of the images often associated with Pompilia, for example, is the general image of the growing plant. According to the demands of structural and logical necessity this image appears in a number of forms, such as: the branch, leaves, bud, flower, and fruit. Similarly, for Guido, the general image of a voracious beast may be seen in a number of forms, such as: the wolf, scorpion, hound, serpent, fox, and hawk. The function of these images of the third rank is to provide a running accompaniment, both picturesque and specific in its symbolic effects, to the main outline of the poem.

> So you may paint your picture, twice show truth,
> Beyond mere imagery on the wall,—
> So note by note, bring music from your mind,
> Deeper than ever e'en Beethoven dived,—

It is difficult to decide which of these three ranks[11] of images in Browning's logical hierarchy is the most effective from a purely artistic point of view, the general image of the poem, the dominant images of certain books, or those images that have been subordinated to the third rank. In composing *The Ring and the Book* the poet has been so successful in his integration of various poetic elements as to give each element, or each group of elements, an artistic significance, as distinct from a logical significance, wholly necessary to the full expression of his ideas and his vision. Consequently, while responsive to the demands of a basic design of logical or critical origin, even the images of the third rank compose of themselves a pattern in every way essential to complete expression. It is true that their influence is confined, apparently, to subdivisions within the books in which they occur, but, on the other hand, it does not follow that the appearance of any number of these images in one book prohibits their reappearance in another, or in several others. Consequently, they produce what Dr. Spurgeon, in her studies of Shakespeare's imagery, has called an "undersong," the music, in this instance, of themes ever recurrent and interestingly modified, that helps to give descriptive interest to a fundamentally critical, or philosophical composition.

It should be noted, furthermore, that from book to book there are a number of intentional changes in the ranks of images. For example, the dominant red

---

[11] A more searching analysis would undoubtedly reveal further degrees and distinctions in rank among the images of this poem. For the purpose of present study, however, it has seemed unnecessary to make this discussion any more complicated.

and white of *Pompilia* become elsewhere images of third rank; the sub-ordinated stars of Books I, II, III, and IV rise almost to a position of singular dominance in *Pompilia* and in *The Pope*. Even the general image of the ring itself appears variously as an image of the third rank. Therefore, not only in what he says, but also in the way he says it, Browning has achieved in a large measure the long awaited consummation. The interlocking elements of his design are as inseparable as the interrelated episodes in the ring of circumstance upon the examination of which he formulates his judgment of society.

It is perhaps unnecessary to state it at length, but the fact should at least be mentioned that in *The Ring and the Book*, as in *Pauline, Paracelsus,* and *Sordello,* the devices of verbal association[12] are in many instances important to the production of imagistic effects. Without the use of this connotative method, for example, the well-chosen *banquet of briefs* in Book VIII would have had little or no opportunity to become the dominant symbol of the character and the attitude of Dominus Hyacinthus de Archangelis. In Book X, *The Pope,* images have been so arranged as to compose, through verbal association, a pattern of summary and conclusion that is very much like the imagistic design of the first part of Book VI in *Sordello*. Furthermore, it should be thoroughly understood that the effects of both the specific and the verbally suggested images in this poem, particularly their symbolic effects, are always dependent upon the nature of the context in which they are used; that is to say, upon the character or characters with whom they are associated, upon the action that they represent, upon who speaks and what is happening.

In the hierarchy of images, which it seems to me Browning has established in this poem, the star serves chiefly as an image of the third rank. In *Pompilia*, however, it approaches a position of dominance because of its important participation in the dominant color-design of this book, the color contrasts: red and white, and darkness and lustre. Similarly, in the *The Pope,* the star rises to a position of greater influence because it becomes an effective part of a dominant image of "white light." In certain well-marked divisions within these books, and in Book XII, the star singly dominates a notable portion of the total number of verses. In *Pompilia,* for example, the dominance of the star may be observed in approximately one-fourth of the entire book.

The numerical sum of literal occurrences of the star-image in *The Ring and the Book* is thirty-two. A scattering of verbal associations with the star-image does not increase the total to much more than fifty, nor does this sum suggest that the star-image is of very great significance in a poem so vast in its proportions. It is only when it is considered symbolically and structurally, rather

---

[12] "Verbal association" is a phrase used here, and elsewhere, to mean that specific images are often suggested by Browning's choice of words. Thus, at times, without actually using the word "banquet," or "feast," it has been Browning's method to suggest the image by using such connotative words as: *food, sauce, stomach, dish,* thus to keep the dominant image of the banquet continuously in the reader's mind.

than merely numerically, that its true significance is revealed. When it is so considered, one may see clearly that Browning's use of the star-image in this poem follows that principle of artistic integration that has been exemplified very clearly in the designs of such poems as *A Death in the Desert* and *Abt Vogler*. This principle, it will be recalled, permits the poet to use the star-image symbolically, in a manner thoroughly characteristic of his earlier and earliest poetry, to signify truth, aspiration, the approach to perfection, resolution, and poetical beauty; on the other hand, it noticeably restricts and controls his structural use of the star-image. In contrast to his having imposed a heavy structural burden upon the star, and other images, in such poems as *Pauline, Sordello,* and even *Paracelsus*, Browning has kept the star-images of *The Ring and the Book* from supplying anything more than what he now regards as their just share in the production of purely structural effects. Their structural effect now diminishes to equal, approximately, those effects supplied by other elements of his technique, such as the logical, rhetorical, narrative, dramatic, argumentative, and lyrical devices of coordination and unification. The star-image is therefore wholly integral to the basic design of *The Ring and the Book,* even though its symbolic effects retain their force (and a number of familiar meanings) and their apparent freedom from literary restriction.

The distribution of the star-image throughout the poem is interesting. Out of the total of thirty-two literal instances of its occurrence, six are to be found in Book I, five appearing in rapid succession, between lines 527 and 556, and one, in line 633, that stands in solitary contrast to deeds of darkness. In Books II, III, and IV (*Half-Rome, The Other Half-Rome,* and *Tertium Quid*), where what we may call its characteristic symbolism would be with reason inappropriate, the star appears, respectively, once, thrice, and twice. In Book VII, *Pompilia,* its influence increases to dominate approximately six hundred lines, throughout which its six appearances are spaced with symmetrical regularity. The star appears eight times in Book X, *The Pope.* In this book its effects are heightened by a number of verbal associations, by the intentional association of the star with other important images of "white light," and by the occasional blending of the star-image with the image of flowing water. Through these effects, and combinations of effects, the spread of the star's influence in Book X has been widened to dominate, through its association with the general image of "white light," more than half the book. In Book XII there are six literal occurrences of the star-image; they are distributed at fairly regular intervals from the beginning of the book to the end.

The very casual appearance of the star-image in Books II, III, and IV, and its total disappearance from Books V, *Count Guido,* VI, *Giuseppe Caponsacchi,* VIII, *Archangelis,* IX, *Bottinius,* and XI, *Guido,* are artistic phenomena that one would reasonably expect to find. There is one notable exception, however. It is well enough to suppose that an image whose characteristic symbolic effect is to suggest aspiration, truth, and resolution would be dissociated from the personalities of Guido, Browning's lawyers, and his Tertium Quid. But why has the star been withheld from the book of Giuseppi Caponsacchi? This question becomes all the more puzzling when it is observed that at least one-third of the star-images in other books of the poem refer directly, or by implication, to Caponsacchi, especially the stars of *Pompilia*. Images of light abound in *Giuseppi Caponsacchi,* notably the sun, the moon, and fire, which I interpret to signify, respectively, generosity, romantic love, and courage; verbal associations with the star may be observed in *Caponsacchi* but no cases of its specific appearance. The answer, which I tentatively propose, is based upon a comparison of the contents and the designs of Books VI and VII, *Giuseppi Caponsacchi* and *Pompilia*. Pompilia, in telling her story, approaches the episodes of the flight with Caponsacchi with thoughts which translate themselves into visions of light thrown against the dark background of her past. For her, Caponsacchi becomes the lode-star of deliverance. To express her gratitude and her ideal love for her deliverer she, in her simplicity, can find no image more fitting than the very stars of heaven. But Caponsacchi's love for Pompilia is romantic rather than simply ideal; his is the courageous passion of knightly adventure, the errantry of rescuing a beautiful and mysterious lady from distress and torture. His whole life, his courtly training, his aristocratic tastes, and his priestly eloquence dictate the style of his rhetoric. For him the lyric simplicity of Pompilia will not do as a mode of expression. The·language at his command must form itself into sentences not only clear, but powerfully persuasive as well; the images with which he adorns his speech must be not only descriptive, but also emphatic. To convince the court he cannot depend upon the insinuating influence of the star; he must call upon the direct brilliance of the sun and the wide radiance of the moon. Again and again he repeats the name of his lady, Pompilia, who, in his romantic mind, is a vision of radiant light:

> But she—
> The glory of life, the beauty of the world,
> The splendour of heaven.

Nor, as we discover when we read the Pope's estimate of him, is Caponsacchi concerned so much with the white star of truth as he is with the fair moon of romance, or the red fire of adventure.

In general, the symbolic meanings of the star-image that are characteristic of Browning's earlier poems are the same for *The Ring and the Book*: the lode-star, the star of hope and aspiration, the stars of poetry, truth, and resolution. Associated with these familiar meanings, there are at least three others which are peculiar to this poem: (1) the star signifies Caponsacchi, especially in *Pompilia,* and to some extent in *The Pope*; (2) it signifies Truth in the particular form in which truth is known to the Pope; (3) as the "Wormwood Star" of Book XII, it refers particularly to the "rocket" of

Guido's "brilliant usurpature." In addition to these three special uses of the star-image, there are several other delicacies of exception to the general rule, and in particular, one in which the star stands for Guido himself, in the cluster of five stars in Book I:

> Because, you are to know, they lived at Rome,   (I, 527)
> Pompilia's parents, as they thought themselves,
> Two poor ignoble hearts who did their best
> Part God's way, part the other way than God's,
> To somehow make a shift and scramble through
> The world's mud, careless if it splashed and spoiled,
> Provided they might so hold high, keep clean
> Their child's soul, one soul white enough for three,
> And *lift it to whatever star should stoop,*
> What *possible sphere of purer life than theirs*
> Should *come in aid* of whiteness hard to save.
> *I saw the star stoop, that they strained to touch,*
> *And did touch and depose their treasure on,*
> As *Guido Franceschini* took away
> Pompilia to be his forever more,
> While they sang "Now let us depart in peace,
> "Having beheld thy glory, Guido's wife!"
> *I saw the star supposed, but fog o' the fen*
> *Gilded star-fashion by a glint from hell;*
> Having been heaved up, haled on its gross way,
> By hands unguessed before, invisible help
> From a dark brotherhood, and specially
> Two obscure goblin creatures, fox-faced this,
> Cat-clawed the other, called his next of kin
> By Guido the main monster,—cloaked and caped,
> Making as they were priests, to mock God more,—
> Abate Paul, Canon Girolamo,
> These who had rolled *the star-like pest* to Rome
> And *stationed it to suck up and absorb*
> The sweetness of Pompilia, rolled again
> That *bloated bubble,* with her soul inside,
> Back to Arezzo and a palace there—

In quoting this passage I have taken the liberty of italicizing those words and phrases that present the image of the false star either directly or by verbal association. Guido is the "fog o' the fen" that would absorb the "whiteness" of Pompilia. However, a detailed interpretation of these verses is hardly necessary. Of more interest is the poet's deliberate use of an image which characteristically suggests aspects of goodness to imply here aspects of evil. Actually there is no aesthetic contradiction in Browning's having thus ostensibly departed from his habitual practice. The false stars of *Sordello*, and the "diminished" stars of *A Death in the Desert* and the *Epilogue* to *Dramatis Personae* are instances of the poet's having elsewhere employed the image of the star to call attention to the enticing lustre of illusions that take their origin in ignorance, as distinct from knowledge, or in partial investigation, as distinct from complete realization. What more natural than that the helpless Comparini should, in their ignorance, mistake "fog o' the fen" for a "possible sphere of purer life"? It was the same fundamental error that led them to open their door to a spurious and dreadful "Caponsacchi":

> "Open to Caponsacchi!" Guido cried: (I, 622)
> "Gabriel!" cried Lucifer at Eden-gate.
>
> . . . .
> . . . . Close eyes! And when the corpses lay
> Stark-stretched, and these the wolves, their wolf-work done,
> Were safe-embosomed by the night again,
> I knew a necessary change in things;
> As when the worst watch of night gives way,
> And there comes duly to take cognizance
> The scrutinizing eye-point of some star—
> And who despairs of a new day-break now?
> Low the first ray protruded on those five!
> It reached them, and each felon writhed transfixed
> Awhile they palpitated on the spear
> Motionless over Tophet:

The contrast of light and darkness represented in these lines is an imagistic theme that runs through the entire poem, so that the star-image here displayed may be regarded as one with the images of light that, in Book X, throw down their spears to transfix the infamy of Guido and his hopeless accomplices. The "scrutinizing" power of the Pope's wisdom, born of his vision of Truth, pronounces the final judgment that these lines foreshadow. Book I is, after all, introductory; it states the variety of themes that are to receive further elaboration and development in the following divisions of the poem.

With Book II this general development of the several themes of the poem begins. Half-Rome favors the cause of Guido; "he" is therefore not particularly concerned with the discovery of truth, but rather with the expression of an argument that supports an opinion founded upon the popular prejudice that a husband's honor must be defended at all costs. Neither artistically nor logically can "he" or "his" argument be illuminated with images of light. Consequently the poet has eliminated the use of the star-image and other images of light from Book II, except in one interesting instance. Half-Rome prefers, for the sake of "his" argument, to distort the evidence by attempting to associate the spurious love-letters of Pompilia with a "love-star" which implies their authenticity:

> For Guido's first search,—ferreting, poor soul,   (II, 1068)
> Here, there and everywhere in the vile place
> Abandoned to him when their backs were turned,
> Found,—furnishing a last and best regale,—

All the love-letters bandied 'twixt the pair
Since the first timid trembling into life
O' the love-star till its stand at fiery full.
Mad prose, mad verse, fears, hopes, triumph, despair,
Avowal, disclaimer, plans, dates, names, . . .

The Other Half-Rome of Book III is sympathetic to Caponsacchi and
Pompilia, sentimentally thrilled with the thought of a romantic adventure.
For "him" the love of Caponsacchi and Pompilia is the meeting of two stars:

. . . . the *courtly Canon*: see in him   (III, 845)
A proper star to climb and culminate,
Have *its due handbreadth of the heaven at Rome,*
Though mean while *pausing* on Arezzo's edge,
As modest candle does mid mountain fog,
To rub off redness and rusticity
Ere it sweep chastened, gain the silver sphere!

Anyhow, whether, as Guido states the case,   (III, 1052)
Pompilia,—like a starving wretch i' the street
Who stops and rifles the first passenger
In the great right of an excessive wrong,—
Or whether the strange sudden interview
Blazed as when star and star must needs go close
Till each hurts each and there is loss in heaven—
What ever way in this strange world it was,—
Pompilia and Caponsacchi met, in. fine,
She at her window, he i' the street beneath,
And understood each other at first look.

But like Half-Rome, The Other Half-Rome is not concerned fundamentally
with the search for truth; "he" is preoccupied with the emotions of romantic
sympathy, a fact which hardly makes him a reliable judge of human behavior
or of social conduct.

Tertium Quid, in Book IV, is a select group of people who abjure what they
consider to be the complacency of Half-Rome, as successfully as they refuse
to have anything to do with the romantic sentimentality of The Other Half-
Rome. They, Tertium Quid, are conscious of their elect superiority; they
are careful, eternally on guard, even against each other, lest any expression
suggesting an enthusiasm should give them away. Their tolerance, their middle way, becomes for them an excellent means of diverting the energies of
making real decisions into the exhilarating pleasures of clever conversation.
The man who could sum up the whole, rather entertainingly scandalous
affair with a phrase like,

Hell broke loose on a butterfly!   (V, 1601)
A dragon born of rose-dew and the moon—

could go home from the chamber-music at the Countess's feeling rather proud
of himself. The phrase would be remembered. It so happens that the lines
just quoted are the words of the poet speaking ostensibly in his own character,

but actually assuming the rôle of a member of Tertium Quid, as for the moment, he attempts to see through their eyes the attitude of The Other Half-Rome. Consequently, when two literal instances of the star-image occur in *Tertium Quid,* one must be on guard against accepting them at their full symbolic value. The "best stars Hymen brings above" in line 712, and the "light o' the morning star," in line 1031, as the rather conventional form of the poet's phraseology suggests, are merely the ornaments of polite conversation.

With the exception, then, of the single star of line 633 of Book I, which foreshadows the Pope's final judgment of Guido and his accomplices, and with the possible exception of those occurring in the discourse of The Other Half-Rome, "who" is sympathetic, at least, to the poet's hero and heroine, all the star-images of the first four books of the poem may be regarded as symbols of questionable "truth," for they are associated with the expressions of the ignorant Comparini, the prejudiced Half-Rome, and the conventionally sophisticated Tertium Quid.

Browning evidently intended that the truth of his story, the correct interpretation of the events in his ring of circumstance, should be realized through the intuitive insight of Pompilia, and the discriminating wisdom of the Pope. Pompilia's "truth" is personal, individual, and uncomplicated by any attempt on her part to see herself disinterestedly, or to evaluate her particular experience in its relationship to the general pattern of society. The Pope, on the other hand, desires to see a whole truth, and his judgment of Guido is presented as the result of a dispassionate evaluation of the facts of the tragedy in the light of their effect upon society as a whole. An estimate of the value of Pompilia's "truth," therefore, depends entirely upon one's belief in the innate purity of her soul and in the possible universality of her character. The decisions of the Pope, however, are fortified by the power of great learning, and by the wisdom of a magnificent devotion to the ways of God. Youthful Pompilia has never forgotten the intimations of truth and goodness with which she was born; the aged Pope has attained to a conception of truth and goodness that fills the hours before his death with serenity.

It is therefore natural to the poet's conception of Pompilia's character that, in Book VII, he should cause her to associate the image of a guiding star of truth with a person, Caponsacchi, rather than with an abstraction. For her, Caponsacchi *is* truth; the truth that she cannot realize philosophically. In this book there are six literal appearances of the star-image; the first marks the limit of Pompilia's endurance of torture in Guido's house:

> When misery was most,   (VII, 1137)
> One day, I swooned and got a respite so.
> She stooped as I was slowly coming to,

This Margherita, ever on my trace,
And whispered—"Caponsacchi!"
　　　　　　　　If I drowned,
But woke afloat i' the wave with *upturned eyes*,
And found *their first sight was a star!* I turned—
For the first time and let her have her will,
Heard passively, ...

When, at last, the day of her deliverance arrives, Pompilia again looks upon her constant star:

And still, as the day wore, the trouble grew   (VII, 1404)
Whereby I guessed there would be born a star,
Until at the intense throe of dusk,
I started up, was pushed, I dare to say,
Out on the terrace, leaned and looked at last
Where the deliverer waited me: the same
Silent and solemn face, I first descried
At the spectacle, confronted mine once more.
So was that minute twice vouchsafed me, so
The manhood, wasted then, was still at watch
To save me yet a second time: no change
Here, though all else changed in the changing world!

The flight accomplished, Pompilia is deaf to Caponsacchi's warnings of troublesome consequences. Her faith in the star is serene, her hope unchanging.

"The plan is rash; the project desperate: (VII, 1462)
"In such a flight needs must I risk your life,
"Give food for falsehood, folly or mistake,
"Ground for your husband's rancour and revenge"—
So he began again, with the same face.
I felt that, the same loyalty—one star
Turning now red that was so white before—
One service apprehended newly: just
A word of mine and there the white was back!

One of the most interesting elements in the poetic design of Book VII is exemplified in Browning's having clearly identified the star-image with the dominant color-pattern of this division of the poem: red and white, and darkness and lustre—Pompilia's whiteness, her fate's redness, Guido's darkness, and Caponsacchi's lustre. It is these colors which fuse into the complex imagery of the following lines:

The husband there,—the friends my enemies,   (VII, 1551)
All ranged against me, not an avenue
To try, but would be *blocked and drive me back*
On him,—this other, . . oh the heart in that!
Did not he find, bring, put into my arms
A new born babe?—and I saw faces beam
Of the young mother proud to teach me joy,

And gossips round expecting my surprise
At *the sudden hole through earth that lets in heaven.*
I could believe himself by his strong will
Had woven around me what I thought the world
We went along in, every circumstance,
Towns, *flowers, and faces,* all things helped so well!
For, through the journey, was it natural
Such comfort should arise from first to last?
As I look back, all is *one milky way*;
Still bettered more, the more remembered, so
Do new stars bud while I but search for old,
And fill all gaps i' the glory, and grow him—
Him I now see make the shine everywhere.
Even at last when the bewildered flesh,
The cloud of weariness about my soul
Clogging too heavily, sucked down all sense,—
Still its last voice was, "*He will watch and care*;
"Let the strength go, I am content: he stays!"
I doubt not he did stay and care for all—
From that sick minute when the head swam round,
And the *eyes looked their last and died on him,*
As in his arms he caught me, and, you say,
Carried me in, *that tragical red eve,*
And laid me where I next returned to life
In the other red of morning, two red plates
That *crushed* together, *crushed the time between,*
And are since then *a solid fire* to me,— . . .

A phrase like "new stars bud" exemplifies another familiar characteristic of
the poet's artistic practice, the blending of two images, the star and the flower,
a characteristic of his technique that may be seen again and again from
Pauline to *Asolando.* Another of his favorite imagistic associations appears
in these lines; that is, the association of the divine or human face and the
star. This imagistic relationship is most effectively illustrated, perhaps, in
a poem like *A Face,* in which the star does not appear literally, but in which
it is clearly suggested. The same association may be observed in *A Death in
the Desert,* in *Saul,* and in the final stanzas of *Pictor Ignotus.* However, the
most interesting artistic fact that is illustrated by the lines quoted above is
the complete integration of the star-image with the dominant color pattern of
the total or enveloping design of Book VII.

The sixth and final image of the star in Book VII appears near the end
of Pompilia's lyric story. It occurs in a context in which she is again represented as thinking of the generous love and friendship of Caponsacchi:

The heart and its immeasurable love   (VII, 1779)
Of my one friend, my only, all my own,
Who put his breast between the spears and me.
Ever with Caponsacchi! Otherwise
Here alone would be failure, loss to me—

How much more loss to him, with life debarred
From giving life, love locked from love's display,
The day-star stopped its task that makes night morn!
O lover of my life, O soldier saint,
No work begun shall ever pause for death!

For reasons which have been mentioned previously, the image of the star
does not appear in *Dominus Hyacinthus de Archangelis,* nor in *Juris Doctor
Johannes-Baptista Bottinius.* In Book X, *The Pope,* it is a significant element
in the design through which Browning has intended to express the "whole
truth," "the ultimate judgment," of the characters and circumstances which
composed the tragedy.

> Then comes the all but end, the ultimate   (I, 1220)
> Judgment save yours [the poet's readers]. Pope
>   Innocent the Twelfth,
> Simple, sagacious, mild yet resolute,
> With prudence, probity and—what beside
> From the other world he feels impress at times,

Accordingly, Book X is divided into at least three main divisions. The first
division, lines 1-398, which is concerned primarily with the Pope himself,
makes an elaborate statement regarding the Pope's integrity, his prudence, and
his capacity for judging with authority. The second division, lines 399-1252,
represents the Pope reviewing the case and pronouncing judgments upon each
of the principal characters; judgments that are in a sense preliminary to the
announcement of his final decision. The third division, lines 1253-2135, sets
forth the Pope's vision of ultimate truth, shows his attempt to relate the
facts of the case before him to the larger conception of truth and justice that
has come to him through his vision of "the other world"; this third division
also sets forth the Pope's moral interpretation of the case, his speculations
regarding the connection of the case with the state of Christianity, his "ultimate judgment," and the pronouncement of his sentence. The matter of
Book X is of utmost importance, therefore, as a conclusion to Browning's
investigation of the murder-case, for it is his own judgment of the affairs of
human society, in relation to his own vision of "the other world," that he
wishes to communicate through the words of his Pope.[13] Furthermore, it is
the social order and the religious doubt of the nineteenth century, rather than
the seventeenth, that Browning here attempts to analyze and evaluate.

Some of the most interesting examples of the poet's acquired skill in artistic
integration may be noted among the eight instances of the occurrence of the
star-image in Book X. Before proceeding to a more detailed examination of

[13] A. K. Cook, p. 203, "It is a serious defect of the Yellow Book as a record of a trial in which
the balance was, as Browning said, hard to strike that it contains neither summing-up nor verdict.
Book X fills the gap. It contains, the poet tells his readers, 'the ultimate judgment save yours,'
and this judgment was no doubt in substance the judgment of the real Innocent; but in all details
it is Browning's only."

the use of these images, we may well remark that all these stars appear, in accordance with the outline I have suggested above, in the second and third divisions of the book; that is, (2) the review of the case and the announcement of preliminary judgments, and (3) the "ultimate judgment" and verdict.

In his review of the case, lines 399-1252, the Pope speaks first of Guido, and incidentally of Pompilia, Caponsacchi, and the Comparini; second of Pompilia; third of Caponsacchi; fourth, by mere suggestion, of the Comparini. As he proceeds in this methodical manner, he attaches a preliminary judgment to each character, thus preparing the way for the expression of a larger vision of universal truth and justice.

The first star-image of Book X appears at line 663, in a passage that is concerned chiefly with the character of Guido. At first glance, therefore, this fact seems to contradict opinions previously stated[14] in this study. Closer examination reveals, however, that at the point in this passage at which the star occurs, the Pope complicates his meditations on Guido by introducing a momentary consideration of the effect of Guido's character upon Pompilia and Caponsacchi:

> Whereby the man [Guido] so far attains his end   (X, 657)
> That strange temptation is permitted,—see!
> Pompilia wife, and Caponsacchi priest,
> Are brought together as nor priest nor wife
> Should stand, and there is passion in the place
> Power in the air for evil as for good,
> Promptings from heaven and hell, as if the stars
> Fought in their courses for a fate to be.
> Thus stand the wife and priest, a spectacle,
> I doubt not, to unseen assemblage there.

As the principal thesis of the moment, the character of Guido, has become slightly more complicated, so the imagery of the passage has become somewhat more complex. The poet here introduces elements of imagery that, in other divisions of the poem, have been regularly associated with Pompilia and Caponsacchi. Professor Gordon Hall Gerould in commenting upon this passage has suggested, for example, that the stars which "fought in their courses" are evidently intended to represent the evil star of Guido and the good star of Caponsacchi which fought to decide Pompilia's fate. In other words, we may see here an intentional imagistic echo of the "fog o' the fen" (Guido) from Book I and of the star of hope (Caponsacchi) from Book VII.

It will be seen, however, that the stars of good, the "promptings from heaven," in these lines do not represent for the Pope quite the same thing that the stars of hope in Book VII represented for Pompilia. For Pompilia they became not only the promise of salvation, but also the image of truth, which,

<hr>

14 See above, pp. 197-198.

for her, Caponsacchi personified. The Pope, who is wiser in his judgments, does not identify Caponsacchi with truth, but merely with good as opposed to evil intentions.

To return to the more interesting observation of the moment; that is, the occurrence of an imagistic echo, we should agree, I think, that there is another passage in which the detail of the stars fighting in their courses is important. This is a passage in *The Other Half-Rome* that represents the meeting of Pompilia and Caponsacchi as lovers:

> Anyhow, whether, as Guido states the case,   (III, 1052)
> Pompilia,—like a starving wretch i' the street
> Who stops and rifles the first passenger
> In the great right of an excessive wrong,—
> Or whether the strange sudden interview
> Blazed as when star and star must needs go close
> Till each hurts each and there is loss in heaven—
> Whatever way in this strange world it was,—
> Pompilia and Caponsacchi met, in fine,
> She at her window, he i' the street beneath,
> And understood each other at first look.

When the two passages under consideration are thus placed side by side, they present evidence that strongly suggests the existing "echo" to be the result of something more than chance. Browning has evidently intended to recall the sentimental opinions of The Other Half-Rome, and to review them in the light of the Pope's conception of truth. The stars still meet in their courses, but with a difference. The Other Half-Rome was capable only of *feeling* the "hurt" and the "loss" in heaven, and of forming "his" opinions accordingly. The Pope, on the other hand, even though he is sensitive to the suggestions of feelings, is capable of seeing beyond and through emotional experience to the essential truth and meaning that the stars proclaim. His interpretation is that "the stars fought in their courses for a fate to be." For him, in other words, the fate of Pompilia was written in the character of heavenly light whose flashes of truth he had learned to read.

Several related aspects of the poet's skill in expressing himself with specific regard for the principle of artistic integration are thus revealed through a detailed examination of the first star-image in Book X. In the first place, he has produced the imagistic echoes of passages in Book I, Book III, and Book VII, but at the same time he has so modified the effects of these images as to make them harmonize with the central theme of Book X; that is, the Pope's conception of, and devotion to heavenly truth. In the second place, Browning has preserved the association of the star-image with the name of Caponsacchi; but, though quite sympathetic to her, he has not followed Pompilia's inclination to identify the star of truth with Caponsacchi. In the third place, Browning has made the artistic move that the enveloping design and the controlling purpose of Book X demand; a restriction of the

use of the star-image to the function of association with other images of
light that, through their cumulative effect, produce the grand image of
"white light" thoroughly appropriate to his principal theme, universal truth
and justice. Thus, since the symbolic force of the star-image is now to be
quite different from what it was in *Pompilia,* or in *The Other Half-Rome,* the
poet has insisted upon making the transition pointedly by recalling earlier
symbolic meanings, and by then making his imagistic transformation before
his reader's eyes. Furthermore, since the poet is here concerned with conclusions, it is to be expected that in Book X he would employ those literary
principles of summary that require the repetition of ideas expressed in preceding sections of his discourse.

An examination of the functions of the second and third star-images in
Book X suggests conclusions similar to those just stated. These star-images
occur in another division of the Pope's review of the case, in a passage that
concerns the character and the actions of Caponsacchi:

> Do I smile?   (X, 1127)
> Nay, Caponsacchi, much I find amiss,
> Blameworthy, punishable in this freak
> Of thine, this youth prolonged, though age was ripe,
> This masquerade in sober day, ...
>
> . . . .
>
> . . . .
> There may have been rash stripping—every rag
> Went to the winds,—infringement manifold
> Of laws prescribed pudicity, I fear,
> In this impulsive and prompt display!
> Ever such tax comes of the foolish youth;
> Men mulct the wiser manhood, and suspect
> No veritable star swims out of cloud.
> Bear thou such imputation, undergo
> The penalty I nowise dare relax,—
> Conventional chastisement and rebuke.
> But for the outcome, the brave starry birth
> Conciliating earth with all that cloud,
> Thank heaven as I do . . . .

The "veritable star" and the "starry birth" of this passage show clearly the
poet's intention to complete the transformation of the image into a symbol
of the heavenly truth that he urges Caponsacchi to see.

This intention becomes wholly apparent in the memorable passage that
introduces the third and final division of the Pope's famous monologue.
Through his speaker, the poet here ascends to the expression of his ardent
belief in God as the ultimate source of Truth and Light:

> What if a voice deride me, "Perk and pry!   (X, 1265)
> "*Brighten each nook with thine intelligence!*
> "Play the good householder, ply man and maid

"With tasks prolonged into the midnight, test
"Their work and nowise stint of the due wage
"Each worthy worker: but with gyves and whip
"Pay thou misprison of *a single point*
"*Plain to thy happy self who lift'st the light,*
"Lament'st the darkling,—bold to all beneath!
"What if thyself adventure, now the place
"Is purged so well? Leave pavement and mount roof,
"*Look round thee for the light of the upper sky,*
"*The fire which lit thy fire* which finds default
"In Guido Franceschini to his cost!
"What if, *above in the domain of light,*
"*Thou miss the accustomed signs, remark eclipse?*
"Shalt thou still gaze on ground nor lift a lid,—
"Steady in thy superb prerogative,
"Thy inch of inkling,—nor once face the doubt
"'I' the *sphere above* thee, darkness to be felt?"

Yet *my poor spark had for its source, the sun;*
Thither I sent the great looks which compel
Light from its fount; all that I do and am
Comes from the truth, or seen or else surmised,
Remembered or divined, as mere man may:
I know just so, nor otherwise. As I know,
I speak,—what should I know, then, and how speak
Were there a wild mistake of eye or brain
As to *recorded governance above?*
If my own breath, only, blew coal alight
I styled celestial and the morning-star?
I, who in this world act resolvedly,
Dispose of men, their bodies and their souls,
As *they acknowledge or gainsay the light*
I show them,—shall I too lack courage?—leave
I, too, the post of me, like those I blame?
Refuse, with kindred inconsistency,
To grapple danger whereby souls grow strong?
I am near the end; but still not at the end;
All to the very end is trial in life:
At this stage is the trial of my soul
Danger to face, or danger to refuse?
Shall I dare try the doubt now, or not dare?

O Thou,—as represented here to me
In such conception as my soul allows,—
Under Thy measureless, my atom width!—
Man's mind, what is it but a convex glass
Wherein are gathered all the scattered points
Picked out of the immensity of sky,
To re-unite there, be our heaven for earth,
Our known unknown, or God revealed to man?
Existent somewhere, somehow, as a whole;

Here, as a whole proportioned to our sense,—
There, (which is nowhere, speech must babble thus!)
In the *absolute immensity*, the whole
Appreciable solely by Thyself,—
Here, by the little mind of man, reduced
To littleness that suits his faculty,
In the degree appreciable too;
Between Thee and ourselves—nay even, again,
Below us, to the extreme of the minute,
Appreciable by how many and what diverse
Modes of the life Thou madest be! (why live
Except for love,—how love unless they know?)
Each of them, only filling to the edge,
Insect or angel, his just length and breadth,
*Due facet of reflection,—*full, no less,
Angel or insect, as Thou framedst things.
I it is who have been appointed here
To represent Thee, in my turn, on earth,
Just as, if new philosophy know aught,
This one earth, out of all the multitude
Of peopled worlds, as stars are now supposed,—
Was chosen, and no sun-star of the swarm,
For stage and scene of Thy transcendent act
Beside which even the *creation fades*
Into a puny exercise of power.

The first division of Book X presents the qualifications of the Pope as judge, the second division presents the Pope's judgment of the characters involved in the tragedy, the third represents the Pope's intention to judge not merely individual characters, but to discern the relationships of these individuals to society as a whole, and to evaluate their actions in the light of universal truth. The final judgment of the Pope therefore transcends all man-made law to found its conclusions upon the law of God. The passage quoted above is the luminous prelude to the final decision.

This change in poetic emphasis, the skillful manoeuvre that shifts the emphasis of the argument from the characters themselves to the idea that what is really important is the relationship of the truth of each character to a conception of universal truth, is clearly implied by the manner in which Browning now uses the image of the star. Whereas the star-image was formerly associated, at least, with the character of Caponsacchi, it now gives up any such suggestion of specific association with a single character to become a thoroughly integrated element in grand image of light that represents universal truth, and the light of Heaven. The poet thus prepares his reader to accept an "ultimate judgment" that will glow with the authority of universal justice, transcend all thought of worldly contradiction, break through the shades of particular time and space to become one with the decision of the eternal Judge.

The images in this passage are composed into a pattern of summary similar in design to the imagistic summary of the first part of Book VI in *Sordello*.[15] Beyond the particular consideration of this phenomenon as an example of the artistic integration of Book X, or, indeed, of the entire structure of *The Ring and the Book*, there remains the general observation that these images of light, together with the ideas that they signify, constitute an implied "summary" of poetic visions that have been expressed in many poems that Browning wrote during the earlier periods of his development. The pattern of summary, which recalls the design of the first part of Book VI in *Sordello*, is only one of several details in the passage that are reminiscent of earlier poems. The "light of the upper sky," for example, recalls the luminous heavens of *Easter-Day;* "Thou miss the accustomed signs, remark eclipse?" through both its imagistic form and function, is reminiscent of the eclipsed star of *King Victor and King Charles*. Here, too, is the radiant sun of *Pippa Passes* and *Luria* with its suggestion of spiritual revelation as distinct from cool, intellectual knowledge. The "poor spark" which "had for its source, the sun" suggests not only the "universal prick of light" and the "more glow outside than the gleams he caught," of *A Death in the Desert*, but also, from *Evelyn Hope*, the "two long rays through the hinge's chink" whose source is the sun of God's truth. "Great looks which compel light from its fount" is a general image characteristic of several poems in which it has been used with appropriate modifications. "Recorded governance above" suggests the lode-star of *Pauline;* "if my own breath, only blew the coal alight" is quite similar in form and symbolic function to

> "A stick once fire from end to end;
> "Now ashes save the tip that holds a spark!
> "Yet blow the spark, it runs back, spreads itself
> "A little where the fire was:"

of *A Death in the Desert*. "I styled celestial and the morning star" produces an intentional contrast to the rather conventional "light o' the morning star" of the sophisticated Tertium Quid, and, at the same time, recalls the morning star of hope in *Fra Lippo Lippi*.

Perhaps the most interesting of these imagistic details are those that occur in rapid succession between lines 1311-1323:

> Man's mind, what is it but a convex glass
> Wherein are gathered all the scattered points
> Picked out of the immensity of sky,
> To reunite there, be our heaven for earth,
> Our known unknown, or God revealed to man?
> Existent somewhere, somehow, as a whole;
> Here, as a whole proportioned to our sense,—
> There, (which is nowhere, speech must babble thus!)

[15] See above, pp. 89-91.

In the absolute immensity, the whole
Appreciable solely by Thyself,—
Here, by the little mind of man, reduced
To littleness that suits his faculty,
In the degree appreciable too;

The two most interesting images in these lines, "a convex glass" and "the scattered points picked out of the immensity of sky," while they are integral to the total design of Book X, nevertheless represent the coalescence of two of the most striking images that Browning has used in earlier poems: the "optic glass" image of *A Death in the Desert* and the *Epilogue* to *Dramatis Personae,* and the "symbols of immensity" of the opening lines of the sixth book of *Sordello.* But, in accord with the assumption that the intentions of the Pope are to explain ever more clearly the single, though complex meaning of universal truth, we may assert that in Book X these images, through their coalescence, have been used to signify a single idea, or a truth, that differs essentially from both of the ideas for which they stood, separately, in *A Death in the Desert* and in *Sordello.* The image of the "optic glass" in *A Death in the Desert*[16] was used to illustrate the inadequacy of mere intellect as an instrumentality for the discovery of universal truth. The poet insisted that, like the reflecting properties of the "optic glass," the power of the intellect was limited, that the intellect, when confronted with "symbols of immensity," let us say, could succeed only in reducing them

"   .   .   .   .   . to plain historic fact,
"Diminished into clearness, proved a point
"And far away:"

The "symbols of immensity," which Sordello beheld, both in their heavenly radiance and in their reflected glory upon the face of the waters of the earth, were an imagistic illustration of Sordello's inability to *diminish* anything into clearness; so that, in effect and in meaning, Sordello's "symbols of immensity" are the virtual opposite of the image of the "optic glass." It was intellectual power that Sordello lacked, the strength of *will* that could reduce the scattered points of immensity into that "littleness" that might have suited his "faculty." Without intellectual power, without will, Sordello was overwhelmed by his own emotional adoration of heavenly beauty. He could see the reflection of scattered lights of heaven in the river at his feet, or, one might conceivably say, in the waters of his own mind. But the surface of the river was flat; it merely repeated the luminous pattern of the heavens; it lacked "convexity"; it could give no meaning, not even a partial meaning, to "the absolute immensity."

The thought of Eglamor's least like a thought,
And yet a false one, was, "Man shrinks to nought
"If matched with symbols of immensity;

16 See above, pp. 178-179.

"Must quail, forsooth, before a quiet sky
"Or sea, too little for their quietude:"
And, truly, somewhat in Sordello's mood
Confirmed its speciousness, while eve slow sank
Down the near terrace to the farthest bank,
And only one spot left from out the night
Glimmered upon the river opposite—
A breadth of watery heaven like a bay,
A sky-like space of water, ray for ray,
And star for star, one richness where they mixed
As this and that wing of an angel, fixed,
Tumultuary splendours folded in
To die.

(Sordello, VI, line 1, ff.)

In effect, then, these images of the "optic glass" and of the "symbols of immensity" say that neither intellect nor adoration, be the emotion of adoration ever so powerful, is alone adequate to the discovery of universal truth. The inferences of the ideas attached to both of these images are negative. In the passage before us, however, the words of the Pope are positive. He says, in effect, that it is true that man's mind is like a "convex glass," but that as such man's intellect is capable (as Sordello's mind was not) of reducing, to a degree compatible with individual faculty, the "scattered points" of immensity to a clear vision that properly may be regarded as the "known unknown, our God revealed to man." Thus, while intellect cannot be expected to reveal the whole truth, the powers of intellect may be said to instigate the search that only love and adoration can do their best to complete. "Absolute immensity," declares the Pope, is appreciable only by God himself. It was absolute immensity, or nothing, that Sordello attempted to understand, for the reflection in the waters before him merely reproduced the vast designs of Heaven. According to Browning, it was absolute immensity from which the Higher Criticism of the nineteenth century attempted to escape by means of diminishing all heavenly mystery into "plain historic fact."

The examination of this interesting example of the poet's transformation of the old into something quite new would not be complete without noting that a third image, again drawn from Browning's experience in composing *Sordello,* has been fused with the figures of the "convex glass" and the "symbols of immensity." This is the image of the ancient river of light. It is suggested, rather than literally expressed, in such lines as,

. . . . . . all the scattered points
Picked out of the immensity of sky,
To reunite there, be our heaven for earth
Our known unknown, our God revealed to man?
Existent somewhere, somehow, as a whole;

The original of this image occurs in the notable passage on the two kinds
of poets, in the first book of *Sordello,* lines 515-521:

> So runs
> A legend; light had birth ere moons and suns
> Flowing through space a river and alone,
> Till chaos burst and blank the spheres were strown
> Hither and thither, foundering and blind:
> When into each of them rushed light—to find
> It self no place, foiled of its radiant chance.

Only twenty-six lines above the passage in *The Pope,* which is our immediate
object of consideration, there is a specific suggestion that this image of the
ancient river of light was indeed running through the poet's mind:

> Yet my poor spark had for its *source,* the sun;   (X, 1285)
> Thither I sent great looks which compel
> *Light from its fount*:

   The artificiality of attempting to extract these elements from a passage
whose imagistic coalescence and logical unity almost deny analytical division
is excusable only as a means of showing the way in which the accumulated
reserves, both artistic and intellectual, of the poet's experience have gone
into the making of *The Ring and the Book.* The very inextricability of these
images, one from another, is in itself a kind of proof of the compact integration of the design of *The Ring and the Book.* In this instance of the fusion
of three images and three meanings into one complex image and one complex meaning, Browning has probably attempted to produce, through the
poet's art, an effect similar to that which Abt Vogler created through the art
of the musician:

> That out of three sounds he frame, not a
> fourth sound, but a star.

   As the passage (Book X, lines 1265-1341), which has been quoted at length
above, reaches its conclusion, Browning's preoccupation with the vision of
universal light continues; it is revealed in such images as,

> *Due facet of reflection,* full, no less
> Angel or insect, as Thou framedst things.
> I [the Pope] it is who have been appointed here
> To represent Thee, in my turn, on earth,
> Just as, if new philosophy know aught,
> This *one earth, out of all the multitude*
> *Of peopled worlds, as stars are now supposed,*—
> *Was chosen, and no sun-star of the swarm,*
> For stage and *scene of Thy transcendent act*
> Beside which even the *creation fades*
> Into a puny exercise of power.

Furthermore, the thoughts associated with these images, if not the images
themselves, cannot but recall the idealism expressed in earlier poems, such

as, *Rabbi Ben Ezra, A Grammarian's Funeral,* and *Abt Vogler,* in which Browning has concentrated his attention upon the serene personalities of high minded men who, like the Pope, have seen the vision of eternal Truth.

Throughout the succeeding sections of Book X, Browning holds to the image of universal light as a dominant symbol. The image of the star appears again, once in line 1549, when it is once more associated with the name of Caponsacchi, and once in line 1685, in a passage that presents the Pope's (or Browning's) opinions on the state of Christianity, combined with his meditations on the meaning of Greek philosophy and Greek tragedy.

> When I perceive . . . how can I blink the fact?   (X, 1538)
> That the fault, the obduracy to good,
> Lies not with the impracticable stuff
> Whence man is made, his very nature's fault,
> As if it were of ice the *moon may gild*
> Not melt, or stone 't was meant the *sun* should warm
> Not make bear flowers,—nor ice nor stone to blame:
> But it can melt, that ice, can bloom, that stone,
> Impassible to *rule of day and night!*
> This terrifies me, thus compelled perceive,
> Whatever love and faith we looked should spring
> *At advent of the authoritative star,*
> *Which yet lie sluggish, curdled at the source,—*
> *These have leapt forth profusely in old time,*
> *These still respond with promptitude to-day,*
> At challenge of—what *unacknowledged powers*
> O' the air, what *uncommissioned meteors, warmth*
> *By law,* and *light* by rule should supersede?
> For see this priest, this Caponsacchi, stung
> At the first summons,—"Help for honour's sake,
> "Play the man, pity the oppressed!"—no pause,
> How does he lay about him in the midst,
> Strike any foe, right wrong at any risk,
> All blindness, bravery and obedience!—*blind?*
> Ay, *as a man would be inside the sun,*
> *Delirious with the plenitude of light*
> *Should interfuse him to the finger-ends—*
> *Let him rush straight,* and how shall he go wrong?

> When out of the old time there pleads some bard,   (X, 1668)
> Philosopher, or both, and—whispers not,
> But words it boldly. "The inward work and worth
> "Of any mind, what other mind may judge
> "Save God who only knows the thing He made,
> "The veritable service He exacts?
> "It is the outward product men appraise.
> "Behold, an engine hoists a tower aloft:
> " 'I looked that it should move the mountain too!'
> "Or else 'Had just a turret toppled down,

" 'Success enough!'—may say the Machinist
"Who knows what less or more result might be:
"But we, who see that done we cannot do,
" 'A feat beyond man's force,' we men must say.
"Regard me and that shake I gave the world!
"I was born, not so long before Christ's birth
"As Christ's birth haply did precede thy day,—
"*But many a watch before the star of dawn*:
"Therefore I lived,—it is thy creed affirms,
"Pope Innocent, who art to answer me!—
"Under conditions, nowise to escape,
"Whereby salvation was impossible"

In both of these passages the emphasis of Browning's (or the Pope's) argument remains clearly fixed upon the question of universal truth. It therefore seems appropriate to pause for the moment to recall that, in all the instances of its occurrence that have been observed up to this point in the examination of *The Ring and the Book,* the image of the star has appeared in passages that have been concerned in one way or another with one of the main themes, if not the principal theme, of the poem: the question, What is Truth? In *Sordello* the star-image clearly marked many of the significant episodes in the "development of a soul," and it therefore appeared in accordance with the requirements of a design that was fundamentally narrative. But since the basic design of *The Ring and the Book* is logical, rather than narrative, it is important to observe that the occurrences of the star-image in this poem are consequently integral to the design of a critical or philosophical argument.

It is of course true that in *The Ring and the Book* many of the passages that contain the star-image possess a distinctly narrative, or even a lyric or dramatic quality; but it is also true that all these passages present either illustrations or considerations of various aspects of truth. In composing the first four books of the poem, Browning was concerned evidently with the representation and analysis of various aspects of questionable "truth," each of which he marked in some way with intentionally specious forms of the star-image. These misconceptions of truth were: the "truth" of the ignorant Comparini, the "truth" of a prejudiced Half-Rome, the "truth" of a romantically sentimental Other Half-Rome, and the "truth" of a conventionally sophisticated Tertium Quid. One star in Book I suggested the contrast of universal truth by introducing the theme that was to be fully developed in Book X. In *Pompilia,* however, Browning moved into the realm of another kind of truth for which he had a most sympathetic and wholesome regard, the truth of native innocence, the unspoiled truth of a beautiful soul. But, with due regard for the critical and philosophical design of his poem, he reserved Book X for the analysis of the form of truth that he considered highest and best, for it was through the voice of the Pope that Browning sought to express his most profound and illuminating meditations on the subject of universal truth. The logical sequence of this order of procedure becomes immediately apparent. Furthermore, it is significant to the conclusions of the present study that the image of the star, although almost inconsequential in the number of its literal appearances in *The Ring and the Book,* should mark, or at least help to point, these important divisions and transitions in the fundamental outline of the poem.

I have mentioned previously what I consider to be the principal reasons for the elimination of the image of the star from Book XI, *Guido,* so that my examination leads immediately to a consideration of the functions of the star-image in Book XII, *The Book and the Ring.* In this book there are six literal occurrences of the star. Therefore, it would seem natural to assume that the star-images of Book XII have been employed with much the same degree of artistic effect, and with much the same purpose, as those observed in *Pompilia* and *The Pope.* But, if I have been correct in the assumption that the stars of *Pompilia* represent, principally, Pompilia's intuitive identification of the personality of Caponsacchi with truth, and if I have been likewise correct in suggesting that the stars of *The Pope* represent the ideal of universal truth, I may conclude that in each of these books the several images of the star merge into a kind of symbolic unity. But no such symbolic unity exists among the star-images of Book XII.

For example, the first star-image of Book XII, the "Wormwood Star" of line 12, is a symbolic device, borrowed from the eighth chapter of the Book of Revelation, to signify the false brilliance of Guido; the second, in line 19, is a symbol of universal truth that the blazing "Wormwood Star" had temporarily dimmed; the third, in line 494, is a "morning-star" of hope; the fourth, the "inmost star" of line 571, is a symbolic reference to the light of Pompilia's purity, which the worldly mists of Guido and his ilk have obscured; the fifth, in line 590, is the "vexed-star," Pompilia, finally set free by the Pope's wisdom; the sixth, again the "Wormwood Star," in the concluding passages of the poem, refers once more to the tragic story of Guido.

The functions of these images, both symbolic and structural, may be seen at a glance to be quite different from those of the star-images of *Pompilia* and *The Pope.* With the exception of the two Wormwood stars of the introductory and concluding divisions of Book XII, the star-images enumerated above possess, severally, individual symbolic meanings. Apparently, the poet did not intend to compose these stars into a pattern that would be symbolically unified. The explanation of this departure from what seemed to be one of the imagistic principles upon which the poem as a whole was composed, may be found by again giving proper consideration to the poet's controlling purpose or design. The evidence drawn from all the elements of poetic form that it has been necessary to study in this examination of *The Ring and the Book* point unmistakably, I think, to the essentially logical, critical, and

philosophical nature of the poet's fundamental purpose. Hence his basic
design is not imagistic, as it was in *Pauline,* but logical. If the question arose
at all as to whether or not he should compose the star-images of Book XII
into a pattern similar to that which he had used in *Pompilia* and *The Pope,*
Browning answered it in accordance with his original assumption that
imagistic patterns were to be subordinated to the enveloping logical design.

The purpose of Book XII is, indeed, quite different from that of all other
books of the poem, although Book I is obviously its structural companion, in
that these two books supply the elements of literary introduction and conclusion. We have noted, of course, that *The Pope* is a book of conclusions,
but the conclusions of *The Pope* are different in kind from the conclusions
of Book XII. They are the conclusions to the main argument or principal
theme of the poem, while those of Book XII are the final summary in which
the many themes of the poem have been drawn together into a finished
whole. Book XII is also the resolution of various elements in a complicated
plot, an epilogue to *The Ring and the Book.*[17] With these several objectives
in mind, it is not strange that Browning adapted his imagistic technique to
the requirements peculiar to the composition of Book XII. If the star-images
of this book do not compose themselves into symbolic unity, it is nevertheless
apparent that they have been integrated and unified structurally in accordance
with the logical outline of an epilogue to the poem.

Consequently, the first two star-images of Book XII represent once more
the contrast between the actions of Guido and the essence of universal
truth:

> Here were the end, had anything an end: (XII, 1)
> Thus, lit and launched, up and up roared and soared
> A rocket, till the key o' the vault was reached
> And wide heaven held, a breathless minute-space,
> In brilliant usurpature: thus caught spark,
> Rushed to the height, and hung at full of fame
> Over men's upturned faces, ghastly thence,
> *Our glaring Guido: now decline must be.*
> *In its explosion, you have seen his act,*
> *By my power—may-be, judged it by your own,—*
> *Or composite as good orbs prove, or crammed*
> *With worse ingredients than the Wormwood Star.*
> *The act, over and ended, falls and fades:*
> *What was once seen, grows what is now described,*
> *Then talked of, told about, a tinge the less*

[17] A. K. Cook, p. 258, "It has been suggested, with a confident 'surely' [by William Sharp in
his *Life of Robert Browning,* p. 126.], that the poet should have ended his whole poem with the
startling invocation with which he ends his eleventh Book, but a measured and controlled ending
is required by acknowledged canons of the poetic art and recommended by the practice of its
greatest exponents. Be that as it may, the suggestion of many critics that Book XII might well
have been dispensed with is altogether unacceptable. For this brilliant epilogue contains some of
Browning's deepest thought and finest verse; much of it is alive with his gayest humor; it displays
throughout his invention in its fullest activity."

In every fresh transmission; till it melts,
Trickles in silent orange or wan grey
Across our memory, dies and leaves all dark,
And presently we find the stars again.
Follow the main streaks, meditate the mode
Of brightness, how it hastes to blend with black!

The lines quoted above constitute the introduction to Book XII. After a brief transitional passage, they are followed by the "four reports" that compose the body of Book XII. The "four reports" consist of three letters, supposed to have been written immediately after the execution of Guido and his accomplices, and the transcription of a sermon said to have been preached by Pompilia's confessor, Fra Celestino the Augustinian, on the day after Guido's death. The first letter was written "to a correspondent at Venice by a lively Venetian visitor at Rome"; the second is a letter from Archangelis to a lawyer friend, Cencini; the third, which contains the transcription of the alleged sermon by Fra Celestino, is a letter written by Bottinius, containing his witty commentary (largely Browning's) on events just past.[18] It will be seen, therefore, that the three letters and the sermon are interesting devices employed to recall and to close several themes previously developed in the poem. The Venetian's letter recalls the matter of *Half-Rome, The Other Half-Rome,* and *Tertium Quid;* the lawyers' letters recall the themes of Books VIII and IX; and the sermon recalls the idealism of the Pope. After submitting these "four reports," Browning drops all pretense of "dramatic" disguise to conclude with an address to his British public, with a defense of his belief in "the artistic way," and with the final imprint of his general symbol, the ring:

> If the rough ore be rounded to a ring,
> Render all duty which good ring should do,
> And, failing grace, succeed in guardianship,—
> Might mine but lie beside thine, Lyric Love,
> Thy rare gold ring of verse (the poet praised)
> Linking our England to his Italy!

From the point of view of structural analysis, if not of symbolic as well, it is interesting that the third, fourth, and fifth star-images of Book XII appear in the sermon of Fra Celestino, the fourth "report," and that the sixth and last star-image in the poem appears in Browning's concluding lines. The star is thus eliminated from the unsuitable contexts of the letters of the Venetian and the two lawyers.

In A. K. Cook's *A Commentary upon Browning's "The Ring and the Book"* there is a collection of evidence[19] that suggests that Browning regarded the sermon of Fra Celestino as an exceptionally important division of Book

---

[18] A. K. Cook, pp. 259-261.

[19] See A. K. Cook, Appendix XI, pp. 324-326. Here Cook records the variations in the second edition and final revision from the wording of the original edition of *The Ring and The Book*.

XII. There is a tabulation of variations in wording among the three editions of the poem. Not only were the revisions in Book XII more extensive than those of any other part of the poem, but they were also more frequent in Fra Celestino's sermon than in any other section of Book XII. The lines containing the image of the star, with the exception of the change, "leave" to "let," in line 590, remain the same, however, in all three editions of the poem.

Although Fra Celestino's sermon recalls the idealism of the Pope, and thereby the theme of universal truth, its emphasis is rather different. The sermon impresses one as an effort to convince the reader, as it was evidently supposed to convince Fra Celestino's congregation, that, in spite of the world's arguments to the contrary, and the world's way to the contrary, truth and justice do exist, and God ultimately controls the life of man. Thus, the thesis of the Pope was to answer the question: What *is* truth? but the homily of Fra Celestino was to persuade his people that truth *is*. He says:

> "But if you rather be disposed to see   (XII, 459)
> "In the result of the long trial here,—
> "This dealing doom to guilt and doling praise
> "To innocency,—any proof that truth
> "May look for vindication from the world,
> "Much will you have misread the signs, I say.
> "God, who seems acquiescent in the main
> "With those who add 'So will he ever sleep'—
> "Flutters their foolishness from time to time,
> "Puts forth His right-hand recognizably;
> "Even as, to fools who deem He needs must right
> "Wrong on the instant, as if earth were heaven,
> "He wakes remonstrance—'Passive, Lord, how long?'
> "Because Pompilia's purity prevails,
> "Conclude you, all truth triumphs in the end?
>
> . . . .
>
> "Romans! An elder race possessed your land
> "Long ago, and a false faith lingered still,
> "As shades do though *the morning-star* be out
> "Doubtless some pagan of the twilight-day
> "Has often pointed to a cavern-mouth
> "Obnoxious to beholders, hard by Rome,
> "And said,—nor he a bad man, no, nor fool,
> "Only a man born blind like all his mates,—
>
> . . . .
>
> "As ye become spectators of this scene,   (XII, 554)
> "Watch obscuration of *a pearl-pure fame*
> "By vapoury films, enwoven circumstance,
> "—A soul made weak by its pathetic want
> "Of just the first apprenticeship to sin
> "Which thenceforth makes the sinning soul secure
> "From all foes save itself, souls' truliest foe,—
> "Since egg turned snake needs fear no serpentry,—

"As ye behold this web of circumstance
"Deepen the more for every thrill and throe,
"Convulsive effort to disperse the films
"And disenmesh the fame o' the martyr,—mark
"How all those means, the unfriended one pursues,
"To keep the treasure trusted to her breast,
"Each struggle in the flight from death to life,
"How all, by procuration of the powers
"Of darkness, are transformed,—no single ray,
"Shot forth to show and save the inmost star,
"But, passed as through hell's prism, proceeding black
"To the world that hates white: as ye watch, I say,
"Till dusk and such defacement grow eclipse
"By,—marvellous perversity of man!—
"The inadequacy and inaptitude
"Of that self-same machine, that very law
"Man vaunts, devised to dissipate the gloom,
"Rescue *the drowning orb* from calumny,
"—Here law, appointed to defend the just,
"Submit, for best defence, that wickedness
"Was bred of flesh and innate with the bone
"Borne by Pompilia's spirit for a space,
"And no mere chance fault, passionate and brief:
"Finally, when ye find,—after this touch
"Of man's protection which intends to mar
"The last pin-point of light and damn the disc,—
"One wave of the hand of God amid the worlds
"Bid vapour vanish,·darkness flee away,
"And *let the vexed star culminate in peace*
"Approachable no more by earthly mist—
"What I call God's hand,—you perhaps,—mere chance
"Of the true instinct of an old good man
"Who happens to hate darkness and love light,—"

The three images of the star, which appear in the quotations above at lines 494, 571, and 590, are undoubtedly reminiscent of the stars that signify universal truth in Book X. But, like the sermon of Fra Celestino as a whole, these stars symbolically emphasize ideas that do not specifically explain or define the nature of universal truth, even though they are closely associated with that general concept. The first of the three is the "morning-star" of hope, which signifies that, even through the mists and the darkness of a pagan age, the light of a true faith in God is clear to those who will open their eyes and see. The second and third are the "inmost star" and the "vexed star," both of which refer specifically to Pompilia. It is she who has been enmeshed by a "web of circumstance"; it is she, "a pearl-pure fame," who has been obscured by Guido's "vapoury films" and apparently transformed "by procuration of the powers of darkness," so that

" . . . . no single ray,
"Shot forth to show and save the inmost star,
"But passes as through hell's prism, proceeding black
"To the world that hates white: as ye watch, I say
"Till dusk and such defacement grow eclipse
"By,—marvellous perversity of man!—"

Of what avail, continues Fra Celestino, is man-made law, that "self-same machine, that very law man vaunts"; of what avail "to dissipate the gloom," to "rescue the drowning orb from calumny"? It is only God's hand, working through the personality of "an old good man Who happens to hate darkness and love light," that can release the "vexed star" of Pompilia's purity to "culminate in peace, Approachable no more by earthly mist."

The "authority" of these images depends in a large measure upon their similarity to, and their close association with, the images of "white light" in the monologue of the Pope, just as the authority of Fra Celestino's sermon depends immeasurably upon the Pope's reassuring discovery of the nature of universal truth. The convictions of the Pope give Fra Celestino confidence, supply him with a sure foundation for his argument. But the Pope is a philosopher, and Fra Celestino is essentially a preacher. Fra Celestino conceives his duty to be the application of the highest wisdom to the business of persuading the multitude to go in the proper way of life. He does not wish, primarily, to reason with his congregation, but, calling upon all the powers of his art, to tell them plainly how to live. The star-images that he uses are therefore related specifically to the examples of living that he discusses, and only generally, though fundamentally, to the inner confidence that he possesses.

But, while Fra Celestino derives his pastoral authority from the Pope, as a good priest should, he has derived the authority of his rhetoric from a poet who did not forget for a moment that he was writing the epilogue to *The Ring and the Book*. If we were to take time to compare the imagery of the lines quoted above with that of other divisions of the poem, we should find that Robert Browning was thinking, as he wrote, not only of Book X, but also of many other parts of his great poem. The "inmost star" and the "vexed star" are surrounded by a cluster of images which specifically recall the themes of Books I, VII, VIII, and IX. Most noticeable of all is the recall of the contrast between Pompilia's whiteness and Guido's darkness, a dominant characteristic in the imagery of *Pompilia*. Here also is the representation of Guido's character as an enveloping mist of blackness, which in Book I is called "fog o' the fen." The reference to the machine quickly recalls the mechanics of legalistic practice, so entertainingly presented in Books VIII and IX. The purpose of the epilogue is to recall and to close the many themes of the poem; it is this purpose which the poet has kept in mind.

Thus, Robert Browning has not permitted his enthusiasm over the introduction of a new device, the sermon of Fra Celestino, to obscure the pattern of his total design, nor has he allowed the opportunity to write a new dramatic monologue to distract his attention from the business at hand; that is, to compose a suitable epilogue to *The Ring and the Book*. He has gone further; he has not merely recalled through his imagery the themes of preceding divisions of the poem, but, like a mathematician, he has written these conclusions in terms of the unknown quantity whose meaning and essence he has attempted to express in Book X. Consequently, he no longer permits Guido to appear, as he did to the Comparini in Book I, a false star which stooped to take Pompilia,

> . . . the star supposed, but fog o' the fen,
> Gilded star-fashion by a glint from hell; . . .
> (Book I, 544-5)

He can present Guido now only as vaporous blackness, and, with fitting regard for the conclusions of Book X, he can now characterize the tragedy as a whole as "Star Wormwood":

> Such, then, the final state o' the story. So   (XII, 827)
> Did the Star Wormwood in a blazing fall
> Frighten awhile the waters and lie lost.
> So did this old woe fade from memory:
> Till after, in the fulness of the days,
> I needs must find an ember yet unquenched
> And, breathing, blow the spark to flame.
>   It lives,
> If precious be the soul of man to man.

For the purpose of drawing together the principal conclusions to this examination of *The Ring and the Book* into a more compact summary, it may be well to recall very briefly some of the general considerations that were stated in the introductory paragraphs of this chapter. We began with the question as to whether or not this poem deserves to be called Browning's masterpiece, and proceeded thence to a consideration of the essential and distinguishing form of *The Ring and the Book*. While it is impossible to answer the first of these questions positively, either on the basis of the detailed observations we have attempted to make, or upon the foundation of our general conclusions, it is nevertheless possible to maintain that the form of *The Ring and the Book* is, like the form of *Abt Vogler,* essentially unique. The evidence in support of this fact is to be found, as we have seen, not only by examining the particular functions of the star-image, but also by weighing the corroborative evidence supplied by other artistic phenomena that have frequently demanded our analytical attention.

From a consideration of form it was only natural that we should proceed to a consideration of the purpose out of which the poet's form grew. This purpose has been defined as Robert Browning's intention to write a criticism of life as he knew it, and as an intention which led Browning to compose the fundamentally logical and philosophical design of *The Ring and the Book*. We have noted, furthermore, that in accordance with this critical purpose the poet has integrated both the structural and symbolic functions of the image of the star within this logical design. The symbolic effects of the image are therefore intentionally false, nearly true, and true, in accord with the deliberate progress of a critical argument, and in the epilogic Book XII the star has been made to conform, both structurally and symbolically, to the requirements of a literary summary of the several important themes of the poem.

With regard to the source of *The Ring and the Book* the evidence that we have found has pointed again and again to the importance of Browning's earlier works, and to his experience in composing these earlier works, as the source of the cumulative force and the vast store of ideas which transformed "The Old Yellow Book" into *The Ring and the Book*. These and other interpretations of the evidence before us show unmistakably that, if it is not Robert Browning's greatest work, *The Ring and the Book* is certainly the culmination of a notable poetic career, a poem that noticeably combines the experience of the past with a new and vigorous intention of the present.

In the present writer's opinion the most interesting detail that this examination of *The Ring and the Book* brings to light is the instance, in Book X, of the coalescence of three images, the "optic glass," the "symbols of immensity," and the ancient river of light, into one complex image whose meaning is quite new, and quite different from the meanings of the original images that have been combined to make it. This imagistic phenomenon is characteristic of the poem as a whole, for it signifies a new, and possibly the last important phase of Browning's artistic development, in which many of the favorite ideas, images, and even personalities of his earlier works have been fused with a new and larger understanding of life itself. Consequently, it is not surprising to find in *The Ring and the Book* the consummation of much that the poet has thought and hoped for during the earlier periods of his career, nor is it surprising to discover that the rival modes of discourse, the dramatic, lyric, rhetorical, argumentative, and casuistic, have been given a new significance and an articulated harmony under the command of a well constructed critical design.

CHAPTER VII

LAST POEMS, 1871-1889

W HEN we turn our attention to the poetry that Browning wrote during the last years of his life, it becomes quite clear that he had reached the last notable phase of his development with the composition of *The Ring and the Book*. It is to this fact, at least, that the evidence drawn from the study of Browning's use of the star-image points. Had we considered, specifically, other elements of Browning's poetic technique, besides this single imagistic detail, it is possible that our conclusions would be somewhat different. Certainly there are qualities in the narrative style of such poems as *An Inn Album, Ned Bratts,* and *Ivan Ivanovitch* that suggest the probability of continued artistic innovation. But with the eye focused directly upon a single imagistic phenomenon, it is impossible to observe in the last poems any peculiarities of function that have not been noted previously. The evidence that comes from the analysis of the functions of the star-image in these poems suggests, indeed, a diminishing poetic force. Of course it is reasonable to suppose that the poet's energy would lose its strength after the strenuous labor of a poetic career which already had run the course of thirty-five years.

The particular nature of this decline in poetic energy is suggested by one of the conclusions we have been able to draw from our examination of *The Ring and the Book*. We have noted that in this poem the image of the star is a poetic detail completely integrated within a total design and that the poet's interest in the use of this image is subordinate to his interest in the critical or philosophical purpose that dominates his thought. The use of the star-image has therefore become ancillary to the expression of a judgment that, in its last analysis, is intended to be the logical conclusion to a series of meditations upon the meaning of human life. We have only to contrast this fact with what we have noted in the study of Browning's early poems, in which both logical purpose and logical design were subordinated to the intention of expressing poetic visions rather than intellectual conceptions, to observe the change that has taken place in the poet's mind and that has modified, inevitably, his artistic form.

With all its remarkable effects of logical and artistic unity, there is noticeable in *The Ring and the Book* a conception of, or a kind of literary form that differs essentially from the characteristic form of the earliest poems, and from that of many of the finest works of the middle period. By following the poet's own most cogent explanation of this difference, in his *Abt Vogler,* we may say that the form of *The Ring and the Book* suggests less the faculty of poetic "improvisation" and more the faculty of intellectual command over *recollected improvisations* that have been skilfully wrought into the fabric of a vast philosophical design. The earliest poems, with the exception of the imitative plays, appear to be much more nearly poetic improvisations, over which the poet did not always attain to complete artistic control, it is true, but over which he did not intend to impose, always, the restriction of a logical design. The poems most characteristic of the middle period suggest an increasing power of artistic control, to the strengthening of which intellectual forces were tributary, but not dominantly formative. In the most striking poems of this period Browning was still concerned, primarily, with the expression of his observations and his visions of life, rather than with the expression of critical or didactic estimates of what he saw. It is true that he did not refrain entirely from making critical or didactic commentary; since he was forever, though casually, pointing the moral in such poems as *Andrea del Sarto, Abt Vogler, The Statue and the Bust,* and *Master Hugues.* But in poems like these his interest in teaching was subordinated to his interest in the creation of character, of lyric tone, narrative situation, or dramatic impact. In *The Ring and the Book* the pendulum had swung far, though not entirely, in the direction of intellectual control as opposed to that power of improvisation which takes its origin in the faculty that we must still regard as the mystery of poetic inspiration.

This opinion is based upon evidence drawn not only from the examination of *The Ring and the Book,* but also from the analysis of the functions of the star-image in all the other poems included in this study, without complete disregard, it is hoped, of the commentary of investigations that have approached the poetry of Robert Browning from many other points of view. If any observation may be said to lead more certainly than others to this statement of opinion, it is that derived from the comparison of the imagistic patterns of *Sordello* and *The Ring and the Book.* The result of this comparison is to reveal the somewhat adventitious appearance of the star-image in *Sordello,* in contrast to the more *methodical* placing of these images in *The Ring and the Book.* In *Sordello* Browning's imagery appears to be the inevitable result of a struggle for expression, an improvisational accompaniment, as it were, that signifies not only the changes in the development of Sordello's soul, but also the poet's changing point of view with regard to his general subject. When we read *Sordello,* we are in the presence of form in the process of emerging; but when we read *The Ring and the Book,* we may behold the results of a poetical composition that was undertaken *after* the fundamental plan of the poem had been clearly and logically established.

This more methodical technique of composition, a consequence of the development of a more highly critical attitude of mind, is revealed not only by the larger aspects of poetic form, but also by small details in the text of *The Ring and the Book.* The elaborate exposition in Book I, for example, of the meaning of his dominant image, the-ring-and-the-book, suggests that.

Browning had turned his critical attention to the details of literary style, as well as to the general interpretation of his subject. It is as if he had decided to refute the charge of obscurity that he took great pains to explain to his British Public just what it was to understand by his symbol, the-ring-and-the-book. Above all he wished to be intellectually clear. On the other hand, in composing *Pauline, Paracelsus,* and *Sordello* he was less, much less, concerned with the possibility of his reader's failure to understand his logical analysis than he was eager to express his poetic vision, to stimulate and to strengthen, thereby, his reader's capacity for imaginative experience. But it is noteworthy that in some of the more didactic poems of the middle period Browning shows the tendency, which we have just noted, to guard against the possible misinterpretation of the philosophical meaning of important poetic images. In *Rabbi Ben Ezra,* for example, he suggests that the point he wishes to make is of greater significance than the famous image of the "Potter's wheel":

XXVI

Ay, note that Potter's wheel,
That metaphor! and feel
Why time spins fast, why passive lies our clay,—

The same desire to be understood logically is even more apparent in some of the expository lines of the longer compositions that follow *The Ring and the Book.* In *Prince Hohenstiel-Schwangau* and *Red Cotton Night-Cap Country* the poet does not hesitate to supply his reader with explanatory admonitions that, like the following, have been methodically worked into his text:

See! having sat an hour, I'm rested now, (34)
Therefore want work: and spy no better work
For eye and hand and mind that guides them both,
During this instant, than to draw my pen
From blot One—thus—up, up to blot Two—thus—
Which I at last reach, thus, and here's my line
Five inches long and tolerably straight:

. . . .
. . . . Analyse with me (76)
This instance of the line 'twixt blot and blot
I rather chose to draw than leave a blank,
Things else being equal. You are taught thereby
That 't is my nature, when I am at ease,
Rather than idle out my life too long,
To want to do a thing—to put a thought,
Whether a great thought or a little one,
Into an act, as nearly as may be.
Make what is absolutely new—I can't,
Mar what is made already well enough—
I won't: but turn to best account the thing

That's half-made—that I can. Two blots, you saw
I knew how to extend into a line
Symmetric on the sheet they blurred before—
Such little act sufficed, this time, such thought.
(*Prince Hohenstiel-Schwangau, Saviour of Society*)

In his *Red Cotton Night-Cap Country*, or *Turf and Towers* Browning insists
that the symbol of "turf and towers" and its meaning be kept in mind:

Are you adventurous and climb yourself?   (II, 107)
Plant the foot warily, accept a staff.
Stamp only where you probe the standing point,
Move forward, well assured that move you may:
Where you mistrust advance, stop short, there stick!
This makes advancing slow and difficult?
Hear what comes of the endeavour of brisk youth
To foot it fast and easy! Keep this same
Notion of outside mound and inside mash,
Towers yet intact round turfy rottenness,
Symbolic partial-ravage,—Keep in mind!
Here fortune placed his feet who first of all
Found no incumbrance, till head found—but hear!

How different are lines like these from the imagistically spontaneous and
"unexplained" verses of Aprile's discourse on the arts in *Paracelsus*, from
which the following quotation has been selected:

Aprile. I would love infinitely, and be loved.   (II, 420)
First: I would carve in stone, or cast in brass,
The forms of earth, No ancient hunter lifted
Up to the gods by his renown, no nymph
Supposed the sweet soul of a woodland tree
Or sapphirine spirit of a twilight star,
Should be too hard for me; no shepherd-king
Regal for his white locks; no youth who stands
Silent and very calm amid the throng,
His right hand ever hid beneath his robe
Until the tyrant pass; no lawgiver,
No swan-soft woman rubbed with lucid oils
Given by a god for love of her—too hard!
Every passion sprung from man, conceived by man,
Would I express and clothe it in its right form,
Or blend with others struggling in one form,
Or show repressed by an ungainly form.
Oh, if you marvelled at some mighty spirit
With a fit frame to execute its will—
Even unconsciously to work its will—
You should be moved no less beside some strong
Rare spirit, fettered to a stubborn body,
Endeavouring to subdue it and inform it
With its own splendour! All this I would do:

And I would say, this done, "His sprites created,
"God grants to each a sphere to be its world,
"Appointed with the various objects needed
"To satisfy its own peculiar want;
"So, I create a world for these my shapes
"Fit to sustain their beauty and their strength!"
And, at the word, I would contrive and paint
Woods, valleys, rocks and plains, dells, sands and wastes,
Lakes which, when morn breaks on their quivering bed,
Blaze like a wyvern flying round the sun,
And ocean isles so small, the dog-fish tracking
A dead whale, who should find them, would swim thrice
Around them, and fare onward—all to hold
The offspring of my· brain.

While these observations may help to account for a general lack of poetic improvisation which is noticeable among many of Browning's last poems, they do not fully apply, paradoxically, to the very poem from which they have been principally drawn. In other words, methodical though it may be in its logical design, *The Ring and the Book* is vastly different in effect and in genuine poetic force from many of the less stimulating poems of later years. I attribute this important difference to a fact that has been previously, and I trust correctly, stated: that the characteristic quality of *The Ring and the Book* is derived from the coalescence of former experience with a new and consuming purpose. This is the "alloy." Even though the full power of poetic improvisation may have been already in a state of decline as Browning composed, the definitive vigor of his critical purpose, the energy of his will, accomplished the recall of former improvisations in a manner that was sufficiently powerful to create new forms out of recollected poetic visions. In no sense, therefore, is this recollection a mere repetition of earlier successes, but, in most instances of its occurrence, a transformation of the old into the new.

It is this power of transformation that distinguishes *The Ring and the Book* from much of the poetry of Browning's last years. As he continues to write, Browning's inclination to recall moments of inspiration is ever noticeable. Whenever the power of transformation deserts him, he must be content to repeat himself without being able to renew himself. In other words, the poet often returns to the imitative technique of the years in which he wrote his imitative plays, but with the distinct and inevitable difference that he now becomes an imitator of himself.

The approach to the complete integration of his powers, which is represented in the composition of *The Ring and the Book,* was an achievement that would have worn out a lesser man. It cost Browning heavily. Many of the poems of these last years suggest that the limits of his "reach" had become coincident with the limitations of his "grasp."

During the last years of his career Browning was to depend more and more upon his ever active taste for inquiry and upon the power of an alert memory. These forces, rather than the visions of mysterious inspiration, were to supply the subjects and the forms of his poetry. His fondness for inquiry was so strong, however, and his recollection so vivid that, even in *Asolando*, he could repeat the thoughts of a lifetime with a freshness that is almost new. Among several of the last poems[1] that contain the image of the star, *La Saisiaz, The Two Poets of Croisic*, the *Dramatic Idyls, Asolando*, and "New Poems,"[2] there are distinct echoes of the lyric and dramatic improvisations of better days. The star-images of *Reverie*, from *Asolando*, are an interesting example.

The very title of the poem, *Reverie*, is significant. Its thesis is the restatement of one of the principal themes of *Paracelsus*, modified, to be sure, by echoes from such poems as *Saul, Rabbi Ben Ezra*, and *A Death in the Desert*. It is a restatement of the theme of Knowledge versus Love, modified by the interfusion of the accompanying themes of pride versus humility, head versus heart, flesh versus spirit, intellectualism versus revelation. As a result *Reverie* becomes one of the final attempts of the poet to understand the reconciliation of the forces of Knowledge and Love, or the perfect union of the manifest results of these two forces, Power and Beauty, in the personality of God. The imagistic echoes in *Reverie* are no less interesting, for here are the "shy buds"

---

[1] Because it would simply increase the length of these remarks without adding much that is significant, I have not attempted to give a complete enumeration of instances of the occurrence of the star-image in this last group of poems. The quotation of every passage containing the star-image is unnecessary to prove what a few illustrations will indicate. In order to make my record complete, however, I shall include in this note the following tabulation of instances of the occurrences of the star-image among Browning's last poems:

Pacchiarotto			*Jocoseria*	
Shop	2		*Ixion*	1
Pisgah-Sights II	1		*Jochanan Hakkadosh*	3
Bifurcation	1		*Ferishtah's Fancies*	
La Saisiaz	1		*Shah Abbas*	1
Two Poets of Croisic	3		*The Sun*	1
Dramatic Idyls, 1st Series			*Mihrab Shah*	2
Ivan Ivanovitch	1		*Cherries*	2
Ned Bratts	1		*Plot Culture*	1
Dramatic Idyls, 2nd Series			*A Bean Stripe*	1
Pietro of Abano	5		*Asolando*	
Parleyings			*Bad Dreams III*	1
Daniel Bartoli	2		*The Pope and the Net*	1
Christopher Smart	2		*Beatrice Signorini*	2
Francis Furini	5		*Imperante Augusto*	1
Gerard de Lairesse	1		*Development*	1
Charles Avison	2		*Rephan*	6
Fust	1		*Reverie*	6

[2] *New Poems, The Complete Poetical Works of Robert Browning*, edited by Augustine Birrell, New York: Macmillan, 1917, Appendix, pp. 1327-1351.

and the "chains" of *Pauline,* the "veil" between man and reality, "wearing its thickness thin," of *A Death in the Desert,* the "flames" and "orbs" of *Sordello,* the "book," "scroll," or "record" of man's life of *The Last Ride Together,* the "clods" of *Saul* and *Rabbi Ben Ezra,* the "potter's clay," the "potter's act," the "potter's shape" of *Rabbi Ben Ezra,* the "barriers (or prison) of flesh" of *Paracelsus,* besides the familiar images of the star.

There are six literal images of the star in *Reverie,* none of them exactly the same as its original,.but all reminiscent of star-images in earlier poems. They are distributed within the poem at fairly regular intervals. The first,

> Is it up amid whirl and roar (11)
> Of the elemental flame
> Which star-flecks heaven's dark floor . . . ?

stands for the primal evidence of heavenly Knowledge; the second, "Try the clod ere test the star!" suggests how Knowledge should proceed, and at the same time indicates its earthly and heavenly limits; the third, "For you dominate, stars all!" represents the informing radiance of God's power; the fourth, "Eclipse of the star bid stay," is a warning against misconception and confusion; the fifth,

> Do I seek how star, earth, beast, (127)
> Bird, worm, fly, gain their dower
> For life's use most and least?

represents the manifest power of God in the greatest of heaven and in the least of earth; the sixth, "Forth flashed knowledge: from Star to clod Man knew things:" like the second, represents the bounds of knowledge. Besides the literal images themselves, there are numerous instances in which the diction of *Reverie* connotatively suggests the light of the stars. For this reason, and also to show the distribution of the literal images, I shall quote this poem in its entirety:

I know there shall dawn a day
 —Is it here on homely earth?
Is it yonder, worlds away,
 Where the strange and new have birth,
That Power comes full in play?

Is it here, with grass about,
 Under befriending trees,
When shy buds venture out,
 And the air by mild degrees
Puts winter's death past doubt?

Is it up amid whirl and roar
 Of the elemental flame

* Occurrence of the star-image.

**Which star-flecks heaven's dark floor,*
 That, new yet still the same,
Full in play comes Power once more?

Somewhere, below, above,
 Shall a day dawn—this I know—
When *Power, which vainly strove*
 My weakness to o'erthrow,
Shall triumph. I breathe, I move,

I truly am, at last!
 For a veil is rent between
Me and the truth which passed
 Fitful, half-guessed, half-seen,
Grasped at—not gained, held fast.

I for my race and me
  Shall apprehend life's law:
In the legend of man shall see
  Writ large what small I saw
In my life's tale: both agree.

As the record from youth to age
  Of my own, the single soul—
So *the world's wide book*: one page
  Deciphered explains the whole
Of our common heritage.

How but from near to far
  Should knowledge proceed, increase?
*Try the clod ere test the star!
  Bring our inside strife to peace
Ere we wage, on the outside, war!

So, my annals thus begin:
  With body, to life awoke
Soul, the immortal twin
  Of body which bore soul's yoke
Since mortal and not akin.

By means of the flesh, grown fit,
  Mind, in surview of things,
Now soared, anon alit
  To treasure its gatherings
From the ranged expanse—to-wit,

Nature,—earth's, *heaven's wide show*
  Which taught all hope, all fear,
Acquainted with joy and woe,
  I could say, "Thus much is clear,
Doubt annulled thus much: I know.

"All is effect of cause:
  As it would, has willed and done
Power: and my mind's applause
  Goes, passing laws each one,
To Omnipotence, lord of laws."

Head praises, but heart refrains
  From loving's acknowledgment.
Whole losses outweigh half-gains:
  Earth's good is with evil blent:
Good struggles but evil reigns.

  * Occurrence of the star-image.

Yet since Earth's good proved good—
  Incontrovertibly
Worth loving—*I understood*
  How evil—did mind descry
Power's object to end pursued—

Were haply *as cloud across*
  Good's orb, no orb itself:
Mere mind—were it found at loss
  Did it play the tricksy elf
And from life's gold purge the dross?

Power is known infinite:
  Good struggles to be—at best
Seems—scanned by the human sight,
  Tried by the senses' test—
Good palpably: but with right

Therefore to mind's award
  Of loving, as power claims praise?
Power—which finds naught too hard,
  Fulfilling itself all ways
Unchecked, unchanged: while barred,

Baffled, what good began
  Ends evil on every side.
To Power submissive man
  Breathes, "E'en as Thou art, abide!"
While to good "Late-found, long-sought

"Would Power to a plenitude
  But liberate, but enlarge
Good's strait confine,—renewed
  Were ever the heart's discharge
Of loving!" Else doubts intrude.

*For you dominate, stars all!
  For a sense informs you—brute,
Bird, worm, fly, great and small,
  Each with your attribute
Or low or majestical!

Thou earth that embosomest
  Offspring of land and sea—
How thy hills first sank to rest,
  How thy vales bred herb and tree
Which dizen thy mother-breast—

Do I ask? "Be ignorant
  Ever!" the answer clangs:
Whereas if I plead world's want,
  Soul's sorrows and body's pangs,
Play the human applicant,—

Is a remedy far to seek?
  I question and find response:
I—all men, strong or weak,
  Conceive and declare at once
For each want its cure. "Power, speak!"

"Stop change, avert decay
  Fix life fast, banish death,
*Eclipse from the star bid stay,
  Abridge of no moment's breath
One creature! Hence, Night, hail, Day!"

What need to confess again
  No problem this to solve
By impotence? Power, once plain
  Proved Power—let on Power devolve
Good's right to co-equal reign!

Past mind's conception—Power!
  *Do I seek how star, earth, beast,
Bird, worm, fly, gain their dower
  For life's use most and least?
Back from the search I cower.

Do I seek what heals all harm,
  Nay, hinders the harm at first,
Saves earth? Speak, Power, the charm!
  Keep the life there unamerced
By chance, change, death's alarm!

As promptly as mind conceives,
  Let Power in its turn declare
Some law which wrong retrieves,
  Abolishes everywhere
What thwarts, what irks, what grieves!

Never to be! and yet
  How easy it seems—to sense
Like man's—if somehow met
  Power with its match—immense
Love, limitless, unbeset

By hindrance on every side!
  Conjectured, nowise known,

   * Occurrence of the star-image.

Such may be: could man confide
  Such would match—were Love but
    shown
Stript of the veils that hide—

Power's self now manifest!
  So reads my record: thine,
O world, how runs it? Guessed
  Were the purport of that prime line,
Prophetic of all the rest!

"In a beginning God
  Made heaven and earth." Forth
    flashed
*Knowledge: from star to clod
  Man knew things: doubt abashed
Closed its long period.

Knowledge obtained Power praise.
  Had Good been manifest,
Broke out in cloudless blaze,
  Unchequered as unrepressed,
In all things Good at best—

Then praise—all praise, no blame—
  Had hailed the perfection. No!
As Power's display, the same
  Be Good's—praise forth shall flow
Unisonous in acclaim!

Even as the world its life,
  So have I lived my own—
Power seen with Love at strife,
  That sure, this dimly shown,
—Good rare and evil rife.

Whereof the effect be—faith
  That, some far day, were found
Ripeness in things now rathe,
  Wrong righted, each chain unbound,
Renewal born out of scathe.

Why faith—but to lift the load,
  To leaven the lump, where lies
Mind prostrate through knowledge
    owed
  To the loveless Power it tries
To withstand, how vain! In flowed

Ever resistless fact:
  No more than the passive clay
Disputes the potter's act,
  Could the whelmed mind disobey
Knowledge the cataract.

But, perfect in every part,
  Has the potter's moulded shape,
Leap of man's quickened heart,
  Throe of his thought's escape,
Stings of his soul which dart

Through the barrier of flesh, till keen
  She climbs from the calm and clear,
Through turbidity all between,
  From the known to the unknown
    here,
Heaven's "Shall be," from Earth's "Has
  been"?

Then life is—to wake not sleep,
  Rise and not rest, but press

From earth's level where blindly creep
  Things perfected, more or less,
To the heaven's height, far and steep,

Where, amid what strifes and storms
  May wait the adventurous quest,
Power is Love—transports, transforms
  Who aspired from worst to best,
Sought the soul's world, spurned the
  worms'.

I have faith such end shall be:
  From the first, Power was—I knew.
Life has made clear to me
  That, strive but for closer view,
Love were as plain to see.

When see? When there dawns a day,
  If not on the homely earth,
Then yonder, worlds away,
  Where the strange and new have
    birth.
And Power comes full in play.

As Professor DeVane has pointed out in his excellent study, *Browning's Parleyings, The Autobiography of a Mind,* the *Parleyings with Certain People of Importance in Their Day*[3] are rich with explanatory reminiscences of a long poetic career. Of particular interest, because of its lively discussion, once again, of the subject of realism in painting, and, therefore, of its relationship to any consideration of Browning's imagery, is the parleying with *Francis Furini.* The temper of the five images of the star in this poem may be tested in the following quotations:

III

. . . .
That one appreciative creature's debt
Of thanks to the Creator, more or less,
Was paid according as heart's-will had met
Hand's-power in Art's endeavour to express
Heaven's most consummate of achievements, bless
Earth by a semblance of the seal God set
On woman his supremest work. I trust
Rather, Furini, dying breath had vent
In some fine fervour of thanksgiving just
For this—that soul and body's power you spent—
Agonized to adumbrate, trace in dust
That marvel which we dream the firmament
Copies in star-device when fancies stray
Outlining, orb by orb, Andromeda—

[3] Published in 1887.

God's best of beauteous and magnificent
Revealed to earth—the naked female form.

. . . .

V

You the Sacred! If
Indeed on you has been bestowed the dower
Of Art in fulness, graced with head and hand,
Head—to look up not downwards, hand—of power
To make head's gain the portion of a world
Where else the uninstructed ones too sure
Would take all outside beauty—film that's furled
About a star—for the star's self, endure
No guidance to the central glory,—nay,
(Sadder) might apprehend the film was fog,
Or (worst) wish all but vapour well away,
And sky's pure product thickened from earth's bog—
Since so, nor seldom, have your worthiest failed
To trust their own soul's insight—why? except
For warning that the head of the adept
May too much prize the hand, work unassailed
By scruple of the better sense that finds
An orb within each halo, bids gross flesh
Free the fine spirit-pattern, nor enmesh
More than is meet a marvel custom blinds
Only the vulgar eye to.

. . . .

VII

"Bounteous God,
Deviser and Dispenser of all gifts
To soul through sense,—in Art the soul uplifts
Man's best of thanks! What but Thy measuring-rod
Meted forth heaven and earth? more intimate,
Thy very hands were busied with the task
Of making, in this human shape, a mask—
A match for that divine. Shall love abate
Man's wonder? Nowise! True—true all too true—
No gift but, in the very plenitude
Of its perfection, goes maimed, misconstrued
By wickedness or weakness: still, some few
Have grace to see Thy purpose, strength to mar
Thy work by no admixture of their own,
—Limn truth not falsehood, bid us love alone
The type untampered with, the naked star!"

. . . .

IX

. . . . Make survey
Of Man's surroundings, try creation—nay,
Try emulation of the minimised
Minuteness fancy may conceive! Surprised

Reason becomes by two defeats for one—
Not only power at each phenomenon
Baffled, but knowledge also in default—
Asking what *is* minuteness—yonder vault
Speckled with suns, or this the millionth—thing,
How shall I call?—that on some insect's wing
Helps to make out in dyes the mimic star?
Weak, ignorant, accordingly we are:
What then? The worse for Nature! Where began
Righteousness, moral sense except in Man?

. . . .

Although Browning's poetic technique shows signs of becoming "methodized," it is not altogether necessary, as the examples cited above tend to show, to regard this change with complete despair. There is nothing particularly disgraceful in *method* itself, and there is little chance that a poem like *The Ring and the Book* will ever be condemned utterly, because of its superior and methodical organization. It is only when method has been reduced to the lowest terms of an automatic formula that we may look for the signs of real weakness in a poem that pretends to be a work of art. In the composition of the last poems of a prolific career, one might expect the habits of a life-time to have become mere formulae of production. There are some poems that look very much as though this change had actually taken place, but the more obvious examples of them are rather hard to find. Most of these poems are sufficiently reminiscent of earlier successes, or sufficiently animated with quick and often amusing argument, to free themselves from the category of the lifeless. To paraphrase, and to change slightly one of the comments of Professor DeVane, one may say that, if inspiration had departed after *Balaustion's Adventure,* in 1871, vivid recollection, as well as argument, was left to fill its place.[4]

It was his taste for inquiry, his alert memory, and his love of argument that, in a large measure, kept Browning's poetry alive to the end, and that preserved the function of the star-image from being reduced to a mere imagistic formula. As early as the year 1836, when he composed *Johannes Agricola in Meditation,* Browning had devised a method for using the star-image to illuminate and to strengthen the points of an argument. It is interesting to see this same technique employed in the casuistically tortuous passages of *A Bean Stripe* from *Ferishtah's Fancies.* The poet always had something to say; apparently something that he wanted to say; so that one does not get the impression that he wrote his last poems merely to keep going. The result is that one of his favorite images, the star, continues to appear, to achieve several of its characteristic structural effects, and to hold to its familiar symbolic associations.

[4] W. C. DeVane, *Browning's Parleyings,* p. xiii, "Inspiration had departed after Balaustion's Adventure, in 1871, and only argument was left to fill its place."

It remains only to speak very briefly of four of the longer poems of Browning's last years: *Prince Hohenstiel Schwangau, Saviour of Society*, 1871; *Fifine at the Fair*, 1872; *Red Cotton Night-Cap Country, or Turf and Towers*, 1873; and *The Inn Album*, 1875. In *The Inn Album* there are four literal instances of the star's appearance, but none is of sufficient importance to deserve particular comment. As it was in the composition of poems like *Ivan Ivanovitch* and *Ned Bratts*, Browning's chief interest in the composition *The Inn Album* was in the grotesque plot, although images of much greater consequence than the star in this particular poem, like the "Album" itself and the "elm," suggest his continued regard for the imagistic method of expression. In each of the other three poems mentioned the star-image occurs three times, but it never becomes prominent in comparison to such images as the-line-twixt-blot-and-blot in *Prince Hohenstiel-Schwangau*, the sea in *Fifine*, and the-turf-and-towers in *Red Cotton Night-Cap Country*. As it may be surmised from their very limited appearance in poems of such length, the structural effects of these star-images are negligible. Their symbolic meanings are nevertheless characteristic of the scores of examples that have been previously observed.

In *Red Cotton Night-Cap Country*, however, the star-images are exceptional in their function in that they have nothing to do with the thesis of the poem proper. They appear in an *envoi* where they represent, rather, Browning's conception of his *Red Cotton Night-Cap Country* as poetry. In a larger sense, therefore, like the stars of poetry in *Sordello*, they may be said to signify Browning's idea of the art of poetry. For this reason it seems proper to close this discussion of the use of the star-image in Browning's last poems with the quotation of this *envoi*:

> How say you, friend?
> Have I redeemed my promise? Smile assent
> Through the dark Winter-gloom between us both!
> Already, months ago and miles away,
> *I just as good as told you, in a flash,*
> The while we paced the sands before my house,
> All this poor story—*truth and nothing else.*
> *Accept that moment's flashing, amplified,*
> *Impalpability reduced to speech,*
> Conception proved by birth,—no other change!
> *Can what Saint-Rambert flashed me in a thought,*
> *Good gloomy London make a poem of?*
> *Such ought to be whatever dares precede,*
> *Play ruddy herald-star to your white blaze*
> *About to bring us day. How fail imbibe*
> *Some foretaste of effulgence? Sun shall wax,*
> *And star shall wane: what matter, so star tell*
> *The drowsy world to start awake, rub eyes,*
> *And stand all ready for morn's jóy a-blush?*

BROWNING'S POETIC DESIGN

T HE study of a detail in poetic design, if it is intended to be reasonably complete, must necessarily run into many of the by-paths of literary analysis. Here and there the going may be tedious for both reader and writer, even though each detail of the analysis may be said to have its importance. Furthermore, the very nature of such an investigation imposes restrictions upon the writer's desire to say things for which his evidence does not provide adequate proof, though, in his opinion, it may supply illuminating inferences. On the other hand, the value of any literary study depends largely upon its success in clarifying and enlarging the general view of the works that have been the object of particular study. In the present instance, therefore, it would seem well to look beyond the several conclusions that arise properly upon the evidence of analysis in order to see something of the relationship between Browning's use of the star-image and the general nature of his art and genius.

Among the various objectives towards which this study was directed, there is one that seemed to lose significance as work progressed. This objective was indicated as the intention to observe the frequency of the occurrence of the star-image. It soon became clear that the mere *count* of star-images in Browning's poetry, or in a single poem, was relatively unimportant. What really mattered was the study of Browning's structural and symbolical uses of these images. These aspects of style could be looked upon as tangible elements of poetic design, and, as such, proper objects of analysis. Further investigation tended to show that, by giving close attention to these details, one might understand more clearly the essential conflict in the mind of the poet. As he prepared to write a poem, Browning always faced the problem of what he should do to bring his *idea* and his *structural pattern* into harmony. He seems never to have been able or willing to solve this problem in terms of a technical formula. It seemed important, therefore, to follow a route of investigation which promised to lead to a better understanding of the relationship between Browning's use of the star-image and his general theory of poetry. Furthermore, if this route were followed chronologically, the investigation might disclose much of the nature of Browning's development as an artist.

For Browning totality of poetic form meant the wedding of what we may call *idea* and *structural pattern*. In this respect his theory of poetry accords with the traditional and most highly approved criterion of fine art. But unlike the more ready craftsman, or the academically trained artist, Browning seems never to have been able to apply this theory without some difficulty, or even a strenuous conflict within his own mind. On the other hand, he seems never to have questioned the validity of his theory, for even beneath the obscurities of his earliest works one may see him progressively approving it. The difficulty arose because his *idea* characteristically ran ahead of his knowledge of *structural pattern*; so that his powers of technical invention were continually strained to keep pace with his swift imagination.

How great was the pressure to achieve this union of *idea* and *structural pattern* is most clearly revealed in *Sordello;* for it is in this poem that Browning set forth a theory of poetry that became the fundamental aesthetic law of his literary life, and it is in this poem that he attempted to write for the first time in full accord with his theory. It was a theory that paid much less attention to the details of literary craftsmanship than to the questions: what is the nature of poetry? what is the nature of the poet? and what is the function of the poet in his relation to other men? These questions were answered in *Sordello* in a manner never calculated to make the future labors of Robert Browning any the less difficult. Poetry, he decided, was the light of Heaven transformed into words, images, meters; the poet was a man of "regal nature," to the manner born, but always in danger of assuming either of the excessive attitudes: a too luxurious, and therefore enervating adoration of beauty, or a too self-centered, and therefore limited conception of truth; the function of the poet was to reveal Man to men, and in so doing to resolve the apparent contradictions of life, the good and evil of the world, into a larger unity. In other words, poetry is the compression of the "starriest into one star"; the poet is king of men; the poet's function is to shed light upon the "wheelwork" of "collective man."

Browning's design for poetry, thus restated even in the thinnest of outlines, may be regarded as a definition of great value in a time like the present when the manifestoes of new poets and new critics demand for poetry some things that it was never intended to do or be. A consideration of Browning's theory, whether or not one can agree with it in every detail, cannot but redirect and focus attention upon first poetic principles. Browning does not conceive of poetry as sociology, nor of the poet as a propagandist, nor of the production of poetry as the work of a partisan whose art is to be valued for its conformity to political, social, or even intellectual doctrine. Sordello's romantic failure to throw his energy into Palma's political cause resulted in his belated decision to know the true function of the poet.

A theory such as Browning's imposes upon the poet an insuperable task. A less energetic poet than Robert Browning might have been forgiven and praised for resigning himself finally to the more sensible plan of composing his works within the limits of his self-discovered abilities. But for Browning a poetic theory was so close to, as to be indistinguishable from a religious conviction. As a result his reader cannot readily ignore the strain, the driving impulse to succeed in his poetic theory, which shows unmistakably in many of Browning's poems. Even in *The Ring and the Book,* composed when his powers of poetic integration had reached their full strength, there is observable the strain, the hope, and the energy of the man whose reach still exceeds his grasp. *Idea* and *structural pattern* still cannot unite in perfect and finished harmonies. There is so much "white light" that cannot be transformed into the "C-major of this life."

To be sure, there are moments of composure, represented by such poems as *Andrea del Sarto* and *Abt Vogler,* when the elements of poetic form are held in aesthetic equilibrium. But there are many other poems in which the marks of internal conflict are visible, in which the union of *idea* and *structural pattern* is not perfect. It is for this reason that the reader of Browning's poetry is often called upon to compose into clearer form what the poet himself has suggested; and, according to his tastes and in response to this necessity, to become either a depressed or a stimulated interpreter. Perhaps Browning came nearest to working out a formula for poetic expression when he wrote his several imitative plays for the London stage. But we have noted that as a group these plays were among his least effective works.

If only that evidence which comes from an examination of the structural uses of the star-image is considered, we are confronted with a strange phenomenon. This evidence points to the infinite *variety* of Browning's methods of composition, and it contrasts sharply with the evidence drawn from the study of the symbolical effects of the star-image which ever suggest the *unity* of idea pervading Browning's poetry as a whole. Structurally considered, even the dramatic monologues, among which one would expect to find a striking similarity of pattern, may be seen to represent many separate schemes of design. Each has been cast in a mould peculiarly suited to its subject; structurally, *My Last Duchess* is quite different from *Soliloquy of the Spanish Cloister.* In other words, while the temper of these poems is produced by a singular motive, there is nothing to indicate that the dramatic monologues collectively represent the formulation of a scheme for production. In writing them the poet did not try to invent an ingenious container which he needed only to refill, often enough, to assure himself literary success.

Among Browning's lyrics there are confusions of dramatic and argumentative motives as well as many varieties of stanza-form; so that it is practically impossible to classify these poems according to fixed standards of structural design. The didactic poems, or the argumentative, may be presented in the shape of lyrics, and the dramatic poems often admit passages of lyric charm or didactic import. Even the last poems, with the possible exception of the several *Parleyings* (which in a sense constitute but one poem), resemble one another in temper and motive much more than in structural design. Structurally considered, there never was a second *Pauline,* a second *Porphyria,* a second *Pippa, Love Among the Ruins,* or *Caliban.* It is not surprising, therefore, that Robert Browning never became distinguished as a writer of sonnets. It is a characteristic of Browning's artistic method that once he has invented a particular structural design, he abandons it to create new designs.

Browning's was evidently a mind which, in so far as *structural pattern* was concerned, was ever in search of a specifically good pattern for the expression of the particular *idea,* or the particular intention of the moment, a mind whose peculiar forte, as the poem *Abt Vogler* suggests, was improvisation. It was a mind restless in its energy, impatient for improvement and development, repelled or dismayed by the thought of perfunctory repetition. It produced a continuously new and unfamiliar kind of poetry; it rarely paused to consider the easier methods of skilled craftsmanship. We who read his poems may pause; we may put down the book to meditate upon lines of quick illumination. The poet himself seems rarely to have paused, but rather to have been eternally in motion, heart and brain, ever changing, reordering, transforming that which might have become fixed form into what he considered the appropriate design for every new poem. It was evidently, for all its faults, an honest mind, possessed of a conviction that real perfection was both an artistic and an intellectual delusion.

The evidence drawn from the analysis of the symbolical uses of Browning's star-image sets over against this impression of variety and change the impression of a continuous unity of motive. It is the unity of a developing idea, however, rather than the unity of a fixed intellectual opinion. It is the unity of the poet's social purpose, to reveal Man to men; of his artistic purpose, to "compress the starriest into one star"; of his philosophical purpose, to spend his life in the quest of ultimate wisdom; of his religious purpose, to permit the expansion of his soul into one "consummate orb" of truth. When a motive of this kind takes possession of a restlessly energetic mind, it is only logical to suppose that growth and development will be the results and that these results will be complex. The different stages in this development, each producing its peculiar and its increasing variety of interests in man and nature, would bear the fruit of constantly modified and frequently enlarged ideas of the world. For these renewed thoughts new patterns of expression would be ever in demand. On the other hand, the growth of all these ideas can be traced to the single, animating force of the poet's dominant motive.

In several divisions of this study we have noted that, whatever the variations may be in the structural functions of the star-image, the symbolical uses of the image remain much the same throughout the poet's career. This image is ever the fixed light of resolution, aspiration, hope, intellectual and poetic decision; it is an image of man's will in action. In its intentionally false forms, the stars of mere fancy and erroneous presumption, it is intended to represent the glittering enticements of illusion and the will-o'-the-wisp of ignorance.

This apparent paradox of variation and unification is symptomatic of the perpetual conflict within the poet's mind, for Browning's conception of the poetic art cannot be separated from religious conviction. He was determined that in some way his poetic practice should be forced, if necessary, or "willed" into accord with his religious faith, and all that his faith implied for Man and Society. A belief such as this does not point the easy way to literary success.

To have reduced his poetic theory to a clear intellectual formula would have been as difficult for Browning as to have become a first-rate theologian. He has been praised for his "theology," to be sure, but never, by acceptable definition did he become a theologian. The formulation of systems of thought and the inclination of the formulators of systems to diminish truth into fine points of demonstrable fact were, in his opinion, to be mistrusted, for to prove the point was to remove the mystery. For him the essential fact, in both poetry and religion, was the immediate presence of the mystery, the flowing river of light of his poetic and religious vision.

On the other hand, Browning thought of himself as a member of that class of poets whose tendency is to impress their own personalities and their own thoughts upon the world; so that, by natural inclination, the formulation of poetic, theological, or even philosophical systems may have been more congenial to Browning's nature than he ever allowed such undertakings to become in his works. It is to protect himself against this, which he considers to be the excess of "the second class of poets," that he "wills" to see ever before him the mystery, rather than the dialectical clarification of the mystery. Again and again, by word and act, he states his conclusion that the poet and Man must approach the mystery, if any degree of creative power is to be attained, and he insists that the evolution of Man consists in growing more like God, Who is the Mystery. For Browning the hints, the suggestions, the impenetrable or only partially understood evidences of the mystery are the most fascinating elements of existence. These are the proofs that we cannot prove. Browning's war with "higher criticism" is that it is a delusion to suppose that purely intellectual man, be he ever so competent, can reduce truth to "plain historic fact." Only the poet, king of men, can catch now and then glimpses of ultimate truth; because he has confessed frankly his analytical inadequacy, and because he depends ultimately upon his vision of white light to dispel the darkness of his mind.

If it has had no other value, we may assume at least that an interest in the frequency with which Browning employed images of light has perhaps led us to focus attention upon one of the most significant images in his poetry. For the star is an image of light which, like his suns, moons, meteors, and rainbows, is profoundly associated with the dominant motive of Browning's genius. When the uses of the star are compared with the uses of other images of light, it becomes clear that the source of all Browning's imagery of light was a spiritual, rather than a realistic vision of the white light of eternal truth. It was this vision that sprang naturally, but with severe effort, from a mind that was preoccupied with the quest of ultimate reality. In his poetry it broke into a hundred heavenly forms of stars, suns, moons, rainbows, meteors; and when it reached the earth, into reflections upon the face of the waters, into all the colors of the spectrum, upon plant and rock, animal and insect. All Nature, heaven and earth, was seen in the poet's imagination to partake of the great white light beyond. Therefore, not only light, but the clouds, the mists, and the fogs of earth became important to the poet's expression, for in them he saw the vision of forces which fought to obscure the white light of heaven. Furthermore, he saw in the powerfully clear colors of Nature a vision of the enticing loveliness which often distracted man's attention from the God beyond Nature. He did not deny their beauty, he almost adored it, but he strove to remember always that it was the pure white light that he was seeking. Even the clear points of distant stars, he thought, might frequently delude man's thinking, because of the misleading clarity implicit in their remoteness.

It is clear that the vision of white light is something that Browning saw only in his imagination. Nature gave him hints and suggestions which he transformed into the conviction that beyond stars and sun existed the eternal light of truth. Nature might reflect the light of truth, but only because nature had been so created by the power of God, whence came all original beauty. Of itself Nature is careless of man's welfare, disinterested, impersonal. Nature affects man's actions only when man wills to see in Nature a reflection of ultimate truth and power. The star itself is not an influence upon the poet, except as he may have the power to see the star in its relationship to the white light of his imagination:

> . . . . light had birth ere moons and suns,
> Flowing through space a river and alone,
> Till chaos burst and blank the spheres were strown
> Hither and thither, foundering and blind:
> When into each of them rushed light—

For Browning Nature is an ever-present though incomplete manifestation of ultimate beauty, ultimate perfection, ultimate unity, truth, and wisdom. In the poet's imagination the objects of Nature are images of this conviction. As they are used in his poetry, the sun and stars become effective images only because Browning has willed to see beyond their physical radiance. They are thus loaded with the fact of his imagination; each has been made over, transformed from a physical object into a sign of spiritual reality, and charged with the energy of a deep conviction.

The true function of a poet and of poetry, which Browning tried to see clearly during the years in which he wrote *Sordello,* is finally manifest in the decision to know God. It is only by attempting to come nearer and nearer to this fact, Browning decides, that the poet may reveal Man to men, may discover the secrets of artistic creation, or may judge with authority upon the elements of human society. God, he concludes, is the supreme poet and artist, for He is of the essence of power and beauty. There are clearly marked stages in the development of this ideal. In *Pauline* Browning declares the object of his quest. In *Paracelsus* he debates as to whether he shall obtain wisdom through Knowledge or through Love, and decides that it shall be through a combination of both. In *Sordello* he examines the excesses of Love and the excesses of Knowledge and prepares to avoid them. By the time he has reached *Abt Vogler* his opinion has been translated into the assurance that "God has a few of us whom he whispers in the ear." With full confidence he undertakes to write, in *The Ring and the Book,* a criticism of life in which he believes he can speak with some of God's authority. Paracelsus' failure ended in the victory of self-realization; Sordello struggled to find a cause, a motive, to which he could give himself and thus rid himself of the excesses of his own nature; Abt Vogler tuned his heart and brain to the music of Heaven.

Mere love, Browning concludes, loses itself in emotional adoration, in sheer wonder at the beauty of Nature, and thus fails to perceive the God beyond; mere Knowledge becomes involved in the making of intellectual distinctions, which, as they become sharper, translate the mystery of God into a diminished clarity, prove Him a point, "and far away." Thus mere love and mere knowledge refuse to have anything to do with the truth that transcends man's powers of appreciation and analysis. True love can therefore be only the love of the source of all beauty; true knowledge can only be the attempt to understand the power that can never be fully known. The poet, or the artist, must yearn upward toward God if he would hear God's whispers in his ear. It is this belief that accounts for the differences among various stages of Browning's development. At the same time, an attempt to understand this belief may help to explain the essential unity of Browning's *idea* and his genius. It is a development in which the poet's constant renewal of himself is implicit; it is a progress in poetry in which the poet rarely pauses by the way with sufficient time to achieve what we may call a classical perfection of poetic structure. It is a pattern of growth in which the personality flourishes, and always remains essentially itself.

Browning's devotion to this way of life and of poetry was the result of both a spirtual and an intellectual necessity. When, in *Sordello,* he made his critical evaluation of the nature of the two kinds of poets and poetry, he found himself, in the main, a member of what he called the second class of poets. They were the poets endowed with vigorous minds and lively personalities. They impressed their individualities upon everything they observed, and in excess of egoism became objects of flattering self-esteem. Browning did not attempt to change his nature, but he prepared himself early in life to guard against the excesses of that nature. His decision to look ever towards his lode-star was necessary; it was a means of guarding against his admitted weaknesses, a means of finding protection against himself. And in this realization and consequent decision lie the elements of evidence which explain something of the conflict that must have possessed his mind continually, and which, incidentally, accounts for the characteristically congested style of many of his verses. It was a conflict waged wholly within himself, lest he should mistake his personal convictions for the truth of God. Only by yearning upward toward God, he concluded, could he hope to speak the truth and at the same time increase the authority of his personality. He realized that he could not withhold his mind from impressing itself upon what he saw, but he could try to tune his mind to the music of the eternal spheres.

The nature of Browning's poetry is compact of a devotion to a consuming motive and of a constant transformation and renewal of that motive. Totality of form in his poetry is, therefore, not merely the harmony of *idea* and of *structural pattern;* it is the result, in each unique instance of composition, of an attempt to create harmony between particles of an expanding idea and a technique that struggled to keep pace with the swiftness of the poet's vision; it is an attempt to reconcile literary structure with the vision or the purpose of the moment.

Browning's development in poetry and personality is never marked by abrupt change, or a definitive alteration which leaves behind all marks of his former self. It is a cumulative development which keeps piling up vision upon vision. Instead of emerging, let us say, from the confusions of youth into a world of fixed judgments and fixed structures, Browning went from confessed confusion into an ever clearer but an ever enlarging knowledge of the complexities of life. His technique improves; his understanding of the proper uses of diction, imagery, stanza-form, meter, and rhythm increases measurably. But the poet invariably moves onward with such rapidity, and his range of vision enlarges so quickly, that even in many of his greatest poems there are signs of restless haste. It is a mistake to regard the observable imperfections of the great middle period of his career, or of the period of *The Ring and the Book,* as one and the same with the confusions of youth. They are imperfections of a totally different order. An analysis of the technical details of the great poems reveals a mastery of form that, when considered against an understanding of the poet's nature, often seems to be nothing short of miraculous. It is a mistake to suppose that the complexities of insight into human character, which are revealed in the great dramatic monologues and in *The Ring and the Book,* are of the same piece with the obscurities of *Pauline* and *Sordello.*

In the period of maturity all elements of the poet's technique are required to conform, in the instance of each poem, to accomplish as nearly as possible the expression of a dominant vision or purpose. It is true that the vision sometimes overtaxes the poet's technical strength, or his patience. Nevertheless, Browning's technical versatility is ever manifest, if only in his invention of meters and stanza-forms, and in his resourceful use of images. Utter formlessness is never a characteristic of Browning's poetry. Analysis of his technique would seem to show that Browning had a livelier sense of artistic form than he ever dared realize. Had he stopped to perfect it, he might have become, almost rightly, the most self-satisfied artist of his age.

But his *technique* is ever the servant of his *idea,* and with his *idea* he could never be satisfied. His total form in a given poem, therefore, becomes as nearly as possible the shape of his genius at a given moment in his development. We may see in Browning's poetry a great number of what may be called first attempts in *idea* and *structural pattern.* It is only the eternal quest for truth which unifies his work, and from which flashes of insight split off to form the constellations of his poetical universe.

The unity of Browning's poetry is strengthened further by the theory of poetry that he came to possess, and which is most succinctly stated, perhaps, in his *Abt Vogler.* This theory emerges from the self-conscious self-analysis of *Pauline,* from the more dispassionate analysis of the nature of Love (beauty) and Knowledge (power) in *Paracelsus,* from the struggles of composing *Sordello,* when the conception of the two kinds of poetry is formulated, and the poet's function defined as the "cause" of revealing Man to men. As a logical result of these definitions the great poems on men and women followed. Then came *Abt Vogler,* a study of a man who, as Browning presents him, knew the secret of artistic creation. It is the theory of an artist who began his work as a painter-musician, who essayed to write poetry, who then strove to know the peculiar limitations of the art he had adopted as compared with the powers and the limitations of the other arts. It is the theory of a poet whose devotion to a transcendent ideal prompted him in later life to turn the devices of poetry towards the expression of a philosophy and a criticism of life.

For literary criticism in general the nature of Browning and his poetry is interesting. Browning is absorbed from the beginning of his career in the attempt to work out that theory of poetry which is compatible with his genius. He does not formulate, as did some of his predecessors, a theory of poetry which he wishes to force upon his literary generation; he spends no time in attacking the theories of the poets of the past. He absorbs the past. He does not self-consciously advocate "the new poetry" of his age. He acknowledges the necessity of form and discipline; the older poetry comes to his hand not for condemnation, but for revitalization, just as his own earlier poetry comes later to his hand for transformation and renewal. He belongs to no "school," but to as many "schools" as he can absorb into his art. He uses hundreds of images without becoming a professional "imagist." He is concerned chiefly with proving himself to be a poetic force and a light in the world of men and women.

BIBLIOGRAPHY

Line references in this study are to the *Centenary Edition* of Browning's works. The works referred to in this study are listed below:

CAMBERWELL EDITION
The Works of Robert Browning, 12 vols., edited by Charlotte Porter and Helen A. Clarke. New York: Crowell, 1898
CAMBRIDGE EDITION
The Complete Poetic and Dramatic Works of Robert Browning. Boston: Houghton Mifflin, 1895
CENTENARY EDITION
The Works of Robert Browning, 10 vols., edited by Sir Frederic G. Kenyon. London: Smith, Elder and Co., 1912
FLORENTINE EDITION
Robert Browning's Complete Works, 12 vols., edited by Charlotte Porter and Helen A. Clarke, containing an Introductory Essay: "Browning's Place in Literature," by William Lyon Phelps. New York: De Fau, 1910
MACMILLAN EDITION
The Complete Poetical Works of Robert Browning, New Edition with Additional Poems First Published in 1914, edited by Augustine Birrell. New York: Macmillan, 1915

Bonnell, John Kester, "Touch Images in the Poetry of Robert Browning," *P.M.L.A.,* XXXVII (Sept., 1922), 574-598
Browning, Robert, "Shelley and the Art of Poetry," *The Prelude to Poetry,* edited by Ernest Rhys. New York: E. P. Dutton, 1927 (Everyman's Library Series)
Browning, Robert, and Barrett, Elizabeth, *The Letters of Robert Browning and Elizabeth Barrett Browning, 1845-1846.* New York: Harpers, 1899
Cook, A. K., *A Commentary Upon Browning's "The Ring and the Book."* London and New York: Oxford University Press, 1920
de Reul, Paul, *L' Art et la Pensée de Robert Browning.* Bruxelles: Maurice Lamertin, 1929
DeVane, William Clyde, *A Browning Handbook.* New York: Crofts, 1935
DeVane, William Clyde, *Browning's Parleyings, the Autobiography of a Mind.* New Haven: Yale University Press, 1927
DeVane, William Clyde, "Sordello's Story Retold," *Studies in Philology,* XXVII (Jan., 1930), 1-24
Duckworth, F. R. G., *Browning, Background and Conflict.* New York: E. P. Dutton, 1932
Elliott, G. R., "Shakespeare's Significance for Browning," *Anglia,* XXXII, 90-162.
Gest, John Marshall, *The Old Yellow Book, Source of Browning's "The Ring and the Book,"* A New Translation with Explanatory Notes and Critical Chapters upon the Poem and its Source. Philadelphia: Univ. of Penna. Press, 1927
Griffin, W. Hall, and Minchin, H. C., *The Life of Robert Browning.* New York: Macmillan, 1910 (London: Methuen and Co., 1910)
Hatcher, Harlan H., *The Versification of Robert Browning.* Columbus: Ohio State Univ. Press, 1928

Herford, C. H., *Robert Browning*. New York: Dodd, Mead and Co., 1905

Hodell, Charles W., *The Old Yellow Book, Source of Robert Browning's "The Ring and the Book."* New York: E. P. Dutton, 1911 (Everyman's Library Series)

Hood, Thurman L., editor, *Letters of Robert Browning Collected by Thomas J. Wise.* New Haven: Yale Univ. Press, 1933

Lounsbury, Thomas R., *The Early Literary Career of Robert Browning.* New York: Scribner's, 1911

Machen, Minnie Gresham, *The Bible in Browning.* New York: Macmillan, 1903

Naish, Ethel M., *Browning and Dogma, Seven Lectures on Browning's Attitude Towards Dogmatic Religion.* London: George Bell and Sons, 1906

Nicoll, Allardyce, *A History of Early Nineteenth Century Drama.* Cambridge: Camb. Univ. Press, 1930

Orr, Mrs. Sutherland, *A Handbook to the Works of Robert Browning.* Sixth Edition. London: George Bell and Sons, 1892

Parrott, Thomas M., *An Examination of the Non-Dramatic Poems in Robert Browning's First and Second Periods* (Dissertation). Leipzig: Schmidt, 1893

Raymond, William O., "Browning and Higher Criticism," *P.M.L.A.,* XLIV (June, 1929), 590-621

Snitslaar, Louise, *Sidelights on Robert Browning's "The Ring and the Book"* (Dissertation). Amsterdam: "Pronto," 1934

Swinburne, Algernon Charles, "Essay on the Poetical and Dramatic Works of George Chapman," *The Works of George Chapman,* Vol. II. London: Chatto and Windus, 1875

Wallis, N. Hardy, editor, *Pauline, by Robert Browning, The Text of 1833, Compared with That of 1867 and 1888.* London: Univ. of London Press, 1931

Whyte, Rev. Arthur J., editor, *Sordello, by Robert Browning.* New York: E. P. Dutton, 1913

In addition to those listed above, the following works, among the many studies of Browning's poetry, have been most helpful for their suggestions and information:

Berdoe, Edward, editor, *Browning Studies, Being Selected Papers of the Browning Society* (London). New York: Macmillan, 1895

Berger, Pierre, *Robert Browning.* Paris: Bloud et Cie., 1912

Broughton, Leslie N., and Stetler, Benjamin F., *A Concordance to the Poems of Robert Browning,* 2 vols. New York: G. E. Stechert and Co., 1924

Browning Society (Boston), *Papers Selected to Represent the Work of the Society from 1886-1897.* New York: Macmillan, 1897

Browning Society (London) *Browning Society Papers.* London: 1881-1891

Chesterton, Gilbert Keith, *Robert Browning.* New York: Macmillan, 1903

Dowden, Edward, *The Life of Robert Browning.* New York: E. P. Dutton, 1915

Raymond, William O., "New Light on the Genesis of *The Ring and the Book,*" *Mod. Lang. Notes,* XLIII (June, 1928), 357-368

and

"Browning's First Mention of the Documentary Sources of *The Ring and the Book,*" *Mod. Lang. Notes,* XLIII (Nov., 1928), 445-450

Russell, Frances Theresa, *One Word More on Browning.* Stanford Univ.: Stanford Univ. Press, 1927

Santayana, George, "The Poetry of Barbarism," *Interpretations of Poetry and Religion*. New York: Scribner's, 1900

Sharp, William, *Life of Robert Browning*. London: Walter Scott, Ltd., 1897

Shaw, J. E., "The 'Donna Angelicata' in *The Ring and the Book*," *P.M.I..A.*, XLI (March, 1926), 55-81

Symons, Arthur, *An Introduction to the Study of Browning*. New York: E. P. Dutton, 1923

Wenger, Christian N., *The Aesthetics of Robert Browning*. Ann Arbor: G. Wahr, 1924

INDEX

OF THE POEMS DISCUSSED OR REFERRED TO IN THIS STUDY